AF600468

The Cinematographer's Voice

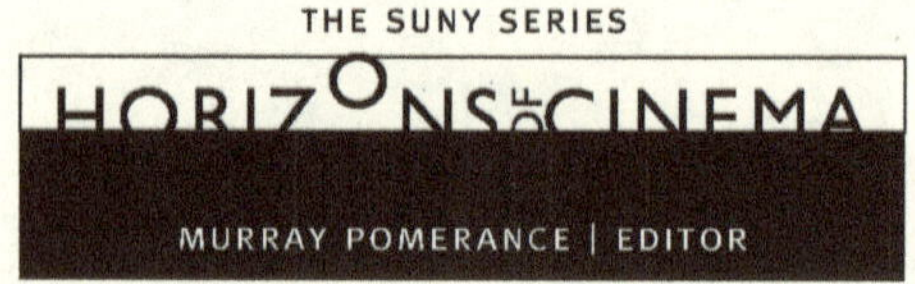

RECENT TITLES

Fareed Ben-Youssef, *No Jurisdiction*

Nolwenn Mingant, *Hollywood Films in North Africa and the Middle East*

†Charles Warren, edited by William Rothman and Joshua Schulze, *Writ on Water*

Jason Sperb, *The Hard Sell of Paradise*

William Rothman, *The Holiday in His Eye*

Brendan Hennessey, *Luchino Visconti and the Alchemy of Adaptation*

Alexander Sergeant, *Encountering the Impossible*

Erica Stein, *Seeing Symphonically*

George Toles, *Curtains of Light*

Neil Badmington, *Perpetual Movement*

Merrill Schleier, editor, *Race and the Suburbs in American Film*

Matthew Leggatt, editor, *Was It Yesterday?*

Homer B. Pettey, editor, *Mind Reeling*

Alexia Kannas, *Giallo!*

Bill Krohn, *Letters from Hollywood*

Alex Clayton, *Funny How?*

Niels Niessen, *Miraculous Realism*

Burke Hilsabeck, *The Slapstick Camera*

Michael Hammond, *The Great War in Hollywood Memory, 1918–1939*

William Rothman, *Tuitions and Intuitions*

A complete listing of books in this series can be found online at www.sunypress.edu

The Cinematographer's Voice

Insights into the World of Visual Storytelling

Edited by

Lindsay Coleman

and

Roberto Schaefer, ASC-AIC

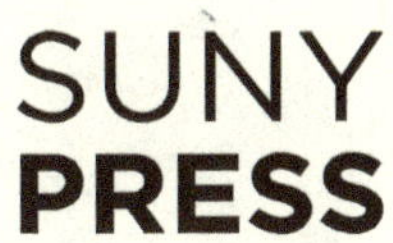

Published by State University of New York Press, Albany

Printed in the United States of America

For information, contact State University of New York Press, Albany, NY
www.sunypress.edu

Library of Congress Cataloging-in-Publication Data

Names: Coleman, Lindsay, 1978– editor. | Schaefer, Roberto, editor.
Title: The cinematographer's voice : insights into the world of visual storytelling / Lindsay Coleman, Roberto Schaefer.
Description: Albany : State University of New York Press, [2021] | Series: SUNY series, horizons of cinema | Includes bibliographical references and index.
Identifiers: LCCN 2021024195 | ISBN 9781438486413 (hardcover : alk. paper) | ISBN 9781438486420 (ebook)
Subjects: LCSH: Cinematographers—Interviews. | Cinematography.
Classification: LCC TR850 .C475 2021 | DDC 777—dc23
LC record available at https://lccn.loc.gov/2021024195

10 9 8 7 6 5 4 3 2 1

This book is dedicated to the great cinematographer Robby Müller

Contents

List of Illustrations ix
Preface xiii
Acknowledgments xv
Introduction 1
Peter Suschitzky 19
Agnès Godard 37
Dean Cundey 47
Rodrigo Prieto 65
Mauro Fiore 87
Peter Deming 97
Dion Beebe 115
Christopher Doyle 127
John Mathieson 137
Luciano Tovoli 153
Rajiv Menon 161
Russell Carpenter 173
Martin Ruhe 185
Javier Aguirresarobe 195
Claudio Miranda 207

Seamus McGarvey 221

John de Borman 229

Affonso Beato 239

Ellen Kuras 247

Uta Briesewitz 261

Roberto Schaefer 273

John Seale 285

Anthony Dod Mantle 297

Index 311

Illustrations

Image 1	Nancy (Chloe Webb) approaches Sid (Gary Oldman) at the end of his performance of the cover version of Frank Sinatra's "My Way" in *Sid and Nancy* (Cox 1986).	6
Image 2	K (Ryan Gosling) confronts Rick Deckard (Harrison Ford) in the darkened foreground while a hologram of Elvis stands atop a set of stairs in *Blade Runner 2049* (Villeneuve 2017).	6
Image 3	Through a small aperture a lecherous Jack Soames (Trevor Howard) peers at a woman bathing in *White Mischief* (Radford 1987).	7
Image 4	Alex Jones (Paul Dano) is tortured and trapped, with a tiny aperture his only source of light in *Prisoners* (Villeneuve 2013).	7
Image 5	Assorted men on horseback travel across the ice in *The Revenant* (Iñárritu 2015).	8
Image 6	*Knight of Cups* (Malick 2015).	8
Image 7	Joe Black (Brad Pitt) in *Meet Joe Black* (Brest 1998).	9
Image 8	Hawk (Forrest Goodluck) surveys the forest in *The Revenant* (Iñárritu 2015).	9
Image 9	Carl Fogarty (Ed Harris) threatens Tom Stall in front of his house in *A History of Violence* (Cronenberg 2005).	19

Image 10 A figure is dwarfed by the Djiboutian landscape in *Beau Travail* (Denis 1999). 37

Image 11 Roger Rabbit and Eddie Valiant are in big trouble in *Who Framed Roger Rabbit* (Zemeckis 1988). 47

Image 12 Ennis Del Mar (Heath Ledger) in *Brokeback Mountain* (Lee 2005). 65

Image 13 The use of long lenses in virtual cinematography lends a veracity to images of the Na'vi in *Avatar* (Cameron 2009). 87

Image 14 A building explodes into flames in *Lost Highway* (Lynch 1997). 97

Image 15 The winter light produced above illustrates the silking required for the set in *Memoirs of a Geisha* (Marshall 2005). 115

Image 16 A woman (Maggie Cheung) in *In the Mood for Love* (Kar-Wai 2000). 127

Image 17 A wide shot of nobles in the Colosseum illustrates the lighting of the set in *Gladiator* (Scott 2000). 137

Image 18 An illustration of contrast in *Suspiria* (Argento 1977). 153

Image 19 Shaila Banu (Manisha Koirala) in an early musical number from *Bombay* (Ratnam 1995). 161

Image 20 Rose (Kate Winslet) and Cal (Billy Zane) enter the ship in *Titanic* (Cameron 1997). 173

Image 21 Clara (Violante Placido) in *The American* (Corbijn 2010). 185

Image 22 Lydia González (Rosario Flores) awaits her bull in *Talk to Her* (Almodóvar 2002). 195

Image 23 Daisy Fuller (Cate Blanchett) dances for Benjamin in *The Curious Case of Benjamin Button* (2008). 207

Image 24 Mi (Saskia Reeves) holds the dead body of Eu (Amanda Plummer) as the tide comes in in *Butterfly Kiss* (Winterbottom 1995). 221

Image 25 CCTV footage of Hamlet (Ethan Hawke) in *Hamlet* (Almereyda 2000). 229

Image 26 David (Javier Bardem) has a guilty secret in *Live Flesh* (Almodóvar 1997). 239

Image 27 The memory light is focused on Clementine (Kate Winslet) and Joel (Jim Carrey) in *Eternal Sunshine of a Spotless Mind* (Gondry 2004). 247

Image 28 Bodie (J.D. Williams) and Poot (Tray Chaney) stand over the dead body of their friend Wallace (Michael B. Jordan) in *The Wire* (Simon 2002–2008). 261

Image 29 The first jailhouse scene from *The Paperboy* (Daniels 2012). 273

Image 30 Katherine (Kristen Scott Thomas) lies dead in front of her lover Almásy (Ralph Fiennes) in *The English Patient* (Minghella 1996). 285

Image 31 Jamal Malik (Dev Patel) and Prem Kumar (Anil Kapoor) on the set of *Who Wants to Be a Millionaire?* in *Slumdog Millionaire* (Boyle 2008). 297

Preface

Almost ten years have passed since the early interviews in this book were conducted, and advancements in digital cameras and post-production have changed the cinematography landscape. What many cinematographers have commented on here about their experiences in shooting digital in the early 2010s must be contextualized on the basis of the production and post-production realities of that time period. The reader should take this into account when noting what is said regarding digital image acquisition, and the quality of the digital cameras versus film cameras. With that in mind, it is still up to the cinematographer (and director and producer) to decide the best medium for their particular project, knowing that digital cameras of the 2020s in the hands of talented and creative crews can give surprisingly great results, competing favorably with 35mm film.

Acknowledgments

I must thank two people for making this book possible: Ron Johanson and Roberto Schaefer. They have become good friends of mine, and throughout the years of putting this text together, they have been tireless collaborators and cheerleaders. I offer them my profound thanks. In addition I thank a number of cinematographers for their guidance and advice throughout. The late Conrad Hall advised me many years ago that I needed to come up with better questions than the ones I was asking during our interview, and I hope that I have succeeded in improving them. Roger Deakins offered me helpful advice very early on and was in fact the first cinematographer I ever interviewed, many years ago. Thank you. Likewise, very helpful and encouraging were Richard Bluck, Darius Khondji, Seamus McGarvey, Ricardo Aronovitch, and John Seale. Although we have only spoken on occasion over the years, Steve Pizzello has always been a voice of real encouragement. Ellery Ryan has been a wonderful collaborator over the past several years and provided invaluable assistance on this book. Murray Pomerance has been a steady and loyal champion of the book. I am indebted. Above all, I thank my loving and patient family. I cannot tell how often my daughter, Audrey, would crawl into my lap to say hello to whichever cinematographer daddy was Skyping with that week. Sarah, my lovely wife, thank you for putting up with my regular nattering on the interview of the day before. You are a marvel.

—Lindsay Coleman

I thank my talented and loving wife, Caroline Eselin-Schaefer, for inspiring me every day and wowing me with her costume design talents. I thank all my friends who are members of the ASC and AIC, past and present, who challenge us every day to excel and try harder to find our voice (sight).

—Roberto Schaefer

Introduction

The Current Place of Cinematography in the Visual Language of Storytelling

The inception of this book occurred around the start of the 2010s. A number of trends in cinematography—including new questions around the authorship of the image, the influence of digital capture technology, and alternating pessimism and optimism in the cinematography community on the future of the profession—had seemed to coalesce around this time in the form of academic commentary, journalistic coverage, and broader debates in the film community. As such, this book was founded on a number of key questions.

Who Claims Authorship of the Image?

Since around 2000, an increasing number of high-level director/cinematographers have come to prominence. Where Ridley Scott aided with framing and operating in previous decades, the likes of David Fincher, Steven Soderbergh, David Lynch, and now, debatably, Paul Thomas Anderson act as their own operators and direct the lighting of their shots. In the age of digital cinema, the director/cinematographer is no longer the hungry amateur looking to save money, filling a position with himself (Robert Rodriguez is a fine example of this), but established auteurs with the financial resources and artistic cachet to hire the best cinematographers in the world. Of course, they often do. Lynch and Peter Deming created stunning imagery in the 2017 *Twin Peaks* season, the continuation of a two-decade partnership. Anderson has created memorable imagery with Robert Elswit. What once was an essential partnership in filmmaking, the cinematographer and director collaborating hand in glove, is now no longer the case. Frequently, the work produced may be described as serviceable. *Logan Lucky*, Soderbergh's comeback and shot by him, was vivid at times, exempting the odd bit of overexposure. Just as often, it may not. Critics noted the look of Lynch's *Inland Empire*, on which he served as cinematographer, was crude and amateurish. The argument could be made this was his intent, but equally, the argument might be made that a similar aesthetic aim in the hands of a professional cinematographer might have yielded some digital visual delights like Anthony Dod Mantle has provided to audiences over the past twenty-odd years. Somewhere in the middle is arguably Anderson's work on *Phantom Thread*: tasteful but nondescript. But could it be pointed out that authorship, rather than beauty or craft, is the key to understanding this choice?

In the behind-the-scenes documentary *Perspectives on "Othello": Joseph McBride on Orson Welles*, film historian McBride points out the unusual fact that during *Othello*'s lengthy, tortured production a total of eleven cinematographers worked on the film. "The unifying factor," he observes, "was in Welles' style. He was the auteur" (McBride 2014). This is a simple statement of fact and speaks directly to the profound question of who may claim authorship of the image in cinema. As this book goes to print, there is, on the part of some of the more major filmmakers and some of the more significant cinematic, streaming, and television output, an increasing drive toward auteurs seeking a greater role in crafting the image. *Roma* has seen director Alfonso Cuarón stepping in as his own cinematographer. In doing so much of the long, virtuosic takes and complex choreography that featured in his collaborations with Emmanuel Lubezki on *Children of Men* and *Gravity* have translated precisely into his own work as cinematographer. The director-as-image-author is not unique, as can be seen from McBride's acknowledgment of Welles, yet it might be safe to say that some of the more major productions of recent times have forgone the classic notion of a cinematographer who crafts images as a member of a larger team including the director, producer, production designer, and costume designer.

This observation is neither an endorsement of nor an overt critique of this trend. By all accounts, Cuarón's work as a cinematographer is as virtuosic as one would expect of a filmmaker of his pedigree. Equally, one could quibble with the visual sameness of the template Soderbergh created for his series *The Knick*, which he also shot, or quietly acknowledge that although *Magic Mike* and its sequel have plenty of razzle dazzle, a full-time, life-long cinematographer may have brought greater finesse to the enterprise. There have been upstart productions that entirely transcend the relative debates that might surround a director/cinematographer. *Sin City* was directed, adapted, edited, and shot by Robert Rodriguez. This film ranked as the thirty-third best-shot film of the 2000s, as voted for by the subscribers of *American Cinematographer*. In the case of Rodriguez, his specific work as a cinematographer exceeded sterling work on films such as *Zodiac* and *Gangs of New York*, by the likes of cinematography titans Harris Savides and Michael Ballhaus. Visual talent has always been the province of the best directors, of visualists; with the increasing availability and accessibility of cameras and filmmaking equipment, coupled with the ever-expanding technical acumen of the best directors, it is little wonder that what was once the exception for the likes of Welles is increasingly becoming a norm.

Where does this leave the role of the classic director of photography? In the tenth *American Cinematographer Manual*, the cinematographer's role is defined by the following statement:

> The cinematographer's initial and most important responsibility is telling the story and the design of a "look" or visual style that faithfully reflects the intentions the director, or the producer/show runner if the project happens to be an episodic television series. It is mandatory for the cinematographer to accomplish that primary goal within the limitations of the budget and schedule. Other collaborators who are generally involved in this creative process with the cinematographer and director include the production designer, art director, and occasionally the visual effects supervisor and/or producer. . . .
>
> The cinematographer is responsible for executing the vision for the "look" of the film, while helping to keep production on budget and on schedule. On many feature films, the day begins with the cinematographer viewing dailies during early morning hours at the lab to verify that there are no technical problems and nuances in the "look" are working. They frequently watch rehearsals of the first scene with the director, and suggest whether modifications in lighting or coverage are needed. (Goi 2013, 3–5)

These are not recommendations of the cinematographer's role from some bygone decade but can be traced to 2013. Cinematographers are their director's right arm in relation to the visual aspects of a production, and tending to its details is a responsibility they regard with profound solemnity.

At this moment, it is opportune to return to Rodriguez's achievement. In the first half of his career, he worked with respected cinematographers such as Enrique Chediak and Guillermo Navarro. Direct testimony on the character of those collaborations is scant, but it might be inferred from Rodriguez's opining in the 2012 documentary *Side by Side* that he felt disconnected from the image-making process and forced to trust that his cinematographer was carrying out his vision. In further outtakes from that film, Rodriguez elaborated that at a screening held by George Lucas in the early 2000s introducing digital capture technology to a crowd of directors—including Steven Spielberg, Martin Scorsese, Rodriguez, and Oliver Stone—the *Sin City* director found himself enthused by the possibilities of the new technology, particularly the ability to directly see on a monitor what was being captured. It meant less "guessing," as he put it. Interestingly, Jerry Lewis is apocryphally credited with the 1960 invention the video assist, which allowed directors to see what they were shooting in real time (still in use today). Lewis certainly assisted with popularizing this technology. In contrast, the likes of Oliver Stone passionately defended the conventional role of the cinematographer, and symptomatically, a schism has persisted in the film world of those filmmakers who seek to reinforce the classic role of the cinematographer, such as Stone, Quentin Tarantino, Christopher Nolan, Alejandro G. Iñárritu, and those who have taken a more active role in image-making, such as Soderbergh, Rodriguez, James Cameron, and David Fincher.

While the more obvious instances of this trend of directors acting as their own cinematographers are mentioned earlier, the most famous instance is from 2009. James Cameron frequently acted as his own operator, and worked extensively crafting the lighting and ambience of digital environments during the post-production of *Avatar*. His ubiquitous stamp on the visuals of that production was so profound that some have questioned the relative presence of Oscar-winning cinematographer Mauro Fiore on the film, the relative input of conventional cinematography in that production. In addition to this, Vince Pace's contribution to the cinematography on *Avatar* has often been overlooked. In short, in film the conventional sense of the director of photography as key author of the images has become contested.

In the early 2010s, American Society of Cinematographers (ASC) president Michael Goi acknowledged the controversy surrounding the Oscar awarded to Fiore for his work on *Avatar*:

> A few months ago, a firestorm of controversy erupted as a result of *Avatar*'s cinematography win (for Mauro Fiore, ASC) at the Academy Awards. Almost overnight, it seemed cinematographers and cinematography societies all over the world were calling for some voice of reason as to what was in store for the future of "traditional" cinematography, and what our place was in the emerging virtual-production world. . . . I think there's a kind of chaos of perception at work in these shifts, a chaos born from the belief that because a technology is capable of expediting an artistic vision with more clarity and precision than was previously possible, that technology must inherently be a threat to the human elements of collaboration and artistry. As we've seen with all of the innovations I mentioned, the nature of how we use these tools might change, but the spirit of collaboration and creativity is actually enhanced in the process. (2010, 10)

In the intervening years the debate has not subsided. *The Life of Pi*, in the wake of its twin Oscar wins for cinematography and visual effects, was beset by controversy with respect to who could and should claim authorship of its visual triumphs, which were bountiful. *Gravity* similarly won major plaudits for its cinematography and visual effects, as did *Blade Runner 2049*. The latter's win was less controversial and was seen as overdue recognition for cinematographer Roger Deakins. The earlier wins provoked further debates about how such visual achievements—those that blended photorealistic visual effects and lighting with expert cinematography, frequently under the guidance of visionary directors—could easily be parsed into relative domains of aesthetic achievement. Similarly, if the works contained a "look" that cohered well, the question might be "was this luck, teamwork, or the dominant vision of a single individual?" In part, this book seeks to investigate these tricky questions.

How Does a Cinematographer Evolve?

Examine these four images. They are from four different films and feature seven different actors. The first image is from the mid-1980s, from the film *Sid and Nancy*. The second is from 2017's *Blade Runner 2049*. The third is also from the mid-1980s, from *White Mischief*. The fourth is from the 2013 film *Prisoners*. Their respective genres are a punk biopic, a philosophical science fiction epic, an erotic courtroom drama, and a grisly thriller. Not much is shared in common between them, right? But look at the first two images. In the foreground are the active figures. These figures are central to the film's drama. Nancy (Chloe Webb) surveys her lover Sid Vicious (Gary Oldman) and Deckard (Harrison Ford) and K (Ryan Gosling) engage in a tense standoff in from of an Elvis hologram. Interestingly these key foreground figures are in silhouette. The background figure is contemplative, yet more brightly lit. There is, in short, an aesthetic link between the two, with the drama set in a sillouetted foreground with the passive figure lit more brightly in the background. Then consider that all images were filmed, lit, and framed by Roger Deakins.

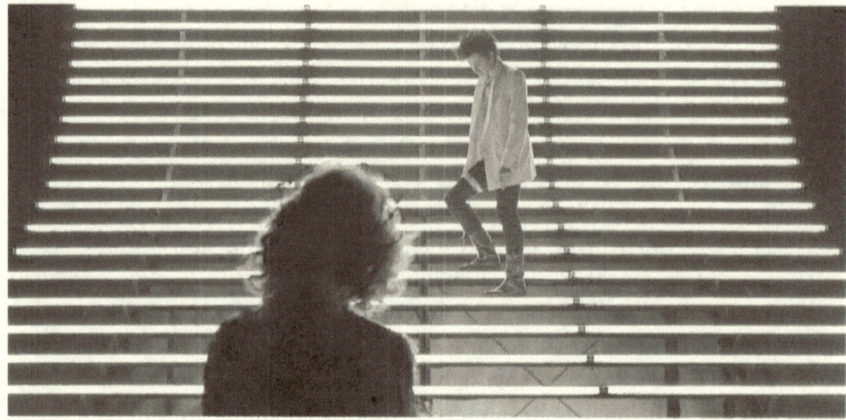

Image 1. Nancy (Chloe Webb) approaches Sid (Gary Oldman) at the end of his performance of the cover version of Frank Sinatra's "My Way" in *Sid and Nancy* (Cox 1986).

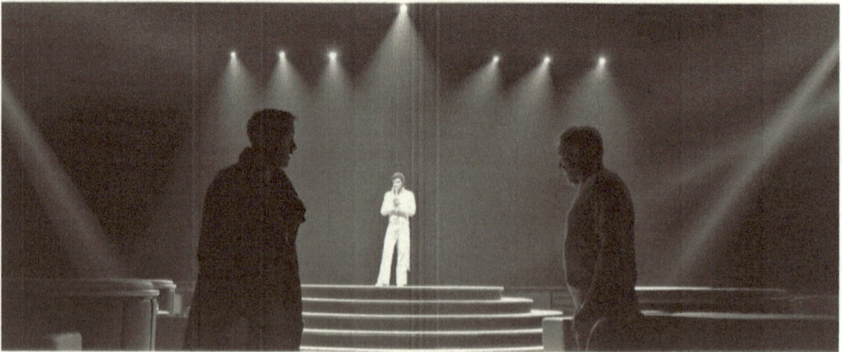

Image 2. K (Ryan Gosling) confronts Rick Deckard (Harrison Ford) in the darkened foreground while a hologram of Elvis stands atop a set of stairs in *Blade Runner 2049* (Villeneuve 2017).

Examine the following pair. In the first image, from *White Mischief*, an aging character played by Trevor Howard spies the film's heroine as she enjoys a bath through a peephole. In a very different scene, Paul Dano's character in *Prisoners*, tortured by Hugh Jackman's character, languishes in a cupboard following his beating, a tiny slit of light his only contact with the world outside. The context, again, is entirely different, by the visual idea is the same: a character, surrounded by darkness, engages with some intense vision on the other side of a barrier, that vision being their only source of light.

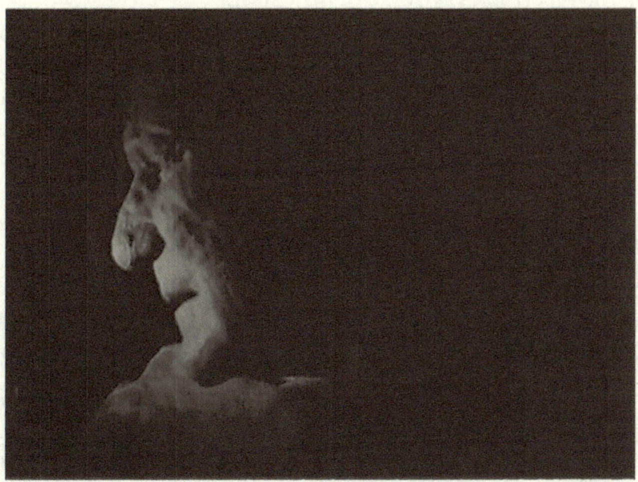

Image 3. Through a small aperture a lecherous Jack Soames (Trevor Howard) peers at a woman bathing in *White Mischief* (Radford 1987).

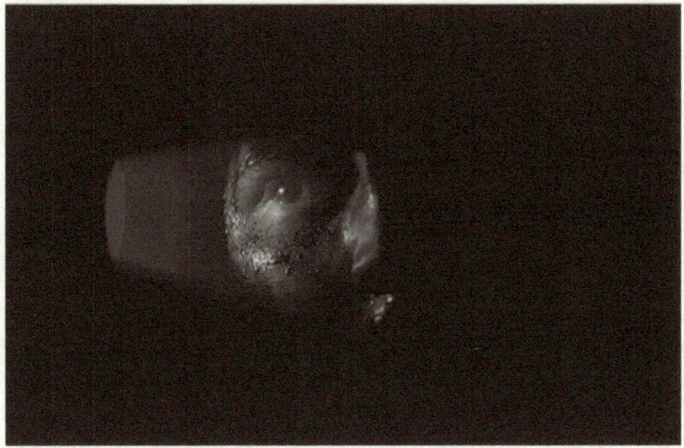

Image 4. Alex Jones (Paul Dano) is tortured and trapped, with a tiny aperture his only source of light in *Prisoners* (Villeneuve 2013).

Close inspection of these images will testify to Deakins's skill at crafting imagery and his ability to convey complex visual storytelling in a simple, graphic style. Equally, his growing mastery of technique, the sensitivity of his lenses, and his ability to direct light are attested to in the noted differences seen in the thirty or so years that separate each pair of images.

The next two pairs are from the work of Emmanuel Lubezki. Three distinct lighting environments are found in the frame of this shot from 2015's *The Revenant*. The is the bright torchlight of the foreground, the darkness of the forest in the middle-backround, and the dying light of the sky of the deep background of the shot.

In 2015's *Knight of Cups* the same visual predilection may be found, but now Lubezki is playing with exposure and time of day. In the background, the sun's final rays are touching the horizon. In the foreground, to screen left, is the darkness of empty houses, to the right a swarm of traffic. Again, three distinct lighting environments appear in the same shot.

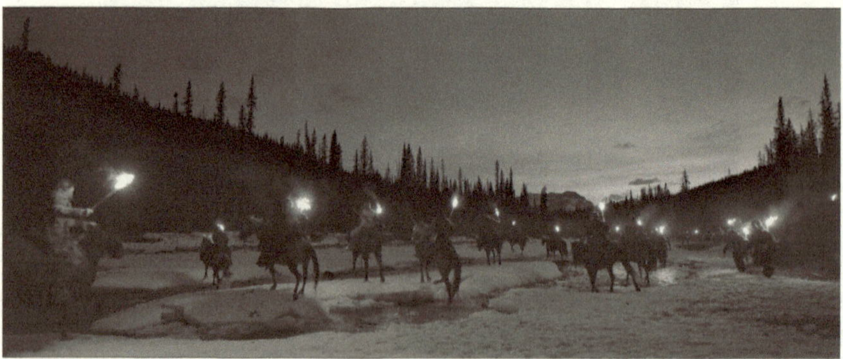

Image 5. Assorted men on horseback travel across the ice in *The Revenant* (Iñárritu 2015).

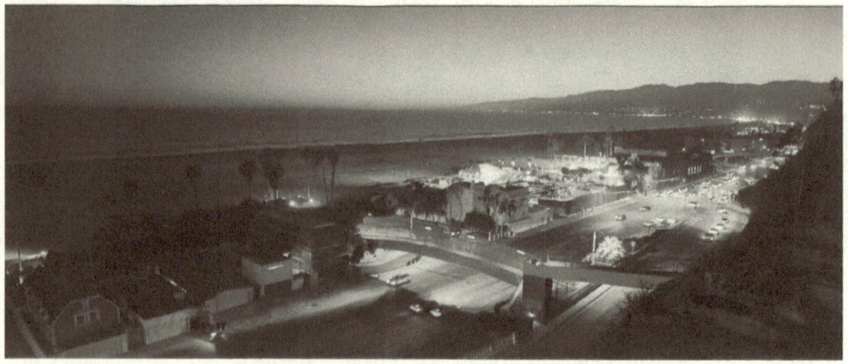

Image 6. *Knight of Cups* (Malick 2015).

In the following pair of shots Lubezki uses a shallow depth of field to highlight the intimacy of a close-up. In the first shot, Brad Pitt in *Meet Joe Black*, specifically during a love scene, the idea is clear and the focus appropriately shallow, yet the blocking and framing seem unclear, undecided. Seventeen years later, a moody closeup of an actor, in *The Revenant*, features the same shallow depth of field, the same feeling of a subjective, intimate point of view, but now the framing seems more confident.

Such casual observations, and a registering of the attendant shifts in technique while maintaining the salient visual ideas from film to film, seem to suggest that cinematographers experience a notable evolution in

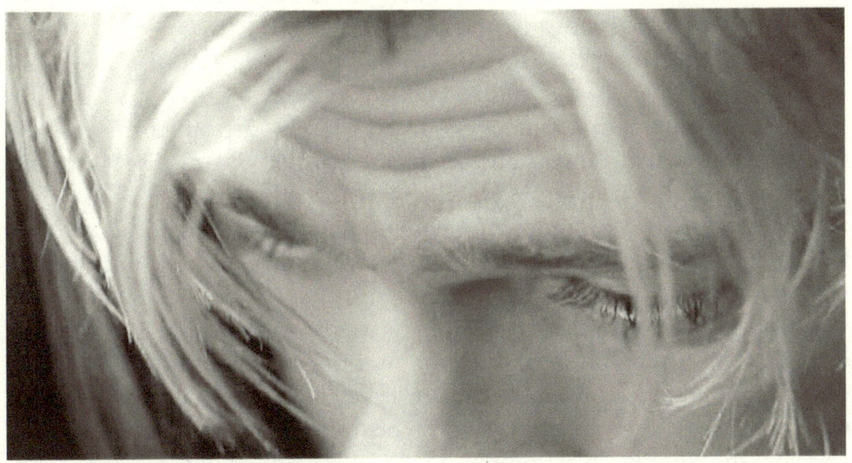

Image 7. Joe Black (Brad Pitt) in *Meet Joe Black* (Brest 1998).

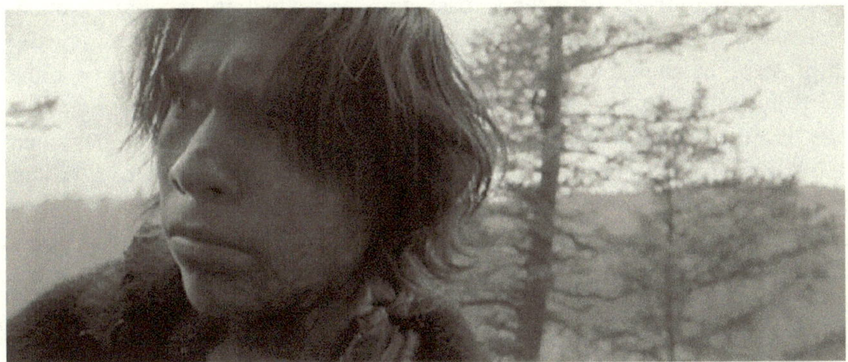

Image 8. Hawk (Forrest Goodluck) surveys the forest in *The Revenant* (Iñárritu 2015).

their style over decades of working. The growing of this style constitutes a kind of authorship frequently overlooked in what is a more auteur-focused theory of what sets a film's style, specifically the notion that the director originates the visual design, the visual ideas of the film. The stamp of the cinematographer can weave from film to film in their oeuvre, irrespective of who the director may be. The eight films cited above were made with six different directors. The shots are separated by genres and sometimes decades between their production, yet the visual glue that holds a cinematographer's output can be, for the very best, unmistakable and in a constant state of evolution—the education of a lifetime.

What Are the New Challenges Cinematographers Face in a Changing Production and Media Landscape?

To discuss contemporary cinematography is not merely to discuss an aspect of filmmaking in a state of change or flux, but to discuss an art and science in the process of cellular transformation. In the digital cinema of the 2010s, the future of cinematography as it has hitherto been known has come into profound question. A number of key notions are consistent throughout this new paradigm.

Never before has the technology used for capturing the moving image been so tangibly accessible to the masses. Arguably, as Christopher Doyle admits, consumers of film have themselves become budding cameramen based on the increasing sophistication and technical virtuosity of even the simple smartphone. The technology of filmmaking, once the province of the technical and artistic elite, is now accessible to the budding amateur editor, effects artist, and even cinematographer. As such, images—striking images, richly colorful images, images technologically impressive in their capture and presentation—are as common as once were flat, dull, utterly disposable Polaroids or grainy home movie footage. Even in the few years spent assembling this volume there has been the advent of 4K capture in cameras that might be attached to a tablet, phone, or stills camera. Super slow-motion in high definition is now a simple gimmick for those capturing footage. Filters or grading tools are now a simple click on a plug-in away from the average possessor of such devices. In the late 2010s, the public has arguably been lulled into the belief by advertisers and tech companies that they have within their grasp the skill and equipment to capture images comparable to those of professional photographers and cinematographers. In a recent podcast for *American Cinematographer*, Spielberg's regular cinematographer Janusz Kamiński noted this trend but bemoans that it has led to a copycat visual culture: "Anyone can take away what you have done once you have created it. . . . Is there anything new created in visual technology due to the advancement of our technology? I don't think so" (Kamiński 2018). To Kamiński, this culture has seen a democratization in film aesthetics offset by a dearth in visual storytelling. The aesthetics he helped pioneer on films such as *Schindler's List* and *Saving Private Ryan* are easily mimicked, and in turn easily accessible technology has made filmmaking more accessible than ever to the masses the core technology of cinematography has failed to evolve:

> Contemporary cinematography has not evolved beyond anything which European master cameramen . . . were doing . . . I don't think aesthetics have evolved to a point where there is now a lack of storytelling . . . the truth is we haven't really evolved. We're still making the movies with the same equipment. It is not evolving. It is beginning to fail. All of the attention is beginning to focus on digital things . . . The lighting units have only really evolved a little bit. (Kamiński 2018)

Ironically, for some major cinematographers, the growth in the accessibility of camera technology has been offset by an encroaching lack of vision in the field itself.

Indeed, prosumer technology and prosumer-level capture technology has crossed increasingly into the mainstream such that, for instance, an ad campaign for the iPhone 13 explicitly focused on how professional-grade cinematography may—according to Apple's claims—be extracted from these tiny phones and multiple apps. Equally, feature films such as *Tangerine*, famously shot on iPhones, have further fostered the notion that the skill—and talent—to create cinematic imagery is now in the grasp of the public. Intriguingly, the explosive innovation found in digital cameras, at a prosumer level and in professional cameras such as the Alexa, and their accessibility has seen the very characterization of the image, of our expectations of what an image should look like if it is "good" or "beautiful" or "professional," be pulled in every direction. Famed colorist Peter Doyle, who has put the finishing touches on films by Peter Jackson and the Coen brothers, in addition to working with many of the world's best cinematographers, is in the most opportune position to comment on these struggles and defines them thus: "I'd like to share some observations about HDR and film. We have distributors and manufacturers pushing for 4K pipelines. We have DPs pushing for the worst piece of glass you could ever imagine in front of the sensors. We have manufacturer and distributors pushing for ultra-wide-gamut color spaces" (Doyle 2018). In this perfect storm of expectation and demand, the typical digital projection technology for most of the world, large-screen televisions on which people stream films and series, is wrenching the work of cinematographers into a garish and supersaturated color space:

> There are manufacturer of projectors and monitors which are pursuing the possibility of displaying what I call fluorescent colors, colors which are of high luminance and high saturation. These colors are not very pleasant to look at. Filmmakers are actually pursuing colors which are beautiful, luxurious, which are, generally, not in fact desaturated, but of low luminance, and of higher saturation. Filmmakers are pursuing images with desaturated highlights, and saturated low lights. Manufacturers, in contrast, are trying to display everything known to mankind in their color space. They are displaying, theoretically, colors beyond what we can even see. The intention of the manufacturer is honorable. They have a shared goal of accurate image representation. What is not happening though is the required etiquette. A film print, produced by the DP, director, production designer, was the display medium for the film. These prints could be damaged. But the etiquette, or the protocol, was that the production would create this visual artifact which represented everyone's intent. We've gone now to a place of manufacturers existing as an equal voice, alongside the production of the film, the studio. They decide if the Barco laser is better than the Sony laser. This creates a general problem because on a laser projector, for instance, all blues look the same. In the past the production company could manage the distribution medium. That isn't the case anymore. It is still being negotiated. (Doyle 2018)

The technology has effectively become an instance of the cart leading the horse. Consumers are being visually educated to expect that the widest color gamut, the sharpest highlights, and the sharpest image are also the "best" image.

In the film and television industry there are also, as never before, the fingerprints of multiple departments on the final images enjoyed by the viewing public. In this climate, the image and its production are subject to the intervention of many kinds of filmmaking technologies. In their specific capture, digital cameras now allow for the relative absence of ambient or artificial light. Where once lighting was explicitly a part of the cinematographer's brief, it is now a quantity open to debate. The calculus is simple. Fewer lights mean more setups, in turn means more footage. It also means lower expenditure of power, less time spent on lighting, and more money saved. Digital cameras, specifically the likes of the Alexa, are arguably setting the agenda and timeline for many productions these days. Equally, in the pre-vising of shots, the image is subject to extensive preplanning and preconceiving before many cinematographers are able to inspect a set or address lighting issues. Frequently the technical specifications that create these images in a computer are not even compatible with the realities of photographic capture. As such, noncinematographers are blocking and framing shots and making lens choices not compatible with real-life technology, which in turn locks cinematographers into choices about these aspects of image-making they are now exempt from. In postproduction the cinematographer's autonomy may be equally compromised. Several years ago the editor of *Life of Pi*, Tim Squyres, was on record saying that the decision to change the aspect ratio of a key sequence in the film, an attack of flying fish, such that the fish would seemingly breach the outside of the frame was an *editorial* decision. The same choice was claimed as a cinematographic one by the film's director of photography, Claudio Miranda. Visual effects may similarly alter, and even distort, the lighting and compositions of a cameraman. Takes may be stitched together, one side of screen one take, the other one filmed hours or days later. Backgrounds may be rendered in such a manner as to make the cinematographer's initial lighting seem flat or misjudged. The workspace in which the cinematic image is created is becoming increasingly crowded with coauthors, all seeking their own type of credit for the final outcome. In this new workspace, cinematographers must work harder than ever to stake out their place.

Methodology

The methodology for putting this text together was, as mandated by its long gestation (around six years) and wide scope, necessarily complex.

Certain major cinematographers were not disposed to contribute. Others were enthusiastic. In specific cases, permissions could not be secured in the time allotted. A wider range of cinematographers representing Indian and Chinese cinema was sought out, but unfortunately, many significant cinematographers from those countries proved elusive. Otherwise inactive and retired cinematographers were sought out, personal favorites of mine, but it became clear that expanding beyond practicing cinematographers meant that the scope of the project became less manageable. I must confess that interviews with some of my personal favorite cinematographers did not always result in material of sufficient quality to print. A number of excellent female cinematographers were interviewed, but it is worth emphasizing that in the period following the collection of all interviews a further number of talented female cinematographers have been given opportunities not open to them before. Among the most notable are Reed Morano, Rachael Morrison, and Natasha Braier, to name a few. These superb cinematographers have inspired many in their profession and future texts are certain to explore their visionary work, work which fell outside of the period of production for this text. The balance was finally struck with what seemed a good mix of those established as key influences of this period of digital cinema, cinematographers with major "brand" recognition based on their celebrated works, expert technicians from the world of television, recognized mavericks, and present elder statesmen of the world of cinematography.

Equally, a marker for inclusion in this volume was based on the ability of the cinematographer to articulate their thoughts on their work and the current cinema. The level of skill (even genius) required for a great cameraperson is hard for most cinema audiences to easily appreciate. This sometimes translates into fluency and infectious commentary on cinematography as a discipline, or it may not, through no fault of the practitioner. The work of a cinematographer requires discipline, calculation, and above all artistry. It is a highly practical and highly reflective vocation. Often cinematographers may be bored reciting the technical details, which to them are boilerplate, and find the act of articulating a process that is personal and emotional, even painful, to be a challenge. Many contributors chosen were hyperarticulate on their process, both practical and creative, in a manner that I believed would be compelling for the reader.

Based on the extent of their influence in modern cinema, certain interviewees were essential. Rodrigo Prieto has worked with Ang Lee, Oliver Stone, Alejandro G. Iñárritu, and Martin Scorsese on some of their more celebrated films of the past two decades. His facility in collaborating with major creative forces deserved further inquiry. Dean Cundey worked with Robert Zemeckis, Steven Spielberg, and John Carpenter on arguably their most iconic films. His ability to construct distinct visual grammars that translated their texts so effortlessly to worldwide audiences speaks to a honed instinct for storytelling using primarily images. Mauro Fiore is the cinematographer of the highest-grossing film ever, *Avatar*, and, with the choice of James Cameron to shoot the film in 3D, Fiore's cinematography kicked off a trend that has seen everyone from Jean-Luc Godard to Ang Lee to Wim Wenders emulate. Anthony Dod Mantle, like many of these figures, is a cinematographer with a gift for collaboration. His work with Lars von Trier, Oliver Stone, Danny Boyle, and Ron Howard is a testament to his versatility. By the reckoning of most, Dod Mantle is also one of the key pioneers in what has become the digital cinema of our modern world.

The particularities of my methodology as interviewer are worth exploring. Typically interviews lasted between 90 and 150 minutes at a single stretch. Occasionally, the interview would be split into two hour-long segments. While numerous bits of industry scuttlebutt and gossip came up, often the cinematographers would come to rue mentioning it and usually requested that I leave such material out. I have obliged. Similarly, the testimony on who said what to whom and why so-and-so was fired from a particular film is easily accessible in other sources who primary focus is not on image-making and the craft of cinematography. My style of interviewing and the particularity of my questions were customized to each cinematographer. Peter Deming, for instance, is technically masterful irrespective of whether the film is *Lost Highway* or the more obviously fun *Drag Me to Hell*. As such, my interview with him was ultimately more technical. Research had indicated that Peter Suschitzky could be terse in his responses if the line of questioning became overly technical, so I endeavored to make it more personal. Martin Ruhe impressed me with the immaculate, cohesive nature of the aesthetic he might develop for a film, so my questions centered on how he might develop this. Research indicated that Luciano Tovoli had an incredible capacity to translate technical decisions into a poetic explanation. Conversely, Claudio Miranda's depth and breadth of technical knowledge was so extensive as to acquire its own poetic rhythm when explained. As such no "format" for questions was devised, but was customized based on the key factors influencing each cinematographer.

Another important point should be made on the content of the interviews. In arranging these interview to be faithful to the statements, language, and points of view of the cinematographers I spoke with, I did not use editorial discretion to excise material. My main goal was always to be as fairly representative as possible of their views in how the interviews were transcribed and presented.

Points of Connection

Cinematographers are frequently loath to admit to influences. They are also critical of themselves and of one another. In 1999 I was drawn into a brief discussion with one of the world's most well-respected cinematographers, who poured scorn on the then recently released, stage-bound *Eyes Wide Shut*, and how it looked nothing like the New York streets it claimed to depict. Similarly, it is interesting to note that the more successful the cinematographer, the more relentlessly self-critical they are, and the more passionately critical they are of a film's images. At times they may be actively engaged in debate and discussion, even competition, with other cinematographers; at other times they may pass by other cinematographers like ship captains nodding across a gulf, each set in their course and briefly recognizing the work of another. Despite this, there are admitted touchstones for the modern cinematographer. These might not be what one would expect. Despite their accolades, the achievements of Mauro Fiore in *Avatar* and Claudio Miranda in *Life of Pi* generated controversy. These have since receded, but the implications of the criticism are well worth exploring in the broader context of the early history of digital cinema. In his interview, Fiore is arguably ambivalent on the 3D legacy of *Avatar*, and this trend, which was prevalent in the early 2010s, has since also receded. The digital camera legacy of films such as *Collateral* and *Miami Vice* is arguable given what Dion Beebe notes to be the lukewarm response of the camera company responsible for the Thomson Viper camera, which was used to shoot those films. Instead, the key themes of this decade could be summed up with a number of significant ideas and technologies: prosumer cameras, the digital intermediate, the Alexa camera, the digital-celluloid debate, and the challenges of filmmaking collaboration (an eternally relevant topic).

The boom of prosumer-level cameras in common, everyday usage has arguably robbed some of the exclusivity and charm from professional cinematography, according to Christopher Doyle. Films, particularly those of the found-footage genre, are getting to look more and more amateurish in their camerawork and lighting. A film might well have a budget in the hundreds of millions, but its aesthetic is closer to that of a kid on YouTube filming their friends. The filmed image is arguably subject to such a range of transformations—from the "capture" phase found in production, to the postproduction phase where it undergoes further changes—that much debate can now occur as to where exactly the majority of the work of the cinematographer is done: in the lighting and filming on a set or location, or in the later phases when the frequently digital image is tweaked, sometimes for far longer, and involving far many more departments, than went into the initial phase in which the image was captured and stored (or converted to) a digital version. One need only look at *Independence Day: Resurgence* to see a prime example of this. A "before and after" comparison show the initial set, lit in flat and glary light, and its final dynamic manifestation, with a bluish tint, shadow and atmosphere added to a what would otherwise be a very flat image.

The digital intermediate, a phase in which the captured footage may be retimed, have new texture mapped in, have colors removed from the image, and so forth, is now *de rigueur* on productions. This allows for the cinematographer to alter any major flaws in the image. More important, it expands the visual toolbox available to the cinematographer and allows them to elaborate on an aesthetic they may have already decided to pursue.

Collaboration

The final word of this introduction must be given to the celebration of effective collaboration. My first collaborator was Australian Cinematographers Society (ACS) president Ron Johanson. A fatherly figure, he welcomed the notion of a book exploring modern cinematography. Over the years, he was tireless in his assistance and encouragement, often directing me toward kindred spirits and future collaborators. My most valued collaborator has been Roberto Schaefer. I always respected his work as a cinematographer, but over time I came to know him as an artist, intellectual, champion of his art form, and now a dear friend. It soon became clear that Schaefer was in a unique position as a respected member of the ASC and AIC, and we agreed that certain interviews would be far better if he conducted them. Without Schaefer, we would not have been able to secure an interview as fruitful and informative as the one with Claudio Miranda. Peer to peer, the conversation was rich, technical, and candid. An important mentor who was engaged with the project from the start was Ricardo Aronovich. My initial interview with the eloquent Javier Aguirresarobe was initially hindered by a language gap and the necessity of a translator. This was remedied when the multilingual Ricardo Aronovich conducted the interview in my stead. On technical matters, Roberto Schaefer was a consistent source of knowledge and perspective, but so was Ellery Ryan, who often stepped in with technical advice. Going back even further, this idea was first encouraged by Darius Khondji in the late 1990s during a series of stimulating interviews and conversations. It is said that it takes a village to produce something, and that is certainly true. I thank all of these cinematographers. Theirs is the essential spirit of shared vision and collaboration.

Bibliography

Doyle, Peter. "Colorist Peter Doyle 1—HDR, Vintage Workflows, Post Etiquette." YouTube, thefilmbook, April 3, 2018. https://www.youtube.com/watch?v=zvTXV5Dh9kI&t=6s.

Goi, Michael. "President's Desk." *American Cinematographer* (June 2010): 10.

Goi, Michael. "Introduction." In *American Cinematographer Manual*, 10th ed., edited by Michael Goi. Hollywood: ASC Press, 2013. 3–5.

Kamiński, Janusz. "Saving Private Ryan—20th Anniversary." *American Cinematographer Podcast*, episode 87, July 2, 2018. https://ascmag.com/podcasts/saving-private-ryan-20th-anniversary-janusz-kaminski.

McBride, Joseph, *Perspectives on "Othello": Joseph McBride on Orson Welles.* Directed by Robert Fischer. DVD, Janus Films, 2014.

Peter Suschitzky

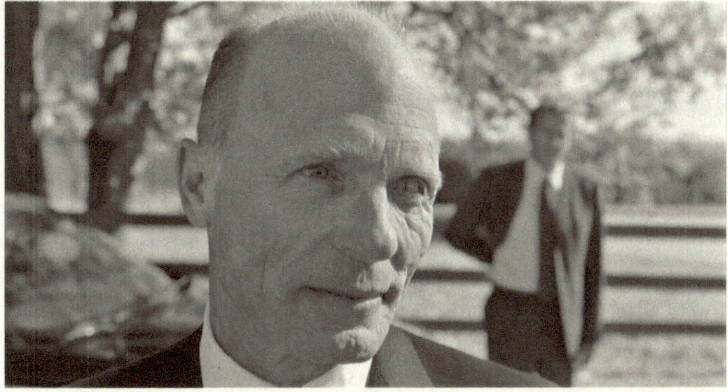

Image 9. Carl Fogarty (Ed Harris) threatens Tom Stall in front of his house in *A History of Violence* (Cronenberg 2005).

Peter Suschitzky ASC has filmed some of the most celebrated genre, cult, and dramatic films of the past forty years. Titles include *The Empire Strikes Back*, *The Rocky Horror Picture Show*, *Lisztomania*, and *Immortal Beloved*. His early work with noted British stylist of the 1960s and 1970s Ken Russell on the films *Lisztomania*, *Valentino*, and equally strong work on the cult classic *The Rocky Horror Picture Show* led to him developing a strong reputation for moody, striking lighting. He was offered the original *Star Wars* but deferred, believing himself not yet experienced enough with effects to do justice to the technical requirements of the film. The second time he received an offer from George Lucas he accepted, working on the Lucas-produced *Star Wars* sequel *The Empire Strikes Back*, notably assisted by the great cameraman, two-time Academy Award winner Chris Menges. This was soon followed by an equally effects-heavy fantasy extravaganza, *Krull*, for British director

Peter Yates. Since the late 1980s Suschitzky has been David Cronenberg's cinematographer, creating films alternately—and often simultaneously—horrific, thrilling, philosophical, romantic, and confounding. Just a few of their more notable works include *Dead Ringers*, in which Suschitzky successfully enabled Jeremy Irons to act with himself in the same frame, playing twin gynecologists. Another is *M. Butterfly*, the story of a male spy masquerading as an actress. Portrayed by John Lone, he was romanced by an unsuspecting diplomat played by Jeremy Irons. Their work on the J. G. Ballard adaptation *Crash* pushed the boundaries of censorship, with a tale of kinky sex and vehicular mayhem. Suschitzky's notable work in the 2000s has included his two biggest hits with Cronenberg, *A History of Violence* and *Eastern Promises*. These films feature a unique sensitivity on Suschitzky's part to the textures of the distinct worlds Cronenberg is creating and an acute understanding of how his lighting and camerawork can enhance the thematic and conceptual concerns of what is frequently challenging material for an audience. In addition to his work with Cronenberg, Suschitzky has often worked on films with a fascinating visual dimension, or scope. Although not the most renowned musical biopic, Bernard Rose's *Immortal Beloved* is nonetheless one of the most visually ambitious works of that genre. Similarly, *The Public Eye* may not be so well remembered as some other films of the early 1990s, but it features immaculate color noir lighting from Suschitzky. In recent years, outside of his ongoing work with Cronenberg, Suschitzky has embraced the possibilities of 4K presentation in his work with M. Night Shyamalan on *After Earth*.

The following interview was conducted between Lindsay Coleman and Peter Suschitzky in June 2015.

Lindsay Coleman: Do you see yourself more as a technician or an artist in your work?

Peter Suschitzky: I have talked about not considering myself to be a technician and here's what I really think about that subject. . . . I am no more and no less a technician than is a director. To accomplish the task of directing really well, the director must understand the craft of directing. The director must be able to shape the film, develop the characters, and deal with 101 nuances in between, as well as understanding how much time there is to do each scene. Is the director then a technician? No, the director needs an aesthetic of his own as well as an understanding of the craft involved with directing, and a certain knowledge and sympathy for the visual side. I also need to call on my own aesthetic senses with a certain understanding and sympathy for directing, as well as of my own craft.

Cinematographers must be in command of their craft in order to be able to get to the desired goal, in every shot, every scene, but the craft, the technique, must take second place to the imagination used.

We directors of photography are often grouped together with the crowd of people called "technicians," and I think that this conveniently and unfortunately downgrades us. Do we wear white lab coats as the word "technician" would seem to demand? Do we use tools, apart from the camera? You won't see many of us wielding screwdrivers or measuring devices. In fact, I use a light meter quite sparingly, only as a guide, using my eyes and visual sensibilities first.

I resist the label "technician" because this is not what my job is about. Of course one could argue that there have been powerful films badly photographed, and of course there is a school of "let's follow the actors whatever they do and wherever they go," and occasionally a strong film may come out of this approach, but I believe that a really fine film will be bound to have its content and its style well integrated, and this includes the visuals.

A badly written novel with a strong narrative may hold your attention, but you probably won't want to visit it again. Similarly, a badly constructed and shot movie but one with a strong story may work for one viewing, but I won't want to see it again.

I never go to the cinema seeking to see beautiful cinematography. I go to see a good movie, and "good" in my book means well written, well acted, and [well] directed. To be really fine, a film needs what we do to be well done, whatever that may mean.

No, I am not a technician. My task is to react with feeling to the script and to try to form a visual style for the film. I believe that our contribution is of vital importance and can affect things other than the visual side of the film, such as the rhythm of the film. This is not technical, but it involves aesthetics and life experience, or the right instincts.

LC: What present trends in cinema would you say are troubling?

PS: I mentioned, I think, how we cinematographers can influence the rhythm of a film. We can, but of course we need to be in accord with the director on this, as far as deciding the number and type of shots in a scene.

So many directors do not seem to understand something very important, and that is that what one cannot see, or what one can only see partially because it is suggested, can be far more powerful than something very clearly visible, in close up, shoved down your throat, because the suggested leaves room for the imagination to fill in the details. Something half lit, or perhaps in long shot, or partly seen through a doorway, can be as strong as a clearly defined close-up.

Most directors want to shoot in close-up most of the time. Perhaps this habit grew up in the early days of TV when the TV sets were small, so that the directors of original work for TV felt that their work would be weak unless it was in close-up all the time, and close-ups became even closer, cropped within the head in a way which the cinema had not done before.

I dislike this kind of close-up because I maintain that first of all it is grotesque to deprive an actor of his hair, and worse with a woman, and secondly, even if in life I go very close to someone with whom I am talking, I am still aware, by my peripheral vision, of the whole head and also the surroundings.

To be able to see two actors interacting in the same shot is a rare pleasure these days because so many films are shot in close-ups by directors who feel that they prefer things this way because it allows them to control things afterward, in editing. How boring and repetitive.

LC: You have made reference to a dislike for too much camera movement. What of the opening sequence of *Gravity*, which features constant movement of the camera?

PS: That is quite different. That is meticulously thought out. I am much less in favor of improvised camera movement, where it just seems to happen for no particular reason. It is found in so many films these days, too many in my view.

LC: Do you feel that the style can be the content?

PS: Ideally the two are inseparable.

LC: Could you address your time as a documentary cameraman?

PS: I was a very impatient young man during the year or so that I shot documentaries and was very eager to get into shooting films. Thanks to great fortune I was able to do this by the time I turned twenty-two.

LC: Do you still feel impatient?

PS: You have to be very patient. We know, as cinematographers, that we are asking for things to be done which take time. But deep down I probably am still impatient. (*Laughs*)

LC: When you declined working on the first *Star Wars* due to your lack of experience with special effects, what made you eventually more comfortable by the time you came to work on *Empire Strikes Back*?

PS: Nothing really had changed. I just was very upfront about the fact that I didn't have experience in visual effects when I went for my interview with George Lucas for the first film. As it happened the studio was also uncomfortable with the idea of a relatively inexperienced director and a cinematographer without any visual effects experience working together on the film. I told them they should go with Geoffrey Unsworth and, as it happened, he was not available.

LC: Yes, but you certainly had started to develop a reputation, even at that point. When people refer to you as the Prince of Darkness, a name you began to acquire then, how do you feel?

PS: I didn't hear that label for many, many years and it's just stupid really. When I feel it is necessary to be light, I can be light, and when I feel it's necessary to be dark, I can be dark.

LC: An interesting aspect of your work are its painterly qualities. There is a very evocative shot in *Shopgirl* of Claire

Danes nude on a bed. Were you influenced by any painting for that shot?

PS: I am an avid visitor to art galleries and exhibitions thanks to my travels. I see more art than most people, but I never try to consciously imitate, or ape, or be influenced by a particular painting or painter. It's a losing game. Painting is not just about light. Lighting is all we can do in cinematography. Painting includes the touch of the brush on the paper or the canvas, and we don't have that. Subconsciously the viewer of the painting or the drawing has a sense of the amount of time that went into its creation. Ours is an instantaneous process. It's a photochemical process, as you know, or a digital, electronic process. I think it is pointless to make a scene in a film look like a painting.

LC: The night scenes in *Shopgirl* seem greenish.

PS: Do they? *Shopgirl* was the only time in my career I was not able to time the film! It was in my contract that I could, but the producers ended up in default on the contract. Damn them!

LC: In looking further at the development and aesthetics of the films you've shot, there is your work on the *Star Wars* films. Looking at all the more recent versions of *Empire Strikes Back*, are you satisfied with all of the more recent transfers?

PS: It was not in my contract. We shot the film prior to the age of DVDs. I was not consulted on the transfer to the current medium of Bluray or DVD. In most cases they've upped the contrast, made it lighter than the original was. I can't say I'm happy about it. I'm very happy otherwise, but I don't see the point in changing the contrast to the degree that they have done.

LC: Richard Edlund's work on *Empire Strikes Back* was really quite stunning, especially the starfields. How did you feel his work complemented your own?

PS: I was thrilled by the work he did! I didn't know what he was doing during the production, but when I saw the final results I thought they were brilliant!

LC: Sometimes you have had to work within tighter budgetary constraints. Working on a set standing in for Tangier on *Naked Lunch* what would you say were the pluses and minuses?

PS: I didn't see any minuses. I felt very stimulated by the script. The difficult side was perhaps doing a lot of it in a small room. That was a challenge. But I tried to make it look different from time to time.

LC: The film has a number of scenes in it where the hero is dreaming or hallucinating. Did you feel you took particular efforts in the film to distinguish scenes which might be considered fantasy from what was real?

PS: No, not really consciously. I don't like to signal changes too consciously. For example, when I have a film that features flashbacks to the past, I never want to use particular filters, or make the image go milky, to show it is the past. I don't think I did anything obvious between scenes, but there are subtle changes, I hope.

LC: Did you respond to the novel of *Naked Lunch*, by William Burroughs, or the script in how you devised to shoot the film?

PS: I only read the script. I try to avoid reading the novel when I am working on an adaptation because I don't want to know what is being missed out on in the script. The film must take on a life of its own. It will never be like the novel. It is a film.

LC: Did you have difficulty lighting the silicone models of the mugwumps, the fantastical alien creatures in the film?

PS: Yes, it was tricky. It's really about bringing the light in from the right angle. The same with the typewriter creatures.

You just have to bring out the shapes and textures as well as you can. You just use your eyes.

LC: Peter Weller was cast as RoboCop because he had a particularly narrow, angular face. What was he like to film?

PS: He was a gift. He had a particularly sculptural face. I always hope to work with a good actor. That comes first. If they happen to have a striking face, in the case of a male, a beautiful face, in the case of a female actor—whether they are twenty-five or sixty-five, it doesn't matter—then it's a big bonus.

LC: Looking at your lighting of John Lone in *M. Butterfly*, a film in which he portrays a transgender [person], how much of your brief was about emphasizing the femininity of his features?

PS: I wasn't given a brief. In attempting to make him look as feminine as possible, it was often very difficult to do, and the end result wasn't always believable. But there we are. I can't change it. There were times when I prepared a lighting setup quickly and John came in, I took David Cronenberg aside and said, "David, I'm going to have to take some more time. I'm going to have to start all over again. He doesn't look like a woman the way I've lit it." It was almost impossible to do. (*Laughs*)

LC: The films you have shot for David Cronenberg always feature very handsome, detailed design. Some cinematographers feel the production designer needs to be amenable to their work and its requirements. Do you agree with this view or take a contrary view?

PS: I don't feel adversarial at all. I feel I'm nothing without the elements in front of the camera. The same applies to my need for the actors. The designer needs to understand the camera and light, and I need to be sympathetic to them in turn. I, as cinematographer, need a good, striking, appropriate design, and the designer need a sympathetic eye, good lighting and a sense of from which angle to best show the set, in a wide shot. We are both nothing without each other. I could, if I were insensitive, ruin a good design, and a designer with little understanding of photography and light can make my job depressing.

LC: Again, going with the fascinating aesthetic requirements of your films with Cronenberg, in the film *Crash* your cinematography often features nudity set against cars and other machines. You have skin tones set against metallic surfaces. Were you shooting to favor the skin tones, or rather the metallic surfaces, or perhaps were you attempting to strike a balance between the two?

PS: My first concern is always the actor; even if I choose to light the scene with a strong color, I'm still concerned about the face of the actor. The feeling of the scene always guides me first, then the actor, then the surface dealt with in the scene.

LC: The film, in addition to depicting quite explicit sex scenes, also depicts the consequences of shocking car accidents. Yes, it is arguably quite matter-of-fact about the physical consequences of these accidents. There is a strong documentary element to Cronenberg's violence, would you agree?

PS: Yes, I would. He also knows that I find it difficult to look at violence. Some of the violent scenes in the films we've made I've had to close my eyes, quite literally, when we are shooting them. I have to believe what is happening in front of the camera is real. If I believe it is real, then it is quite painful to watch. If I don't believe it's real, then the whole film falls apart. Luckily for the films we've made together, I have always believed that the violence we are depicting is real.

LC: Do you believe in the notion of catharsis?

PS: It depends. It is certainly possible to find catharsis as a result of a film, even if it is only brief.

LC: Would you say the ending of *A History of Violence* creates catharsis? That is a film with intense violence presented for precise dramatic purpose.

PS: Yes, I would say that.

LC: What about the decision to film the attack on the lawn in front of Viggo Mortensen's house, where a goon has his nose smashed off his face, with a very wide-angle lens? It is quite confrontational.

PS: That film was shot almost entirely on the 27mm lens.

LC: So, it was just a matter of sticking with the lens and seeing what the lens would give you, depending on your shot?

PS: Yes, I prefer to move the camera—after we've completed a wide shot, or a medium shot—closer to the actor but sticking with the same lens, rather than switching to a longer lens.[1] It's a stylistic thing I prefer to do.

LC: It probably helped on *Dead Ringers* because you were filming the twin brothers with the same lens.

PS: Yes.

LC: Jeremy Irons said he would have to think about which brother he was playing in a scene or shot.

PS: Yes, once I had to remind him that he might have been playing the wrong brother in a given take. He said, "Thank you, yes, you're right."

LC: Do you discuss your lighting much with Cronenberg?

PS: No, he trusts me on the subject of lighting. We discuss the position of the camera and the kind of lens we will use.

LC: Cronenberg's *A Dangerous Method* features an intriguing scene where Jung and Freud are engaged in a dialogue on the importance of intuition. It might be judged a little dry in terms of the dialogue, how would you say you give such a scene cinematic flair?

PS: Well, to start with, there were certain issues with the set. It was an exact reproduction of Freud's study. There was a lot of glass in it, glass cabinets. I had a lot of trouble avoiding highlights and unwanted reflections. Then I went on to the artistic side of it, if I can say that, after I resolved that issue. There was also a lot of dark wood in that set. That was another hurdle I had to overcome.

LC: Looking at the bathhouse battle in *Eastern Promises*, the camera is very sympathetic to the emotional and physical violence of the scene. How is the camera in sympathy with Mortensen in that scene?

PS: That scene was unusual in that David Cronenberg felt it was necessary to shoot in all directions with minimum delays.[2] So I had to light it with that in mind. I knew we were shooting with a Steadicam. So, it's the least formal of all the scenes in the film, the most improvised. I conferred a good deal with both Cronenberg and the stunt director. That was how the scene evolved. I lit it so we would only have to make small adjustments to every angle that we shot, and we would do very long, complicated takes.

LC: I'm not quite sure of the stock you went with on *Eastern Promises*, but the immaculate set design is complemented by a very specific texture. Would you say that was a happy accident, or very much by design?

PS: I really wish I'd shot it digitally! It was probably a bit of a struggle to get it the way that I wanted it to look, and probably I only ended up getting half of the way there.

LC: Why do you think the film is so popular?

PS: Because it has a narrative. It's relatively popular in David Cronenberg's oeuvre. Nearly all of his films are far from narrative-driven. They are films of ideas more than anything else. That film has a narrative. So does *A History of Violence*. Those are the only two films I've made with David which are narratively driven, as well as by ideas.

LC: In a BBC interview, Cronenberg said that he doesn't set out to make films that are about ideas. If the idea is conveyed through the experience of watching the film, he believes that to be a side effect, as it were.

PS: He's not a storyteller, and I don't think he'll mind my saying that. I believe 99.9 percent of us want to be told a story as well as being intellectually stimulated and entertained.

LC: Do you see yourself as trying to capture ideas in your photography with Cronenberg?

PS: No, no I don't. I hope that I'm making each scene visually interesting and appropriate. The work that a cinematographer can do on a film is meaningless unless the context is a good one; in other words, the film must be a good one. Beautiful shots in a terrible film won't have any meaning.

LC: Doesn't the audience make the meaning?

PS: Not if the film's a bad one!

LC: Moving onto some of your more recent collaborators, M. Night Shyamalan has worked with some wonderful cinematographers, including Andrew Lesnie and Christopher Doyle. What do you feel is his particular visual intelligence?

PS: Well, I think it is worth noting that very few of them have worked with him again. I don't know why that is, perhaps the feeling of disappointment on the side of the cinematographer, perhaps the director wanting to move on. He didn't really speak to me very much during preproduction. If I saw him for five minutes in a week, even though we were in the same office, that was a lot.

LC: With your work on *Immortal Beloved*, do you feel you were able to innovate in any way of the visual conventions of the musical biopic?

PS: I was certainly very, very interested in the subject. Music is my first interest in life, my first pleasure. I had to see all the locations before I was able to formulate an approach. We had many, many locations on that film and rather little time to prepare them. Sometimes I felt I was lighting by the square meter. But it was largely an enjoyable film to make.

LC: Did you have any particular say on the music used in the film?

PS: No, Bernard Rose told me beforehand what he had selected for each scene. Sometimes he knew ahead who would be playing. It didn't matter, I loved them all.

LC: How did it stimulate your imagination? Did you listen to the pieces before you shot the scenes?

PS: I didn't have to. I know them all intimately. It was a tough film to make in that the director did not seem to enjoy the process of filming very much. He would only do one take, often when I felt more takes were required. But he would just move on.

LC: The final sequence of the young Beethoven floating in the lake which becomes a sea of stars was considered quite transcendent. Did you share that view?

PS: I did. I really appreciated it. I think the film has really good qualities.

LC: Going to *Krull*, there were a lot of challenges in terms of the rotoscoping on that film.[3]

PS: I suppose there were. There was a lot of it.

LC: Coming straight from *Empire Strikes Back*, was that a technique you were comfortable with?

PS: Yes, I was comfortable with it. Working with a technique like that, you want to be equally confidant in those you are working with, visual effects people. They are always present on the set and I expect a certain amount of consultation on each shot, to make sure they're happy with what we're doing. Really, that film was an unusual blend of fantasy and science fiction.

LC: Do you feel that such a blend can be tricky?

PS: In this case I don't think that they blended at all well. The makers of the film, Columbia, were undoubtedly hoping to make lots of money by putting two genres together. They didn't sit well together. Peter Yates wasn't the right sort of director for it. *Breaking Away* was a remarkably fresh and charming film. So I didn't hesitate when he offered me the job. But maybe he was not the best man for that kind of film.

LC: I feel that the approach with the swamp scenes, which would have been in a studio, a flooded studio at that, had some really amazing variation in the lighting.

PS: It was a very big job, to plan it and rig it. The only thing I really contributed to it was the idea of having two suns on the planet [where] the film is set, creatively. There are moments in *Krull* I felt happy with, other moments where I didn't feel entirely in control of what I was doing. I didn't have the knowledge or confidence I have today, so there are some scenes I was less happy with.

LC: How would you describe that confidence?

PS: It comes from knowing you've got a lot behind you and some of it has worked out quite well. I find I can be more daring, more creative than I used to be.

LC: On *Red Planet*, how much time did you spend familiarizing yourself with Coober Pedy, the location you shot in to stand in for the surface of Mars?

PS: Things changed in preproduction very violently because the director had initially wanted to shoot in Iceland, I think because he had seen photos of it. He thought it was a good stand-in for Mars. When I arrived in Sydney, people on the spot had told him there had been a lot of rain in Iceland and as a result it had become very green. He, and they, decided it would not work. They, he and the producers, were looking at a map of the world on the floor, trying to pick where to shoot. They asked me for my thoughts. They asked about Namibia, but I thought there would be issues in terms of the infrastructure of hotels, so I suggested Jordan or the Negev desert. I don't recall if we got to scout Coober Pedy as stand-in for Mars, but I remember spending a memorable month there.

LC: Finally, a debate exists on whether 4K or 3D is the best direction to go in for films. You recently shot *After Earth* in 4K capture. Do you have a particular view on this, the quest for greater resolution?

PS: I do love definition. It's best to start with the highest definition you can attain. If you want to, you can degrade it after. If you look back at TV broadcast and the use of NTSC, the quality was just ghastly, and has ruined many broadcasts.[4] You should go for the highest definition you can possibly get! 8K, 12K! The present standard is 4K, I don't know why you should shoot anything less. I shot a 4K film a few years ago, but all the effects were being rendered in 2K and you could certainly see the difference on the screen.[5] Whenever I asked the visual effects people why they were still using 2K, they told me that they couldn't afford the upgrade. It's obvious 2K is not sufficient.

~

Suschitzky clearly champions some notion of authorship on the part of the cinematographer. The motive of bringing up the greenish nights of *Shopgirl* was not to criticize Suschitzky's excellent work but to wonder at what seemed like an atypical stylistic flourish, particularly given the rest of his work on that film. His response, one of anger that his right to grade the picture was not enforced, speaks to the pride he places in delivering an image in line with what he had imagined. Suschitzky sought not to simply light his night scenes for that film, to make certain that the actors could be seen but to match the particular hue he hoped for in these scenes. Likewise, he notes the change in the contrast levels of the latest *Empire Strikes Back* transfer, clearly stating that his input was not welcome. Seemingly simple things such as the hue of night scenes—be it cobalt blue, amber, mercury or sodium vapor, tungsten—all can make a major difference in the effect of such scenes on an audience. So does the subliminal effect of a particular level of contrast. Suschitzky's words suggest his innate understanding of this and the desire to see visual work translating effectively for an audience, producing a particular mood. One might perhaps think of the half-light of dawn featured at the end of *The End of Violence*, as Viggo Mortensen's character washes the blood off himself after he has killed his own brother and his cronies. The natural ambiguity of the scene, the character's experience of both catharsis and guilt, play out equally in the specifically murky half-light of that scene.

Notes

1. The cinematographer has a number of options in going from, say, a mid-shot to a close-up of the same subject: (1) Change the lens (from e.g., a 24mm at seven feet subject distance to an 50mm focal length at the same distance). (2) Keep the same lens and move the camera closer (e.g., from a 24mm lens at a distance of seven feet to the same 24mm lens at a distance of around three feet, two inches). (3) A combination of both—say, from a 24mm lens at twelve feet to a 40mm lens at five feet, six inches. Each will result in an (approximately) equivalent subject size, but the look is very different in face shape, background size, and so on. Try it with your still camera and a zoom lens.

2. To shoot in all directions with a Steadicam means that in the course of a long involved tracking shot, the camera will record every angle visible—essentially 360 degrees. Lighting must be very carefully planned if it is not to come into shot as the camera tracks and pans around. See the tour de force Steadicam shots of *Boogie Nights* and *Goodfellas*.

3. Rotoscoping started as a technique (and device) in which individual frames of live action were outlined via projection onto tracing paper and used to create animations. It was and is very labor intensive—at twenty-four frames per second, the frames quickly mount up. The development of digital manipulation and computer graphics have streamlined and automated some of the manual labor involved. Richard Linklater's *A Scanner Darkly* makes extensive use of digital rotoscoping techniques.

4. NTSC (National Television Standard [or System] Committee) is a TV broadcast system that has been used in the United States, much of South America, Taiwan, and Japan. It suffered from some severe compromises largely due to historical factors. Its color fidelity has been criticized, and it has occasionally been referred to as "Not Twice Same Color." See also alternative analogue systems PAL and SECAM. (SECAM has been called System Exactly Contrary to the American Method since it is a French one. PAL has been called Pictures At Last.)

5. In digital capture, a 2K image is around 2,000 pixels wide (2,048 exactly) and a 4K image is around 4,000 pixels wide (4,096 exactly). The number of vertical pixels varies according to the aspect ratio. It can readily be seen that, all other factors equal, a 4K image will have more resolution than a 2K image. Perceived sharpness and resolution are not the only factors influencing the quality of an image: see especially color depth and dynamic range.

Agnès Godard

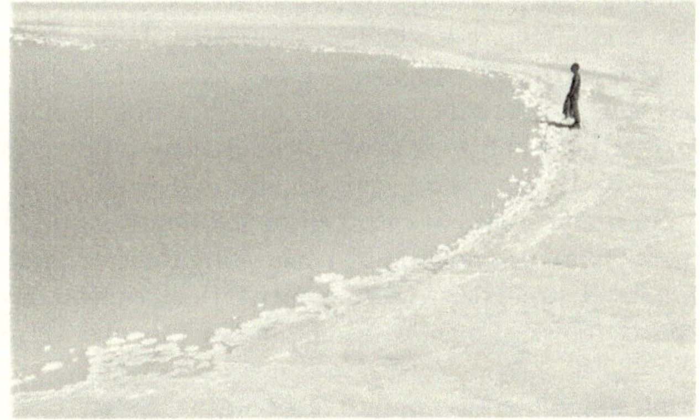

Image 10. A figure is dwarfed by the Djiboutian landscape in *Beau Travail* (Denis 1999).

Agnès Godard AFC, perhaps most famous for her decades-long collaborative relationship with Claire Denis, has achieved a consistent style of poetic naturalism over the years. Her work on the Swiss film *Sister* is subtle and evocative, but her style can be equally bold and formalist. There is as such no defining "Agnès Godard" style. Her camerawork can be limber, seemingly improvised in an era (the 1990s) when such a style was yet to be in vogue. It can also be languid and mesmerizing. As a cinematographer, Godard's great strength is her ability to carefully plan visual textures—which vary greatly from film to film—which match with a unique camera style. Sometimes this approach can lead to an intense and intimate focus on the intricacies of an actor's performance. *The Dreamlife of Angels* is a two-hander between Élodie Bouchez and Natacha Régnier, and Godard's camerawork creates the possibility of the film maintaining a balanced perspective on its two extraordinary heroines. She can equally achieve a style both intimate and epic. She is adept at capturing the natural colors and contrasts of the Djiboutian landscape in *Beau Travail* as she is at dealing with that which is nearly impossible to film well: massive snowscapes in *Sister.* In both cases, her skill is rooting intimate stories, and intimate performances, in overwhelming physical environments, her eye on the human foreground and the background of the natural world. *Beau Travail* is likely her most celebrated work, and rightly so. A nearly wordless adaptation of Herman Melville's *Billy Budd*, it features sublime images of male beauty set against a landscape that she never undersells with cheap exoticism. Her ability to judge framing and proximity to her subjects, specifically lead actors Denis Lavant and Grégoire Colin, is a major contributing factor to this film's unspoken, terrifying struggle. Yet to speak of her collaborations with Claire Denis and only mention this one film would undersell their partnership. One need only look at what would seem to be a conventional horror film, *Trouble Every Day*, and see the two working together to produce a film where scenes of cannibalism and obsession present colors and textures far more psychologically penetrating than a typical gorefest. In short, Godard's strength as a cameraperson comes from a complete commitment to the visual manifestation of a film's themes and emotions.

The following interview was conducted between Lindsay Coleman and Agnès Godard in October 2012.

> **Lindsay Coleman:** It is interesting, looking at your work, to note how you have sometimes adopted a very naturalistic approach. Do you feel the style of *Dreamlife of Angels* is a verité, observational style?
>
> **Agnès Godard:** In a sense, yes. Let's say that the style director Erick Zonca was looking [for] to translate his story could be qualified as an observational one. The script was very thick, full of psychological details. He wanted us to shoot everything, record as much as possible. I was convinced the biggest challenge for the camera was to make the characters believable. We were trying to reach the truth of the drama on every level: social, psychological, emotional. It was meant to represent a documentary truth. The budget was low. We made tests to compare 35mm and super 16mm. I was interested in 35mm for its more powerful response with a small electrical list.

But finally, super 16mm won—less expensive, no limit of film stock. In a way this choice made me happy. I knew I would have to light more. It thus became a door which opened to allow for an interpretation of the very specific atmosphere of the film. So the choice of the tools has been made for both financial and artistic reasons.

LC: How much coverage did you come up with for the film? In terms of the editing, it would certainly seem a lot.

AG: Quite a lot! Master shot, then close-up, two shot, one shot, most of the time both actresses. Everything was covered. Sometimes, I must confess, I thought it was too much coverage. But Erick was very attentive to the long dialogues and he would shoot them all. The first rough cut was very, very long, like two films.

LC: The actresses in the film, was it difficult for them to maintain their emotional intensity given all of the coverage you were shooting?

AG: For Élodie Bouchez, it was not, well I mean it was easy for her. She was very energetic. For Natasha Régnier, it was harder. She was a younger actress, meaning having less experience. Erick Zonca was working hard to get what he wanted. He was pushing her to a kind of exhausted state, trying to drive her to a border of fragility and aggression combined, revealing the difficulty the character was in, a young woman trying to find herself, her place on Earth. So the coverage I was shooting, the time and energy it took, was part of his directing. A benefit of all this material was that the editor had a lot of material to speed up the rhythm of intensity in the film.

LC: Leading up to *Dreamlife of Angels*, how did your ability to sensitively capture performance evolve? I believe your skill is akin to the synthesis of camera and subject Jean Rouch discusses in his own work.

AG: I remember having a good relationship with the two actresses. Laughing one minute with Élodie, tender the next minute with Natasha. I would say that I am always very careful to be discreet. To capture the evolution of a performance, I would work on the placement of the camera and the choice of the lens. Cinematography is definitely a lot about that in addition to lighting, of course. I would try to find the best angle of attack, if I may say so, to reveal more emotion each time, to capture the limits of each actress's limits. I had good relationships with both of them. I always wanted them to sense from me "I have seen what you've done, it's good, I do believe in you as the character of the film." You know, I need to feel the same while looking through the eyepiece. I need to believe in what I see. I do believe you look at people with your feelings as well as with your eyes and the technical tools used to shoot the film. And even knowing the rules, the grammar, the vocabulary of images, the best guide is what you feel when you look through the camera. This is what constituted most of the comments I would share, in a very low voice, with the director Erick. The quality of cinematography lies in faith somehow, faith to share with the director and the actors.

LC: Even so, your craft keeps evolving. How has your relationship changed to the camera as time has gone by?

AG: It has improved, in an intuitive way. I can shoot without rehearsal now. I feel a shiver of discovery the first time I see the action performed through my eyepiece.

LC: When you are filming, and your camera is an active participant in the scene, does it ever feel like a dream or some new kind of reality?

AG: I don't think of it as reality, but I care about the reality of my sensation. It is like a new reality, a different reality, the film's truth!! (*Laughs*)

LC: Do you feel the entirety of *Beau Travail* is captured in this state?

AG: Yes!

LC: How did you succeed in achieving this?

AG: When I first went to Djibouti, I was deeply impressed. Such a spiritual place, astonishing, like the beginning, or the end, of the world. The challenge was how do we put human beings in this powerful scenery? It has to be very, very simple. The human beings were soldiers, all men, sculptural men, beautiful men, and mysterious men. To film the beauty of human beings against this landscape became the goal. The isolation we were in while shooting was probably a great help. While we were filming, we never saw any images, not one! So, every day, we would push further and further into this other reality of the film: abstraction opposed to those deeply and strong human matters of fiction, love, hate, jealousy, betrayal, war!

LC: As a female cameraperson, do you feel your camera is looking at the men in the film as a woman would look at men?

AG: I have never thought about that! As an image-maker, I film with the idea of being a witness, so I do look the same way at both men and women. Is there a feminine specificity in the images I make? If there is, I don't know in which way. I'm looking for the "right" image. I guess the content is more charged by the singularity of each human being, leading in a wide range of the differences you can find in between two persons, differences as much noticeable between a man and a woman as between two women or two men. My hope is to find images fitting the film, which carry a sense and exist beyond questions of identity.

I'd like to think about differences related to the supreme variety of human beings, men and women included, which is enjoyable . . .

LC: Do you feel silent cinema is an influence on you? I certainly see it in sections of *Beau Travail.*

AG: Yes, silence sometimes says more than words. When the actors are far away from the camera, I don't put my headphones on. I want to see if the choreography of the scene means something, independent of words. I remember my feelings when I first saw the silent film *The Wind*, by Viktor Sjöström. Such a noisy film, I was amazed, even though it is of course a silent film. The ability of images can be so strong, and this film is really noisy!

You can hear the sound of the wind during the whole film without any sound!

LC: When you are filming characters, do you like or hate them?

AG: I do love them, I do hate them.

LC: Do you hate the Denis Lavant character in *Beau Travail*?

AG: I can't, I would say I care for him! He is so convincing. That's a main thing, to be convinced! Something must be imposed upon you.

LC: Other cinematographers have spoken to me of this, so I must ask if you have ever been unhappy with your work?

AG: Oh yes! (*Laughs*) With my own work first. The doubt is a companion of work. I will try to find out if I am the only one who is unhappy. I'm very passionate, I'll keep asking questions, striving for a solution, probably much more than I would in my own private life.

LC: So you are passionate in your work, but in your life less so.

AG: (*Laughs*) You see I'm very passionate! Cinema is a part of my life, but life is another kind of story! It lasts more than two months, and you don't know the end of the script.

LC: Looking at *Trouble Every Day*, another film you made with Claire Denis, these are the images of a nightmare. How do you feel about creating such images? It really is an overt horror film.

AG: I was very attracted to find those images. I would say it was less creating horrific images than suggesting something beyond understanding. It really goes back to the power of human face. I think sometimes the simplest images are the best, if they contain what they should contain. When images are resonant they are simple, and to approach that simplicity, it takes a while. This is why silent cinema can be very inspiring. It is all about imagination.

How people use their imagination. As a matter of fact I remember, while looking through the camera, during the cannibalism scene, that it was a "love scene"!

LC: Do you feel everyone uses their imagination when they see a film, and therefore everyone sees a different film?

AG: Probably. That's the chance, or risk, when you do films. They are abandoned to the secret of each one. Let me add: if a film is teasing your imagination, it's a good film!

LC: When you were operating on *Paris, Texas*, what were you learning from people such as Robby Müller?

AG: On *Paris, Texas* I was a focus puller, not camera operator. Robby was operating.

I learned a lot from him. Even though I was very busy with my own job, I spent time watching him handling the camera. I was astonished by the way he was choosing the lens, the framing, the simple way he was moving the camera as if he had no camera in his hands and the perfect harmony he was in with Wim Wenders, the director. I also noticed how well it was working with the new (at that time) kind of fluorescent lights. It was a totally different way of working compared to the other DPs I worked with before. They were older, from another period, if I can say so. When you are in front of an Alberto Giacometti sculpture, it is so impressive it drives you right away from the desire to grow up. I felt the same way beside Sacha Vierny and Henri Alekan, with the additional sensation of having found "fathers," wondering how I would be able to reach this level of knowledge. With Wim Wenders and Robby, as opposed to father's time, I felt I was reaching another time, the present through their contemporary knowledge and work. They introduce me in my time, in a sense.

LC: Do you feel now that you are the mentor, as they were?

AG: No, I don't. To me each film is a new adventure, something to discover, to experience, to learn still. So in a paradoxical way, I feel the same I felt earlier, even getting older. I want to keep away from me the idea of having knowledge because I think it is "dangerous." Research is the stuff of life. I'm sure all the DPs I mentioned probably shared this idea, but I did not know, I was looking at them as a child, wondering about the future, shy to enter it.

LC: Speaking of relationships, how would you describe your relationship with your main collaborator, director Claire Denis?

AG: We've known each other for thirty years. We spent a lot of time, side by side, working on fifteen films. It is quite rare to have such a continuity. Everything is around cinema. We know each other, but we don't speak that much about our private life. We carry on exchanges about scripts, films, books, etc., etc., but in other respects there is a little distance, reserve. We are close around one thing: cinema. Its a "rencontre" of cinema.

LC: You have captured so much beauty, male and female. In *Sister* you worked with Léa Seydoux, who is an unusual beauty. How do you go about capturing that unusual, striking attractiveness?

AG: Nothing special but let myself to be attracted, there was no defense possible!

The film, the drama, the character is a quite unusual casting for her. My effort was concentrated on making believable that she was part of this world. She was tired quite often, because she was working on another film in the States, and also very much involved in the character. She believed the title character, in *Sister*, was very, very tough, very unsympathetic. So sometimes, her suffering was printed on her face while she was entering into this broken and sad part: it would affect her appearance.

I decided not to fight against that with the light or the frame. In other words, I was trying to let her be affected by this hostile environment. But it was not working that well!

Her beauty, her youth, were indestructible. So I let her be beautiful, even kind of "helped!" From time to time, the dark and fragile part of her would raise up, emerge from her far hidden inside. We call this, *en français*, *photogénie*." It is mysterious. It is a part of the mystery of cinema.

LC: What of Grégoire Colin, who has also a very distinctive appearance? What is the relationship of the camera with Grégoire Colin?

AG: I don't feel I had a special way with him, more than with other actors. Gregoire is a singular beauty, he has a special face, a lot of charisma, sex appeal. I just look at him, frankly. In other words, I open myself up to how mysterious he is.

LC: Does a camera see a person's personality?

AG: That's what a camera should try to do all the time!

LC: So is he trying to hide from the camera?

AG: It's very funny with him. He's able to stand in front of the camera, offering all I was describing before. And then, after a while, he sort of . . . stops! It's really strange. As if he's embarrassed to offer himself like that, or as if he says, like a kid, smiling, "Stop, I'm not playing anymore!" So better be fast to capture this moment of abandon before he quits! (*Laughs*)

LC: What about Denis Lavant?

AG: Denis Lavant does not have a narcissistic relationship with a camera, so you can take everything you want! He lets you do it! He wants you to do that. As a normal thing.

LC: Is he open, or is this more exhibitionistic?

AG: He is not exhibitionistic. He is open all the time. He's working, and this work is a gigantic pleasure for him; the rhythm of his work seems to be the rhythm of his existence.

LC: Many times he is a lover in films, of both men and women. How does he reveal his love to the camera?

AG: Denis Lavant is a generous person, very honest, very involved. He is also very proud and simple. Difficult to answer that question. He manages to bring the undefinable impression that his mind and his body make one.

LC: So this is the reality the camera can capture.

AG: It is a wish, the wish: the camera to succeed in showing the essence of existence, of the extraordinary thing of being alive. Denis does that with his whole body, very simply, leaving you alone, speechless. Do you see it also?

LC: Yes, I think I have seen that many times in Denis Lavant's performances. I think you just articulated what he does amazingly.

~

Godard demonstrated a vibrant emotional commitment to her role as a storyteller with her camera, as well as to her duty in capturing the essence of the performers with whom she worked, often perceiving the elements of each actor's personality that contributed so essentially to their performance. This suggests immense sensitivity and the degree to which the personality, the emotional intelligence, of the cinematographer may play an essential a role in their successful image-making. Another important aspect of this interview is Godard's description of her relationship with Denis. Too often the work of artists in collaboration is seen in mystical terms, their souls seemingly melded through their partnership. Admittedly, creative partnerships are frequently intense, but what Godard describes is a long-term professional relationship of great productivity and emotional depth, one that nonetheless has not translated into much of a personal friendship. Intriguingly, this is seemingly a common part of the director–cinematographer relationship. Despite decades collaborating to create sublime films, Ingmar Bergman and Sven Nykvist met very rarely in their personal lives. This ability to connect, intellectually and emotionally, on films such as *Trouble Every Day* and *Beau Travail*, says much for the uniqueness of the professional and artistic bond between director and cinematographer.

Dean Cundey

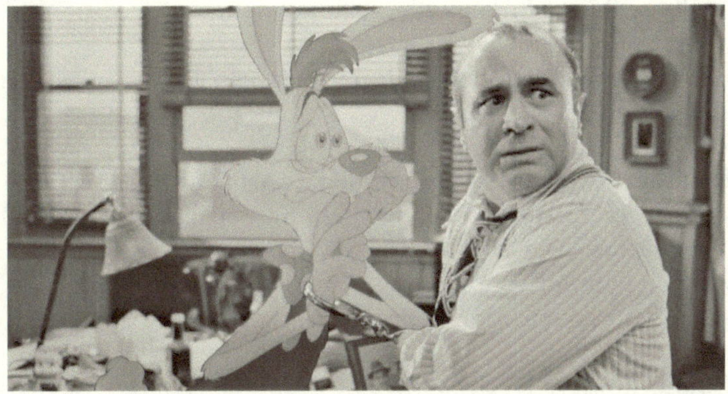

Image 11. Roger Rabbit and Eddie Valiant are in big trouble in *Who Framed Roger Rabbit* (Zemeckis 1988).

Dean Cundey ASC has filmed some of the most popular, entertaining, and technically impressive films of the past forty years: *Halloween*, *The Thing*, *Back to the Future*, *Who Framed Roger Rabbit*, and *Jurassic Park*. A former member of the ASC board, he has taught cinematography and presently stands as one of the major elder statesman in the field of cinematography today. What makes Cundey's work so special is his ongoing commitment to two notions: that commercial Hollywood cinema produces the kinds of stories he wants to tell and has always wanted to tell, and that these stories can be presented with beautiful images and with a degree of technical excellence. His photography in *Halloween* uses blank suburbia as a perfect stalking ground for killer Michael Myers. In his daylight photography for the film, the camera unnervingly trails the heroine. In the fateful night depicted in the film, there are numerous sequences where Cundey lights and frames for the maximum experience of mood and terror, every shadow potentially hiding the killer. Conversely, in a film like *The Fog*, terror and death are to be found in a nebulous cloudy mass, the glaring, thick medium of the fog equally unnerving for the audience. His crowning technical and artistic achievements are likely *Who Framed Roger Rabbit* and *Jurassic Park*. The former features a camera animated by the same sensibility as its manic title character. The latter was a great watershed moment of digital effects, the first time the public became widely aware of the potential of photorealistic digital characters to exist in a frame with actors. All told, much of Cundey's work has passed into the visual shorthand found in big, visually striking blockbusters of Hollywood.

The following interview was conducted between Lindsay Coleman and Dean Cundey in May 2015.

Lindsay Coleman: You have made so many films, with so many major Hollywood directors. In the collaborative process, if you feel your lighting needs to take precedence in a situation, will you fight for your lighting? Or do you compromise? How would you say envision your role as the cinematographer?

Dean Cundey: It's always about the right compromise. My purpose is to serve the vision of the director and the storyteller. Usually you get a sense of what is right for a particular shot to tell a story, how to capture what the director wants. There's always some compromise. If I can't talk a director into something, or talk him through a decision which I feel is better—and a lot of time directors I have worked with are willing to listen and to understand where I am coming from in a suggestion—a lot of the fun and the challenge of filmmaking is in the collaborative process.

LC: Let's talk about a major film you worked on with John Carpenter, a film you shot which has since become notorious for all of the right reasons: *The Thing*. It presented many technical challenges, not the least of which was shooting in real snow, as far as the eye could see. What was your experience shooting in snow with *The Thing*?

DC: Snow was a concern on *The Thing*. Snow, when lit by the sun, can have a little bit of texture. You see highlights, shadow, and so forth. When the light is overcast, the texture kind of disappears. It becomes just a white shape. The concern was how to keep the texture. One of the things I did was to take neutral-density grad filters, glass filters darker along the top.[1] They are usually used for darkening a sky. Bringing out the blue and clouds. I turned them upside down. I used the filters to darken the snow at the bottom of the frame. That kept the presence of the snow from being a white sort of shape. It kept a lot of the texture also.

LC: Did you use actual flame bars on *The Thing*? I ask because you often seem to be lighting the action with flame, and the look is memorable.

DC: We used all kinds of fire. Some of it was chemical. A lot of it flame bars and propane, because it's safe and controllable. I just watched *The Thing* two or three nights ago. I reminisced my way through it. I was struck by the fact that we used dimmers with colored gels to provide flickering in the background,[2] but a great deal of the lighting was done by flame bars, containers with chemical fuel. Also, the red flares which the characters hold for the ice tunnel sequence and outside in the cold and at various other times of course represented lighting with a kind of flame.

LC: Did you feel at all nervous about taking that approach, lighting just with the flares?

DC: I did some testing beforehand. I thought the flares would give a very low tech, but dramatic, source of light. I think we had about two or three different kinds. We did tests and I liked the ones we chose. They are basically road flares that people put out during an accident. So as a result, that was the choice. I knew that at a certain distance from the actor's head, it would produce the right amount of exposure. It turned out to be a comfortable distance from the head. If it was too close, it was too hot and sputtery. I think it was a unique way to make these guys deal with their environment in a very visual way. The color was extremely vivid, very pure. The brightness, the smoke, the sputtering made it a lighting device which was very unpredictable, very unconventional. If we wanted to do that now it would be almost impossible. OSHA, Health and Safety, the Fire Department, everybody gets involved. To say we want to light a movie with these dangerous pyro devices, as they would be viewed now, would have been impossible. I don't know how we would have got permission now.

LC: Do you feel your use of flares was influential?

DC: I'd like to think that the mark I left in film history was that sometimes characters carry flares. I don't know. We're so used to always looking for something new and unusual in visual storytelling that I may have missed some low-budget film in the '50s that used flares, and that cinematographer could claim that he was the originator of the technique. I sort of rediscovered it. I am sure we are always rediscovering one another's secrets.

LC: The final shots of the film are really devastating. Looking at them, I would guess you slightly underexposed the final scene.

DC: Yes, you always adapt the lighting and exposure all of that stuff to what should each scene visually tell you about the story and the mood. In that scene, all that is left is fire, and themselves, and the building burning. Everything else is gone.

LC: It's interesting, critics have speculated on the meaning of that final scene. Many have said it is the ultimate statement of pessimism or nihilism. What were your thoughts on the tone of the final scene?

DC: We had a discussion, John Carpenter, myself, and the crew. What was the ending? Who was the Thing? Was it Childs, or Kurt [Russell]'s character? I don't think we ever came up with it. John wasn't saying. He said "maybe neither of them." Maybe they killed it, and their paranoia is going to finish them off. Rather than finding some way to escape, they are just going to wait there and see what happens. It was an ambiguous ending. It differentiates the film. But it is also a reason why people say it was not successful at the time of its release. People wanted to know what happened. It didn't have all of the tying up that we tend to like in a film.

LC: It's an interesting question that the scene is what makes the film great, but that scene alone may have been responsible for producing a chill in audiences, which they rebelled against. It may have been a contributing factor to problematic feelings toward the film at the time.

DC: I sort of feel that way. As we were finishing up and going home there was a lot of speculation as to the ending, and indeed whether people would respond well to the film. We also wondered, what was the sequel? Did the military come and rescue them? Did they take them back to some military base? Was one of them the Thing? Did it get loose in the army base and create the sequel? We had various scenarios going. What that meant was that nobody had a clear-cut story they could create a sequel with because the ending was so ambiguous.

LC: Looking at Rob Bottin's designs in *The Thing*, they are quite explicit and graphic. There is nothing cuddly about his creature designs. Sometimes your lighting of the creature is very stylized. How did you balance out your horror stylization with more naturalistic aspects of the film?

DC: Rob and I had discussions early on. He had made a test sculpture. He felt if you flat light one of the creatures, it would lack some of the mystique and mystery. It would become a piece of sculpted plastic or rubber. It was a very careful technique of finding those parts of the sculpture which were the most interesting, looking for the weaker areas where the cast line of the mold was. It was necessary to let some of the creature go into darkness so that there was something to imagine. A lot of it was the fact that the whole thing was kept very wet-looking. It was always glistening, and always looked as though it had come from within your body, which of course it did. So it was a very careful balance of what to light, what not light, knowing ahead of time what was going to be necessary—for the dog transformation sequence, and the surgical sequence—how to establish the lighting style or technique in advance, so it didn't become suddenly unusual lighting just because the creature was there. That would of course tip the audience off to its presence and ruin the scare.

LC: What about the scenes with the flamethrowers, how tricky was it avoiding everything whiting out?[3] To some degree, that is the opposite of the more dimly lit scenes, with a bright light and flame exploding onto the screen.

DC: You develop an eye, knowing your exposure range, and determine what the film will capture. I say that part of a thing like that is knowing that the flame, and other areas, may burn out and become overexposed, and other areas less so. Some bits in between are exactly what you want to see. So it's a case of knowing, in the case of the flamethrower, where to shoot it, how long, and so on. That way the area of the frame you want properly exposed is in the range of exposure for the flamethrower. One of the things I look back on with *The Thing* was the fact that we used so much real fire. As a justifiable source of lighting.

LC: Didn't you worry about the model at any point?

DC: I think we protected them, except for the crawling head in the surgery scene.

LC: That's what I was thinking about. I am sure that it was an expensive model.

DC: Sometimes you have to sacrifice for art.

LC: *Apollo 13* was one of the first realistic, naturalistic-looking films to be set in space. How did you envision lighting for the interior and exterior of the space capsule?

DC: There's a certain logic to lighting for space. There's one light source, the sun, bounce from the Earth. The rest is all dark. We as an audience know about this because we've seen real footage from space. There an obligation to do what might not have been done in the '50s or '60s, which was lighting as we imagined space. The interiors of spaceships of '40s and '50s were all brightly lit by cameramen as if they were lighting a room. We've now become more sensitized to the reality of these situations, especially because we know audiences have seen that reality in photographs and filmed footage from space. We wanted to represent that experience as realistically as possible.

LC: How did you approach the use of fill light inside the capsule? The console is lighting itself up, but you also need to really get a good sense of fill light.

DC: When we look at actual footage from space capsules, you realize that what they're relying on is the light in the capsule environment. That's always a very carefully balanced thing because they only have so much power which they can use. It was a case of analyzing that look. We lit the capsule only with the lights that were in it. I had them add a couple of small lights. Then we would pick out areas. I had them add fiber-optic instruments, two or three of them. They were long, fiber-optic cables, with a little lens on the end. They also had a low-voltage light source. This allowed us to create a very bright, but very directional light source. We would poke that through the console, and use it to light a bit of the dark area behind them, or bring out a face, or whatever. So much of the lighting was done within the capsule through the reality of the units. Very rarely did we add any additional lighting. It was all preplanned.

LC: A plot point is the very low voltage they were working off. How did you go about capturing that in your lighting? Naturally, you would have to show that they were using fewer lights in the capsule.

DC: What they did is they shut down all of their lights. The light which was evident came through the windows from the sun. And the light reflected off the earth. So it was a case of building a crane arm with a lighting unit on the end, a rock and roll automated light which you could aim. It was essentially a mirror which reflected very bright light. So by moving the crane arm past the window, you could keep the light aimed in the window. That became a light source, especially in those scenes where the light had been shut down due to their needing to save power in the capsule. Most of the lighting was justified by light coming through the windows. Soft light coming from the Earth side, and bright light coming from the sun side of the capsule as it rotated. The sun was always a moving light source which came through the windows. The capsule rolled, and the light coming through seemed to move, but of course it's really relative to being inside and the capsule moving.

LC: How did you choose to orient the camera for the scenes in Mission Control? How did you pick your angles for this set?

DC: Well, Mission Control, when it was built and Ron Howard and I went to look at it, had all of the various levels and steps with monitors on them. I was concerned that it would limit where we could put the camera. I thought a crane and a remote head would be ideal in that type of environment. The camera could float anywhere we wanted. Ron had never used one before. It became so effective it was the tool we used 80 percent of the time. It gave us a tremendous amount of versatility in terms of where to put the camera. It also became a way to move the camera in an interesting way.

LC: Something interesting came through in your article on *Jurassic Park* in *American Cinematographer*. You were taking a nonintrusive approach in your cinematography and lighting because you wanted to create more of a showcase for the visual effects. Would that be correct?

DC: It sort of goes to my idea that any time you are getting the audience to believe something unbelievable, you need to give them as much believable visual material as you can. We all know the rules of physics. We've seen things explode in the news. It's what Walt Disney called the plausibly impossible. How do you make the impossible plausible? *Jurassic Park* was that. Here's something completely new and different. Yes, we've seen dinosaurs before. But it was always the case that we felt we were being told a story because they did not look absolutely real.

LC: Stop-motion movement is quite limited. That, of course, was the technique used to present dinosaurs before *Jurassic Park*.

DC: Yes, and it was stuttery because they hadn't figured out how to create motion blur.[4] People were used to seeing that. How could you convince people that they were seeing real dinosaurs? To do that, you had to follow the rules the world is run by. In movies, there are certain artifacts, motion blur and so on, which we are used to. So I think the obligation is always to ask, how do we get them to believe the impossible? Get them to say, yes this is an image captured on film, but it seems to be capturing something which is *real*!

LC: The same would have applied to *Roger Rabbit*, where you would have needed to determine the effect a particular lens would have on a cartoon being filmed in the real world of the film.

DC: Subconsciously, the audience understands artifacts of a wide lens as opposed to a telephoto lens.[5] We've created a grammar around that. How to tell the story for dynamic action, or a romantic scene which is out of focus in the background.

LC: Like the kissing scene in *Notorious*.

DC: Exactly. In *Roger Rabbit* we always said, if Roger Rabbit was there in the scene, an actor in the scene, how would you shoot the scene? The Disney company told us the opposite. They said, always shoot your scenes with a nice wide frame so that the animator can move the character around in the frame. Don't pan the camera or tilt it. We had a series of rules we'd been given. We said, "Those are rules of convenience, not necessarily what the requirements are for the storytelling." The audience needs to believe in the characters, so let's treat it as though they are real performers. We can tilt, pan, dolly, and so on. We made the choice about what the shot required.

LC: There's a shot in the film where Roger is in the background and is out of focus. This always struck me as remarkable as he was literally animated to be out of focus. It makes him seem very real in the world of the film.

DC: That's become now more commonplace with the use of computers in animation. It is not necessarily something the audience understands, but they just know that sometimes things are out of focus. They just know that that is how things are in a film.

LC: Highlights and shading for the cartoon characters were provided in their rendering, giving them dimensionality. Did you give visual effects supervisor Ken Ralston much advice on how to light them when he was adding his visual effects to your plates?

DC: Prior to *Roger Rabbit*, as we were told by Disney, because the characters are painted on acetate cells, they become flat surfaces, flat areas. Looking at other films, with minor exceptions of their walking in and out of shadows, characters were always lit flat. It was something we accepted in cartoons. They weren't real, they were moving paintings. Disney said "make sure your lighting is very even," which meant "flat." One of things Ken and director Bob Zemeckis decided was that they needed to create dimensionality. They created this very labor-intensive process of creating light and shadows on the character. It was a very meticulous process which gave a sense of dimensionality in the real world. After that, everybody had to do it and now it is just standard in 3D computer animation. It was the first time on *Roger Rabbit.*

LC: The color grade on *Roger Rabbit* was quite a challenge for you. You had, on your final print, so many layers rotoscoped and scanned in. They all had to balance with one another, in terms of how you went about tweaking the image.

DC: It was. We were dealing with multiple layers on a frame. There was the background plate with the live-action actors. You might do a particular grade on that. But then there were all of the other layers which were added by the animation process. The compositing was done in optical printers,[6] not in computers as it is done now. Now you have a great deal of control over each layer.[7] In those days you would expose the background layer, then the next layer, then the layer on top of that. Sometimes, there would be fifteen to twenty passes of a single piece of film through an optical printer to get all of the layers and components and parts onto a frame. There's always a chance that one of those layers, once the color is adjusted, will be wrong for the background plate or the lighting style of a particular shot. White, as Roger is, is the first color which shows variation. In other words, if it is slightly yellow, or slightly green, you can immediately tell. It'll show up so much faster than skin tones. They did such a brilliant job of keeping Roger white and not changing the backgrounds. I look with great pride at how well that went together, and how much work on the background plates is so well represented without being altered to serve any needs or decisions after the fact.

LC: That seemed like one of the most challenging parts of your work on *Roger Rabbit.*

DC: I think so. We approached the live action component like you would a live action movie. How would you light a set? Which colors of light would you use, how much light and shadow should you set up? That was the main interest when we did it. What happened after that was that the animators were so brilliant to tie the animation to the live action.

LC: What was the main pioneering aspect of motion control on *Roger Rabbit*?[8] It is certainly one of the most significant aspects of that film's cinematography.

DC: Previous to *Roger Rabbit*, motion control was an industrial robot arm which weighed hundreds of pounds, was physically large, and took a long time to program the movement. I remember working motion control on various movies and they'd say, "So much for the dialogue, here comes the motion control shot!" They'd march in with white gloves. There'd be this giant machine they'd taken one whole day to set up and level and program. A one-day thing to do one shot. We said, "There has to be a better way." Working with ILM we developed a very simple motion control dolly, the VistaGlide they dubbed it. It was the panther dolly, which had motors in it, but they put feedback controls in. What it boiled down to was that we could take this dolly, set it on some track, and we could program it very quickly to do whatever shot we wanted. It would do the same as any regular dolly, but it would also repeat.[9] We would set up conventional shots very quickly, using the same lighting, and it was just another shot that was done by us in the camera department, as opposed to being handed off to somebody. As a result, there were a lot of times we would shoot a shot with the device, and then with a clean background plate, so that they could remove a puppeteer. On *Back to the Future II* and *III* we used it also. In the dinner scene in *Back to the Future II* where Michael J. Fox is playing all of the different characters in the one shot, it was feasible for us to do it ourselves just as we would have shot a shot, as opposed to bringing in other outsiders, specialists you might say.

LC: What was the evolution between *Roger Rabbit* and *Casper* do you feel? I ask because this later film, as well as *Looney Tunes: Back in Action*, features extensive interaction of the leads with animated characters.

DC: *Casper* was on the cusp of being able to use the computer a little. On *Roger Rabbit* I had inquired of the studio whether we could use a computer on set in addition to a wireframe rabbit so that we could look and kind of define how the shot would be done. We ended up going very low-tech with possible rubber versions of the cartoon characters. *Casper* was the same. We had the same technology. We would shoot a shot with the rubber figure so that the animators could know the intention of our shot with its particular staging. They had started to develop the ability to do some compositing in computers. I asked that we use a down-shooter—which is a video camera mounted on top of an animator's table—and we can double-expose the image from that onto our video assist. The animator would come in and draw the shape of Casper and it would be superimposed. We would use that for the line-up. Then he would draw where *Casper* would end up and the stages in between. It became evident that as we would shoot it, he would do poses and animation to the real footage. Then he would show it to the other animators and show what Casper was meant to be doing in the shot, and they would have a composite black and white of the animation on top of the live action. That became so useful that we set up two, then three of them. These guys would be animating as we were shooting. Then there would exist a pretty good outline of the requirements of a given shot, which provided the necessary reference for the animators later.

LC: Your camera moves are faster and more complicated on *Casper* than *Roger Rabbit.*

DC: Yes, with the new techniques we developed on *Roger*, and the confidence and experience we gained, it became clear that there was a lot more we could do with the camera. As with anything in this business, it becomes an evolution. Always questing for something which hasn't been done before, some kind of storytelling which is new and unique.

LC: Around that time, even with these successes, there was also some criticism you faced. Film critics felt that the Neverland sets on *Hook* were overlit. How did you feel about that feedback at the time?

DC: Originally, the thought was that the film would be shot on a Caribbean island. As Steven Spielberg, the director, wrote and conceived the film, he said he wanted it more theatrical. There are two sections to the film. There is the reality London stuff, the beginning and ending. I took a much more realistic approach to that. Then, when we were doing research, watching sequences of films in Steven's screening room, one of the things we realized is that much of Neverland would best be shot on stages to achieve the look and feel we were going for. In the past, we noticed that when shooting in studios and when daylight was being replicated, the temptation was always to make the contrast ratio between sun and shadow perfect. Even back in the '40s and '50s when shooting day exteriors in studios they would say, "We don't want that too dark, we can't overexpose that." If you go outside of the studio with film there is a big range of contrast, and quite often there are these anomalies. Some part of sunlight is overexposed, and the shadows are darker than in the background. Those are the cues that let an audience know they are not in a studio. Steven said, "Let's be sure that it's not perfect." One thing we noticed in John Alcott's work on *Greystoke: The Legend of Tarzan* was the use of hot backlight in the jungle scenes they had filmed in the studio. Steven wanted to diffuse it a little bit as well also, so it had that fantasy feel. We chose filters, paired with hot backlights, so as a result there was a look achieved somewhere between reality and theatricality. Steven really liked the look of that.

LC: Something which has always intrigued me is the incredible visual stimulation which can be created from seeing something entirely new: a unique camera move, a new style of film processing, and so on. Looking back at your career it is fascinating so see how often you did that, be it *Roger Rabbit* or *Jurassic Park*!

DC: Well, that is one of the things in recent filmmaking, because we have the DI, because we use computers, which has been found more and more. It gives us a great deal more color palette, contrast, desaturation, other looks which weren't possible in the beginning. When I was first beginning, everything had to be done in front of the lens. As far as contrast and lighting, colors of lights. In the final making of the print you'd take the film you'd exposed, and you'd have a minimal amount of control. Three colors, up and down, that would give you brightness and darkness, and a certain range of color you could come up with. Now the only limits are the imagination and the skill of the guys operating the equipment. So, I think it's a very handy tool. You have to be careful not to just use it for its own sake. I think a lot of special effects are now done just because they can be. I think there are a lot of sequences in the latest *King Kong* that just went on and on. You become desensitized to it. It's about a technique being used correctly, in context. Think of the use of cinematography, and the DI, to evoke Kodachrome in *The Girl with the Dragon Tattoo*. That was a case of recognizing that the audience associated footage of things from the past with the Kodachrome look because that is what it was captured on. Then you have a flashback set perhaps thirty or forty years in the past captured in that manner. So it makes sense to create that particular look.

LC: Given the number of incredibly popular films you have made, it might be interesting to ask what are your influences? Hollywood, or the avant garde?

DC: More Hollywood films. I grew up with Hollywood films and cartoons. That's what I've been immersed in. How to tell a story to an audience and what kind of stories do they like and appreciate. I follow the mainstream end and work in that area.

LC: In *Looney Toons: Back in Action*, there is a scene at the Louvre where Daffy and Bugs are jumping from one painting to another and actually jumping inside the action of each painting. If you love animation, that is true heaven. How do you feel about such iconic pop moments?

DC: I think what drew me into film was that we can take an audience on a journey which they can't go on in real life. How do you make memorable experiences of such stories? I think one of my great satisfactions is that so many of my films have achieved exactly that. They have taken people somewhere they haven't been, even in film. Or they've taken then to a familiar film place, but it is funnier, or more exciting, than it had otherwise been typically. My satisfaction is wanting to do that from when I was twelve at the Saturday matinees and having accomplished that so often in the films I've been part of.

LC: How do you feel about being part of such a major mythical legacy?

DC: Again, the fun of what we do is being able to create these impossible worlds and get the audience to accept them. The great characters—Bugs Bunny, Daffy Duck, Luke Skywalker, Darth Vader—touch something in us which we recognize, or would like to be able to do, or recognize in other people. We attach this humanity to all of these characters who frankly don't exist.

LC: Daffy Duck never lived.

DC: No, he didn't. You go into a dark room with a white wall and shine these colored shadows onto it. Yet somehow you buy into it. Usually willingly. You accept that Daffy is that way, that Vader is that evil, yet you are only looking at colored shadows.

~

In terms of visual storytelling, there is a need for a film's cinematography to support a growth or change in the art of cinematography in general. Such films inevitably become touchstones, and in turn represent a turning point in the expressive capability of cinematography as a medium. *Roger Rabbit* was such a film. The concept of the film required the audience to believe that cartoons and humans could interact. This was part of the film's plot; however, if this concept has not been sold visually, the film and its effects may well have failed. For this to be achieved, Cundey was in a position where he was required to bend or subvert the existing rules for integrating cartoon characters and actors. Such sequences had existed for decades, yet never in the context of cartoon being believably integrated into the real world. In *Mary Poppins*, for instance, Dick Van Dyke dances with and interacts with cartoon penguins. This part of the film is definitely a fantasy and is signposted as such by the filmmakers. The audience is charmed by the interaction, but has no expectations that it follow the rules for physics, or the required dimensionality of real-world interactions between moving, living things. The cinematography had to evolve on established norms for such scenes.

Cundey speaks to the need for coordination between the cinematography department and other departments in large Hollywood productions. By way of contrast, Agnès Godard's famed cinematography in *Beau Travail* provides an obvious showcase for her gifts, melding actors and landscape together through her viewfinder, where Cundey's work on *Casper* and *Roger Rabbit* required a three-way collaboration between his lighting, framing, and camera movements; the efforts of the animators; and the layering of visual effects provided by Ken Ralston and his department. The success of any one of these layers of the image depended on close collaboration between departments and Cundey's ability to have a close understanding of effects and animation, in addition to his work relating to the camera.

Notes

1. Graduated neutral-density filters are rectangular or square glass filters in which about half the area has been made darker and the other half remains clear glass, with a graduated area between the two where the density change occurs. Such a filter is placed in front of the lens and adjusted up or down to selectively darken part of the image. They are often used to darken the sky area of an exterior, which may otherwise be too bright to record correctly. They can be rotated to give an angled grad line if required. In the digital age, they have proved particularly useful in darkening areas that would be too overexposed, resulting in "clipping."

2. Dimmers are electronic controls used to adjust the brightness of individual or multiple lamps. They can be adjusted manually to mimic the flickering effect of fire or candlelight, and specialized flicker versions can provide an automated random flicker effect. Colored gels are sheets or rolls of colored plastic or polycarbonate material, which can be cut to shape and placed in front of light sources to alter the color of the light. A neutral-colored lamp can thus provide the warm gold, yellow, or amber color characteristic of firelight, sunset, candle flame, and so on.

3. The human eye can discern a much greater range of light—from the darkest tone to the lightest tone (i.e., the dynamic range)—than can film or digital recording. Particular care in lighting and knowledge of the range of a particular film stock or digital camera sensor are necessary if one part of the frame is not to be overexposed beyond the capacity of the recording medium to reproduce.

4. Since the 1930s and the introduction of sound, films have traditionally been shot at twenty-four frames per second (fps). The shutter speed that resulted was around one forty-eighth of a second. At this shutter speed, there is still considerable "motion blur" in each frame—we don't consciously perceive it much as the film is projected, but we are aware of it on a nonconscious level—and we have come to accept it as part of the experience. In stop motion, where each frame is recorded as a locked-off motionless shot (see Kong's movements in the 1933 version of *King Kong*), there is no motion blur and we perceive the slightly juddering motion as not quite real.

5. A wide-angle lens creates a different perspective, a different depth of field, and reveals more background than a long lens shot of a subject at a particular distance from the lens. The film audience may not have any idea of the focal

length of a lens, but it knows that a long lens shot of Lawrence of Arabia in the desert has a completely different feel to a close-up of Amélie on a wide angle.

6. Optical printers were used to rephotograph film images by projecting them on to a separate negative roll using mattes to limit the exposed area on the negative. Various layers could thus be built up by using several passes and holdout mattes.

7. Digital compositing does not result in any image degradation through successive generations (unlike the analogue process of the optical printer and film), and the registration and alignment issues of the analogue system do not apply.

8. In motion control, the camera, on a motorized dolly or crane, is linked to a computer so that all aspects of its operation can be repeated as many times as necessary. Panning, tilting, tracking, frame rate, and so on are all controlled. Separate passes can be recorded or filmed so that different elements are created. In their initial forms, these massive machines were operated by highly specialized teams, were highly complex, and were very likely to break down.

9. The panther is a normal and relatively lightweight dolly made in Germany. The fact that it could with some modification achieve similar motion control work as its prototype predecessors illustrates the huge strides that ILM was making in this field.

Rodrigo Prieto

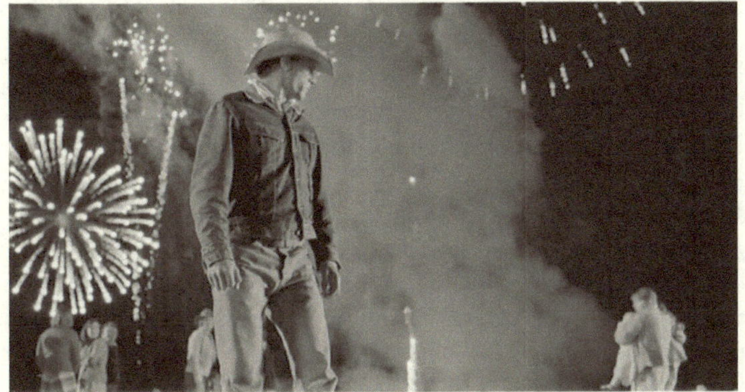

Image 12. Ennis Del Mar (Heath Ledger) in *Brokeback Mountain* (Lee 2005).

Rodrigo Prieto ASC, AMC first came to the attention of cinemagoers worldwide with his gritty work on *Amores Perros* in 2000. Since then, his eclecticism has been startling, alternating between family films such as *We Bought a Zoo*, romantic dramas such as *Water for Elephants*, hip-hop drama *8 Mile*, war epic *Alexander*, and the unforgettable *Brokeback Mountain*. While he is a fine technician, it is arguably Prieto's sense of storytelling that has proven the most distinctive aspect of his career. Scenarios he explores may be tragic, epic, profane, heartwarming, sexual, glamorous, or terrifying. Speaking broadly, he is one of the most flexible, adept cinematographers in the world today. In *The Wolf of Wall Street*, his whirling camera was a justifiable approximation of the drug-addled perspective of that film's antiheroes. In *Brokeback Mountain*, his approach toward the alienated characters placed them in landscapes both beautiful and uncaring, and so in turn he favored a static, highly pictoral approach to the visuals he captured, punctuated periodically by flights of poetic realism.

The following interview was conducted between Lindsay Coleman and Rodrigo Prieto in May 2013.

Lindsay Coleman: If we may, I'd like to start off with a somewhat broad investigation of an aesthetic you created in collaboration with a director, specifically your night exterior scenes in your two films with Ang Lee, *Brokeback Mountain* and *Lust, Caution*. When I spoke with Peter Pau, he discussed having with Ang Lee a very detailed debate on the subject of moonlight, what qualities he wanted moonlight to possess in *Crouching Tiger, Hidden Dragon*. What discussions did you have with Ang on *Brokeback Mountain* about moonlight, and how you would go about achieving it?

Rodrigo Prieto: We had major discussions about it, both on *Brokeback Mountain* and on *Lust, Caution*. He has a lot to say about it. Strangely, it wasn't about hard light or soft light, it was about the presence of moonlight. There were certain scenes on *Brokeback Mountain* where I thought we could get away with campfire light and not have any moonlight at all, but he felt, when you are out in the field, moonlight is much more present than what we as urban-dwellers are used to. Even to us a full moon is very dim, almost imperceptible. The same thing happened on *Lust, Caution*. He again wanted moonlight to be present, and seen, and felt. The film is set in the '30s and most light sources were pretty dim. Moonlight was more visible then. It's one of the hardest things to do in cinematography, to create moonlight. It's hard for many reasons. One is the evenness of it, which is found over a big area. That's very hard to achieve with lighting units, creating just a single shadow, and it is meant to represent only a single light source. When you have multiple sources, you can justify a backlight and a fill light, you can really justify multiple sources of light. Different angles of light, I should say. But with moonlight you can have only one. It's essentially like the sun, yet without the visible ambient fill light that the sun would give you. One of the other characteristics I note in moonlight is that it seems not very colorful, it seems desaturated. That is because the cones in the eyes, at a certain light level, register less color. But it is not that moonlight has no color, it is that the eyes do not register it. Moonlight does have color because it is bouncing light from the sun, and has the same level of color as is found in light from the sun, yet it is being received by our eyes at a much lower level of brightness. Our eyes would register this if they were registered to picking up color at such low light levels. So that's why I tend to like a combination of gels when I am reproducing moonlight, which to me reflects in the tones of the actor's skin. It makes the skin tones seem less red, more pink-red. So, I use a little bit of green, and a little bit of blue. The combination I've come it like is quarter CTB,[1] and one eighth plus green.[2] It all depends if moonlight is on its own, or if it's combined with other light sources. If I'm coming at it with warm light sources, that's a combination I'd use. For example, on *Water for Elephants* I used this combination. I was using an oil lamp, and if I went deeper on the blue and the green, compared with the extreme warmth of the oil lamp, it looked too weird, too much color. When it was just moonlight, like on *Brokeback Mountain*, I would use half CTB,[3] and quarter plus green.[4] But sometimes, on *Brokeback Mountain*, I would try to get that same result but I had to use HMI lighting,[5] but daylight balanced. We were using these weather balloons, hanging on the tops of trees, to bounce light off of. For intensity and throw, we used HMI par lights.[6] 12K and 6K pars.[7] But I gelled them the opposite.[8] I gelled them with quarter CTO,[9] to bring them halfway in the color temperature, but I did use also, in this case, quarter plus green. Yes, moonlight is complicated. I would tend to agree with Ang Lee. Even though real moonlight is quite hard-edged, it's a small bright dot in the sky like the sun, so the shadows are the same, the feeling when you look at the moon, in my perception, is softer. Even though I know it's not in reality. The eye, when the overall brightness level is so low, the perception is not off a high contrast.

LC: Isn't that the emotional state that the moon puts us in?

RP: I guess it is emotional. It is also physical. The eye is trying to raise the light level to capture all of the detail. For moonlight, a lot of DPs make big light boxes, like twelve by twelve cubes with lights inside of them with these combinations of gels I've described, or lighting balloons, where you use it at a distance where it will create a relatively sharp shadow, but not as sharp as the actual moon would create. I did that on several scenes on *Lust, Caution*, for example—we couldn't do it on *Brokeback Mountain*, it was impossible due to the location to move cranes up to produce these soft sources of moonlight—so that's why I was describing this approach that we took with the weather balloons. The trick with that was that I was making it look like one source whereas we had several balloons.

LC: Shooting in Alberta was quite a bit further to the north than the story was set, did that present much of a challenge?

RP: Not really. One thing in Alberta that was striking, and I hear it's like that also in Wyoming—where I haven't actually been, but I have been to Montana—are these huge skies, endless skies, the feeling of endless skies which is really particular. I don't think I've seen that any other place. That matched. The type of topography was also very similar. Ang is very particular about these things. We saw a lot of references of what Wyoming looks like. We were very careful. I believe people from Wyoming would have been fooled into thinking it was Wyoming. I'm not sure if for the whole film. We shot a little piece which was supposed to be Mexico around Calgary also.

LC: You were in that scene? Playing the male prostitute?

RP: That's right!

LC: Are you amused by that casting?

RP: (*Laughs*) That was a surprise, on the day. Originally, I wasn't going to do that part. I started lighting the scene. Ang had already cast that part, but he had only seen him on video and in photographs. Ang liked his acting, but when he saw him he saw that he was short, shorter than Jake Gyllenhaal. Just visually he didn't like that difference of height, especially when they are walking away into the darkness. The backup Mexican, that was me. (*Laughs*) He asked me to do it right then and there. God, it was embarrassing, but in the end it worked out fine.

LC: In an interview with Roger Deakins, I discussed the image in *The Shawshank Redemption* where Andy Dufresne burst out of the pipe into the rain and is free. It was such a great image, and I complimented him on it. He said it was only a great image because of all of the other events in the film which had led up to it. There is an iconic shot in *Brokeback Mountain* of the fireworks exploding behind Heath Ledger. Do you feel similar to Roger, or do you feel that the image does stand by itself?

RP: I would tend to agree with Roger. As cinematographers, we are shooting twenty-four still photographs a second. The value of each image comes because of each preceding image. And the one after. That is for a single shot. But the same applies for a whole movie. You build on the drama, you build moods and atmospheres as the story progresses. I always say I don't shoot movies to beef up my demo reel. In fact, I don't even have a demo reel. (*Laughs*) I'm not looking for shots, or a cool moment of lighting, or an unusual angle which will stand alone. I'm looking for how a given shot will work for that moment in the movie, that emotional moment for the characters, how the scene is positioned in the story. But having said that, there are moments in movies which are memorable. It can be an image, yes. And you can strive to enhance such moments, so that hopefully they touch the audience in a way that is remembered. Sometimes these images can become iconic. That image, specifically, is important, but it is what you were feeling in the context of the film which gives it its value.

LC: There are many memorable images from your career. When you capture an iconic image do you feel it is important when you are shooting it?

RP: Not particularly. For the shot of Heath Ledger, I knew it was going to be a good image, but just like every other shot in the movie. You plow on. You look for the lighting, and the angle, look at the edge of the frame, deal with the complications, and so on. Rarely, in my situation, do I think this is going to be *the* shot. Once you're shooting it, and the camera is rolling, you feel "this is special." For me my favorite ones are when things come together in a surprising way. The performance works, the light hits the eyes just right, when all these things come together, those are my favorite moments. That's one reason I like to operate the camera. I like to see these moments and witness them through the camera right there. I'd rather be watching it through the camera than on a monitor.

LC: When I spoke with Uta Briesewitz, she spoke about how important she found eyelights, how essential they were to her photography. What is your attitude toward eyelights?[10]

RP: I very rarely use eyelights. I'll think about the eyes when I'm lighting. I light an actor in broader strokes, and hopefully a key, or a fill light, will shine toward the eyes. There are certain scenes where I will conscious un-eyelight. I am thinking of *Lust, Caution*, a very simple scene, a dialogue scene. With Ang Lee, he and I agreed that when the two young women are discussing their seduction approach on the couch I just use a key light,[11] and a dinky,[12] near the lens, to just show the excitement in their eyes about what they are going to do. On *Alexander* I actually borrowed a technique from Jordan Cronenweth on *Blade Runner*. It was a scene were Rosario Dawson is getting married to Colin Farrell, and it said in the script that her character had a panther-like quality. So I used a halfway mirror in front of the lens—actually I just used a piece of glass—at a forty-five-degree angle. Then I had a small unit of theater light shining onto the glass, in turn into Rosario's eye, at the exact same axis as the lens. So the light's coming from where the negative is, and the light shines into the pupil and is reflected off the retina back into the camera. So it gives the impression of glowing eyes. That was a very special eyelight I did. I used eyelight on Penélope Cruz in *Broken Embraces*. [Pedro] Almodóvar and I wanted her to look very alluring, so I tested many methods of lighting her. I found that using fill light coming from right on top of, and underneath, the camera with longish but small Kino

Flos,[13] with some diffusion, gave her a nice lighting effect in her eyes and filled her face very nicely.

LC: You are on record about being very alert to the choices of actors in their performances. Do they discuss with you choices they will make in the scene, or is it more a matter of you keeping up?

RP: I would say it is the latter. We do rehearse. Some directors like to shoot the rehearsal. That can be pretty nerve-wracking. Once you put something on film editorially you can't do big adjustments, cutting back and forth. There might be a shot with an eyeline, and one that doesn't have one, and so on. In those situations you have to light and hope for the best. When I know the director will not shoot the rehearsal, I try to get the stand-ins to block their own light. To try to put their heads down, put their hands up or down, and anything which might indicate things that the actor could do which would block the light. When I see what could happen, which generally does happen, in terms of ways the actors might block the light, I then try to prepare for that, and put some light somewhere, hidden in the set to take care of their performance and make certain there is light in their eyes. So to that extent I am conscious of the eyelight, but I don't specifically put what you would call an eyelight. But I am conscious of trying to find ways in which the performance is seen in the best way possible. That's why I'm very aware of actors. I try to keep the paraphernalia as simple as possible. I don't want the actors too conscious of marks and limitation on them, things like that. I try to make them feel there is the least amount of film stuff around. I try to not to tell them things, to stay as invisible as possible, though I do have a good relationship with actors. I try not to distract them, to give them their space.

LC: I'd like to go to a moment of performance you captured, which really resonated for me as a young hip-hop fan, and I am sure for millions of others. When Eminem sits down at the end of his final rap battle in *8 Mile*, how personal did you feel that moment was for him, especially given that he is playing a version of himself in the film?

RP: Very good question. I do remember that very clearly. I do think that moment was very personal. I do think it was taken from his experience. Before *8 Mile* I had always shot-listed with the directors I had collaborated with in Mexico. I tried to do that with Curtis Hanson. I sat down and gave him a list of I was thinking about. He said, "Rodrigo, I'd rather not do that for this film. I want it to be like the battles where they are improvising in the moment." So that was how we did it. It meant arriving every day and not knowing what the shots were, basically. We would see a rehearsal and make our mind up how to shoot it. It was a little scary at first, but I decided to embrace it. You have to be very present, very focused, and very attuned with the performances. You have to ask yourself "what's the best angle to capture what they just did?" Curtis was very open to my ideas on set, so it was really exhilarating! Particularly the rap battles. I didn't know what they were going to say, and being from Mexico I didn't understand it very well anyway! (*Laughs*) I couldn't make everything out, and I had never read it. The people in the audience were not extras, they were brought in and reacting for real to what they were hearing, and doing, and saying. The energy was very special. I was on stage and following whatever. It was just going with the energy. It was like I was performing with them as well. I was improvising with them. When I felt like going to the mic I would do that, when I felt like going to the audience I would do that, then I would whip-pan to Eminem, or stay with him while he is watching the other guy rap. It was like editing, in the moment. We did that several times, I improvised it differently each time, so that was how they got the coverage for editing. But we would do the whole performance each time without cutting. But I remember that moment, when Eminem sat down, and I didn't know he was going to do that, and I got down on my knees and remember framing that in a way which was a little off. I remember putting his face very much in the edge of frame and pushing in close to him. It was like a note! That frame felt just like a note, like music, and he wasn't talking or rapping in that moment! It felt like I had to get in, get close, and I needed to be a little bit daring with the framing, like he was. I had to be daring like he was!

LC: You didn't know he was going to sit down?

RP: I didn't know it was going to happen! In that moment, I took it to a framing which felt good for me. In that moment I felt "yeah, this frame feels right!"

LC: From all the moments in your career are there other times you've felt that, felt completely right, in the moment?

RP: There is a moment in *Frida* where Trotsky has just died, and Frida goes to a bar, and she sees a strange woman with a mask behind her head. So Frida goes and sits with her. When we filmed the scene, we shot on a set in Mexico City. On the outside of the walls on the set they built platforms for musicians, and the old woman, who is a famous actress and singer, sang live. It was all live music that we were filming. I had a gag with the lighting on Salma Hayek where it was a Chinese lantern on the end of a pole,[14] and my gaffer was just moving it around in circles on top of Salma as she was listening to the music. There was this moment of intense emotion where Salma tilted her head back exactly as the light was passing behind her, and her tears catch the light in a very special way. I don't know if you will notice that moment when you are watching it, but when we were shooting it, it was so special that we chose to move the light in circles, in time with the music, and then at the moment the tear spontaneously happened, that wasn't planned, it caught the light in a beautiful way. Another moment which comes to my mind is *We Bought a Zoo*. Matt Damon is looking at the photos of his wife on a computer and he had not dared to do that in the past because his wife had passed away. As he is seeing the images, he has glasses on and he is effectively seeing the memory of the moment captured in the pictures reflected in his glasses. Cameron Crowe wanted something special for that. We brought in the actress for his wife, and the double for the actress who played the daughter. They were running in the foreground, and out of focus, but lit as they would have been when the photo on his laptop was taken, on a bright sunny day outside. Even though the scene where he is watching this takes place inside the reflection on his glasses, the reflections they are casting are lit like a sunny day. You can't really plan on when they cross, and when the light reflects, but it coincided with a very emotional moment for Matt. He got really emotional because the young double was giggling and it really touched Matt, and he started weeping, and then Cameron Crowe was playing this great music in the background, and then everyone started crying. It was that connection between the light, the camera, the story, the performance, the shallow focus, they all come together to make an emotional image rather than just a pretty image. That's the kind of thing which for me is very special, when you achieve an image that transmits an emotion, or at least when it happens on set. The photography is in tune with the emotional moment.

LC: Do you judge any of the characters that you film? I ask because many of the characters in the films you have shot can be very flawed or ambiguous. Examples might be the widow portrayed by Naomi Watts in *21 Grams*, who is a troubled addict, or the Gael García Bernal character in *Amores Perros*, who arguably stalks his sister-in-law.

RP: A good question. I try not to. I think in life I try not to judge. But we all do. I try to approach people in general, try not to prejudge people. I think characters become interesting when they are multidimensional. I find with many of the directors I work with, every character is a facet of that director's personality. For me, it is fascinating. When a character speaks, it is the director speaking through them. So if I judge then a lot of that loses its power. Ang Lee openly admitted that the lead character in *Lust, Caution* is him. He projected so much of himself into a girl, a female character. The scene in the film where she is giving her first theater performance where the curtain opens, that was directly referencing Ang's own first experience in theater. And that is the reason he is a director: theater. He's a shy man, yet when he's creating, and directing, the shyness disappears. He had a point of view shot he wanted to evoke of the experience where as the curtain opened the light reflected off his eyelashes. I tested the fake huge eyelashes in front of the lens. I kept asking, "Was that what you saw Ang, was that what it was like?" In the end we just used a small flare on the lens. We were really trying to produce that subjective sensation from his own life, so that character is definitely Ang Lee. Also, all the other characters.

LC: It's funny because that means he is having sex with himself in the film, as many characters, male and female, have sex with one another.

(*Laughter*)

RP: Imagine that! *Alexander*, that is also a film that is very personal for Oliver Stone. All of the characters are clearly Oliver. When Philip the king is talking, I can hear Oliver talking, I can also hear Oliver's father talking. When the mother is talking, all of these things I have heard Oliver talk about, they are all there. That's what art is. To be a director you have to be a general, marshal the troops, but a very vulnerable general. That is a balance that only the greatest directors achieve.

LC: Do you feel you are an artist alongside them?

RP: I think so. I don't want to be pretentious, but I see my approach as more abstract, with lighting and camerawork, as opposed to directors working with actors and dialogue. It's more clear to your intentions, in the latter case. When I'm lighting, I think I do it from an emotional state. There is a lot of technique involved, a lot of technology, but all of that disappears for me when I'm on set. I forget all that and feel this space, feel the energy, and try to reproduce that energy with the wavelengths of light and color.

LC: How much of your work as a cinematographer is autobiographical?

RP: I would say every shot is autobiographical because you bring a memory of light to it. I am constantly looking at the light, and feeling the light of my surroundings. When I am talking to someone I am always looking at the way that the light is hitting their face. Always. I can't remember a time when I was talking to someone and I wasn't noticing how the light was hitting their face. *Frida* contains a lot of the culture I grew up with, Mexican culture. I always, since I was a little kid, knew the paintings featured in that film. The Mexican side of my family was always very involved in politics. So the beginning of the century, into the '20s, '30s in Mexico, is always something I have in my mind. That was something which was a major part of the film which I really related to. I wanted to reproduce, from my childhood memory, the images I imagined when my grandfather would tell me of that time. In a strange way, *Brokeback Mountain* was exploring my mother's side of the family. My mother was American, and was born in Montana, raised on a sheep ranch. Her brother grew up in this sheep ranch. He wanted to become a ballet dancer. So he was gay, grew up on a ranch, in Montana. In a way, *Brokeback Mountain* was a way to be in touch with that side of my family. I grew up in Mexico, and growing up, the Mexican influence on me was huge, with a huge extended family. I didn't have that on my mother's side because my uncle didn't have any children. So *Brokeback Mountain* was a way to get in touch with my American side. But every film has something in it. When I did *8 Mile*, because I had just done *Frida*, I went to the Detroit Institute of Arts, which has a huge Diego Rivera mural. I had never seen the mural, only photos of it. From *Frida* I knew the mural very well. I saw paintings he had done of factories, and the coloration of these murals was cyan, green. There were shades of yellow and orange for the molten steel, but mostly a lot of industrial lighting was referenced in his murals with this green type of lighting. I incorporated a lot of that into the lighting of *8 Mile*. He took it from what he saw when he was in Detroit, and then I took it from him. So, it was kind of me stealing from another Mexican a perspective on Detroit! (*Laughs*)

LC: Chivo [Emmanuel] Lubezki, your mentor, talks about how he feels that he fails often in what he is attempting in his cinematography. Do you feel similarly about your work?

RP: That's very Chivo. Every time I talk to him about what he is doing, he is always suffering. That's not my experience.

Certainly, I can feel very insecure. I am never quite sure if things are working out. But I do enjoy what I do a lot. I like not being safe, not knowing if you are doing the right thing. I don't mind that. But I can be harsh on myself. I watch work of my colleagues and admire it, and think, "ooh, I'm glad I didn't do that because they did it better than I would have." I don't know what I would have done. All I can act on is what I am feeling in the moment. And not judge it. Let it play out, good or bad. I try to be present in the moment. I don't see myself as a suffering artist.

LC: Some cinematographers discuss alternating beautiful images with ugly images. Is that an approach to which you can relate?

RP: I would say I don't try to produce "pretty" images. That's not my objective. I get irked when people say the cinematography is "beautiful." I try to make images which fit the story and the emotional content. If they are ugly, so be it. I don't judge them for their beauty, I judge them for their effectiveness. Very often, a pretty image is not effective for a story. I do agree, in general, that if every image is beautiful, one after another, they lose their power. If every image has this super powerful framing, lighting, and color, then they will lose that power. I definitely find myself suffering at times with images which do not make par. But I have to remind myself that having a continuous stream of images which have that level of powerful color, framing, lighting, is not always a good or useful thing.

LC: In *Brokeback Mountain* you shot a husband/wife love scene where Michelle Williams and Heath Ledger are naked in bed together. A scene such as this is actually quite rare in modern cinema. What is your process when you are dealing with shooting scenes which are rare or unique, without easy precedent.

RP: I very rarely use cinema as a reference for the films I do. When I bring ideas to a director, I do not bring ideas based on what has been shown in other films. Mostly, I use still photography. Not all still photography, but the type I am attracted to are not lit, they are moments from life which remind me of a moment in the story, maybe it's a texture, or the color, or the light found in the shot. My lighting is always based on real light, rather than artificial light. When I'm lighting, I'm obsessed with making it look as though it is not lit at all. I'd be happy to just use available light! One of the problems with that is continuity, as light is changing all the time. Also, it's not always effective for what you are trying to portray in a scene. Sometimes natural light isn't expressive for the moment. I try to do naturalistic but expressive lighting. My references, to some extent, are things I've done in the past. Every movie you can't say that you are starting from scratch. Your experience always comes into play, as well as my experiences as a cinematographer. The scene in *Lust, Caution*, where the young people all kill the man, Ang Lee wanted me to emphasize that the young people are actors, that they are playing at being revolutionaries. So as the scene begins, Ang wanted me to light the set as if by a theater work light. No fancy lighting, just flat light. As the scene progressed, and things started to get uglier, I changed the light into a darker, more ugly, contrasty lighting. The challenge was to make it seem as though it was the same light. Things are changing emotionally as the scene progresses and thus the light does as well, but hopefully you don't notice that. As the scene progresses, the walls get darker, there is less fill light, the shadows are deeper, but that came from no reference from a book. It was just based on a theory that Ang Lee had. I loved his idea and tried to execute it. Of course, because it is filmmaking everything is shot out of order, so we had to go back and forth with the lighting changes. In *Brokeback Mountain*—(*laughs*) I've done so many sex scenes in my career, I've done everything you can imagine—but *Brokeback Mountain* had to feel mundane.

LC: The scene is all about ambivalence. She's naked, she's beautiful, but there is no love or desire in the scene, just emotional and spiritual exhaustion from the two characters.

RP: He does have sex with her, but he's thinking about being with a guy. She's not happy with it. The scene had to feel mundane, but at the same I didn't want it to look horrible. She had to look okay. At one point, when he turns her around, and she is facing downward, the camera turns around and finds her face and I lit her with moonlight, a hard light on her face. It shifts from this soft lamplight to this harsh, cool moonlight on her face. There is a transition of light within the scene. The other sex scenes I all approached differently because I wanted the spectator to feel involved in it. I wanted the spectator to have a sense of what they are feeling. The first time Heath and Jake are together, they are in the tent and there is just moonlight shining in from the canvas flap. Heath wakes up and starts touching Jake. Then it is happening, fast, and quick, and ugly, really sloppy. It's all one shot. I had the camera on a jib arm to adjust to their positions, but we didn't want it to feel floaty. The camera had to have the energy that they had. It had to move fast, then move slow again, then move fast. The lighting, going with what was very natural at that moment, was murky. It's no direct light, it was filtered through canvas with the combination of gels I was talking about earlier. That is in contrast to another sex scene in the tent where their relationship has grown. It's a scene where there is a campfire lit outside the tent. Jake is outside by the fire and Heath looks out from the tent. They come back in, they are both inside the tent, and the flap was left open so the firelight is still lighting their faces. So it is warm light, flickering. It had a nice contrast. It was romantic light for this moment. It's funny, when I lit Jake for his close-up, I lit him very soft with all of these rope lights,[15] which are inside a plastic tube around the camera. It is very soft, warm light. Heath's character had a more harsh light coming from the fire because their energy, as characters, was very different. I wanted Ennis to be the male in the scene. Jake complained, as a joke, "why do you always give me the girl light!" (*Laughter*) [In] *Lust, Caution* there was a very thought-out design of the sex scenes.

LC: Rumor has it that it was a dozens of hours of shooting for the sex scenes.

RP: I don't know about that, but it was two weeks of shooting for the sex scenes, so you do the math. It was very intense, emotional, and hard. The first scene is where Mr. Yee kind of rapes her. Mr. Yee grabs her, throws her against the wall, throws her on the bed, and whips her. The operating on that was very tough. Ang Lee told me, "The first whip, come down with the whip, wait a second to see his reaction, then come back to see her reaction." It was all split-second stuff. We got it, but it was with a level of precision that was extremely high. The first sex scene was cool in terms of light. It's raining outside, so there was a kind of metallic blue to the image. When he leaves the bed, we had a pink dusk light, combined with some golden sunlight, which is a motif we used later at the end when they are at the jewelry shop at sunset. When she warns him to run, and comes out knowing she will be caught, we used the ambient dusk light, a magenta pink, and the rays of sun were golden, we used that light. But this was the first scene where we used that light. It transitioned from this cool, ugly light in the rape scene to this purple and golden light at the end because she is achieving her objective even if the rape has happened. There is another sex scene where now they are both naked in bed. For that one I used warmer light, suffused through the curtains. Mr. Yee's house was always with big drapes closed. He was involved in espionage so this was a natural consequence. What I did was I created a gap in the curtains so that a slash of sunlight was lighting them as well, crossing over their bodies. That light, like a knife, represented the violence, and also the danger, of the scene. The rest of the light on their bodies was very soft and shiny on their bodies. We wanted to see their sweat, and at the same time show their bodies as attractive, but at the same time with the element of this slash of sunlight. There's another scene where they go to a hotel room somewhere. Ang Lee showed me a Tibetan mandala. The colors were green, and a little bit of purple, and red and black, and a little bit of orange. It was very strong and stark. But he wanted to go for that look, so we incorporated some of those colors into the set, but for lighting we were looking for light based on realistic lighting, but at the same time trying to give it that edge. I asked the production designer to place a lamp with a green shade on it so that would justify a sickly sort of green hue in the scene. At the same time, I asked for the desk it was on to be made of red wood so that the light would bounce off it and you could produce an image with green light, but at the same time a bit of red in it. I was lighting them with a combination of colors which reminded me of that image that Ang showed me. It's a conflict of these two colors which are almost opposites.

LC: Were you taking a bichromatic approach?[16]

RP: Yes, yes I was. I took a similar approach for the scenes in the movie theater where I used lighting that was both red and cyan. So yes, this represented that conflict, both of their conflicts really. He knows he's in danger, and she knows she is in great danger sleeping with him also. He knows that in being with this girl she now has the opportunity to kill him because there is a moment where there is a gun hanging next to them. While they are having sex she puts a pillow over his head, and looks at the gun, and he realizes that is what she is doing. So there was a moment where we ended up with a close-up on her and she needed to be emotional about this realization. Ang Lee wanted her to have a combination of an orgasm, but to also break down and cry. What happened was that she was not achieving that.

LC: It sounds very difficult.

RP: Very difficult! She just couldn't do it. So we cut the camera and then suddenly she started to weep uncontrollably. But she was not crying as a character, she was crying as a person. She started crying very intensely so we started filming her crying like that. That moment was very hard for all of us. I started crying, but not because of the scene, but because it was too intense for all of us, for her as a person. These very intense sex scenes with this man, we were all very conscious of being professional and careful with each other, but still it was very intense. I broke down crying, and she kept weeping, and Ang Lee went over to comfort her. That was the last sex scene we shot, but we were all affected and Ang Lee was affected. It was tough. For me filmmaking is way beyond the technical aspects. You really are dealing with emotions, and there is a big responsibility that comes with that, even when you are doing the lighting you are lighting emotions. You are dealing with people that are in touch with these emotions, and you have to be very respectful of that. But, it is a big joy, it is a big privilege.

LC: For me the group murder scene affects me the most, even more so than the power of the sex scenes. It is quite devastating as a scene.

RP: True, it is very powerful. But in shooting that scene, it was very technical. How do you wield the knife? Now we have to change to the fake knife. How much blood do we put? Oh no, now I can see the protection that the actor is wearing. It became all of these things when we were shooting. When we were shooting it did not become as emotional as it ends up in the movie. The actors had to get to an emotional state, but for me it was more about making it look real. Really the scene is not so much about violence, more about intense emotional violence.

LC: You have filmed almost every kind of person, every kind of character, would you say that is true?

RP: (*Laughs*) Yes, it is true.

LC: Where does that curiosity come from?

RP: If I can, I try to pick projects which are very different from one another. It's also been luck, but I do try to pick projects which are very distinct from one another. I was shooting *Alexander*, and then the next film was *Brokeback Mountain*. You can't get more opposite than that! I just finished *The Wolf of Wall Street*, now I'm going to a western with Tommy Lee Jones. I also like to work with directors who are very different to one another. Julie Taymor, Ang Lee, Oliver Stone . . . my life expands when I work with people who are unique, and uniquely different to each other. Pedro Almodóvar! I don't come in with a set idea, or a way of working which is uniquely mine. I don't say, I'm Rodrigo Prieto and I like desaturated color, etc.

> I try not to do that. I try to understand how the director sees the world. By understanding that perspective, I grow. I give that point of view eyes, and translate it into visuals, and make it mine, and bring my own experiences to their perspective. That's what I find fascinating about cinematography.

~

Prieto's references to color, emotion, and character find easy corollaries throughout his career. Here he discusses how an approach to color allowed him to separate out three distinct visual approaches to the three protagonists of the film *21 Grams*:

> "We were separating each story with colors that we felt were appropriate," explains Prieto. "We pictured Paul's story in cool colors; the [interior] lighting is generally white, and the night exteriors have the cool, greenish look of metal-halide lamps. By contrast, we went for warmer colors for Jack; all of the night exteriors in his story are lit with sodium-vapor lamps, and we gelled lamps indoors with warm colors. The vibration of red-orange light is more intense, which we felt was right for the character. Cristina's story is presented neutrally, as something in between. In general, the lighting is white, but her story mixes so much Paul's that they both have blue-green night exteriors. And when they finally meet Jack, all three color schemes become more red-orange." (Calhoun 2003, 1)

In a similar manner, color and mixing various colors assist the audience in the emotional journey Ang Lee invites them to take in *Lust, Caution*. Mr. Yee and Wong Chia Chi are opaque as characters, both spies, and many of their interactions are a mixture of subterfuge and vulnerability. In such a narrative, with performances of great complexity, subtlety, and little obvious exposition provided to guide an audience through such ambiguous interactions, color may indeed provide an evocative framework to contextualize a character's actions and help elucidate a film's subtext.

For Prieto, color can in turn produce a parallel thematic dynamic to the story. In the case of *8 Mile*, his decision to evoke the murals of Diego Rivera hearkened back to his own cultural and aesthetic heritage. But this is arguably not an indulgence. In fact, it reinforces the themes of the film (the struggles of the working classes and the unemployed, the attempt to transcend one's social setting through art) in its evocation of artwork very much akin to the preoccupations of *8 Mile*, albeit those of an era far removed from the present. The story of the Rivera-influenced green chimes with the narrative of the Eminem film.

Notes

1. Also referred to as 1/4 CTB. CTB is short for color temperature blue, a type of lighting gelatin, or plastic film, that has a blue tint. It comes in various densities of color notated as 1/8, 1/4, 1/2, and full. It is used to raise the color temperature of the light by several hundred degrees. This can be used to do a full conversion of Tungsten light, nominally considered to be 3200K to 5600K, the temperature of mid-day sunlight, using full CTB.

2. Also 1/8 Plus Green. Much in the same way that CTB shifts the color temperature from warm to cool, Plus Green will add varying levels of green to enable color matching of disparate lighting sources. For instance you might use some degree of plus green to make a warm white fluorescent that which tends toward magenta match a cool white tube that tends toward green.

3. Or 1/2 CTB, described in note 1.

4. Or 1/4 Plus Green, described in note 2.

5. HMI is a term used for a particular type of lighting fixture that is made for the film industry based on metal halide. It has been developed to give a full-spectrum daylight balanced color temperature light with high efficiency ratio of power draw to lumen output.

6. HMI PAR lights are powerful HMI lights that have no lens with a very narrow beam and a long throw.

7. Two of the various strengths of HMI PAR lights made. The 12K and 6K refer to 12,000 watts and 6,000 watts.

8. "Gel" is the term for the rolls or sheets of the plastic-like material that come in many different colors and transparencies for lighting control. It is mainly manufactured by Rosco (United States) and Lee (United Kingdom).

9. Or 1/4 CTO. This is one of the temperature warming colors, color temperature orange. It does the opposite of CTB in similar increments.

10. Eyelights are any type of light source that is used specifically to put a desired amount of light into an actor's eyes It can be used to illuminate the area around and including the eyes or just to give a "kick" or reflection of the light itself to be seen in the actor's eyes.

11. "Key light" refers to the main lighting source(s) for the actor(s) in the scene. Each position in a set or different actor may have their own key lights for the moment and position they are in.

12. "Dinky" is a nickname for a very small tungsten light originally called an inky-dinky. It is also often referred to as an inky. It has a Fresnel lens and a bulb of 100–200 watts.

13. Kino Flo is a manufacturer of fluorescent lamps and ballasts made specifically for the motion picture industry. They are full spectrum, color balanced to daylight (5600K) or tungsten (3200K, 2700K), and flicker-free. They are made in various sizes and configurations. The name has come to be used synonymously with all fluorescent lighting in the movie industry. The company now makes many different types of lighting sources, including LED fixtures.

14. The Chinese lantern is a decorative paper lantern made in China. They are made from a bamboo or wooden support of rings that form a ball covered with thin rice paper, which allows them to give a soft even light in all directions. They are extremely lightweight and very flammable. Several companies now manufacture stronger and flameproof versions for safer use.

15. Rope lights are usually found in home lighting stores like Home Depot. They are flexible plastic tubes of varying lengths with small, closely spaced lightbulbs in them. Either tungsten or LED, they can often be chained to give greater lengths. They produce a semi-soft omnidirectional light.

16. "Bichromatic" refers to using a two-color-only lighting scheme. The colors are often but not necessarily opposites on the color wheel.

Bibliography

Calhoun, John. "Heartbreak & Loss." *American Cinematographer*, December 2003, 1. https://theasc.com/magazine/dec03/cover/index.html

Mauro Fiore

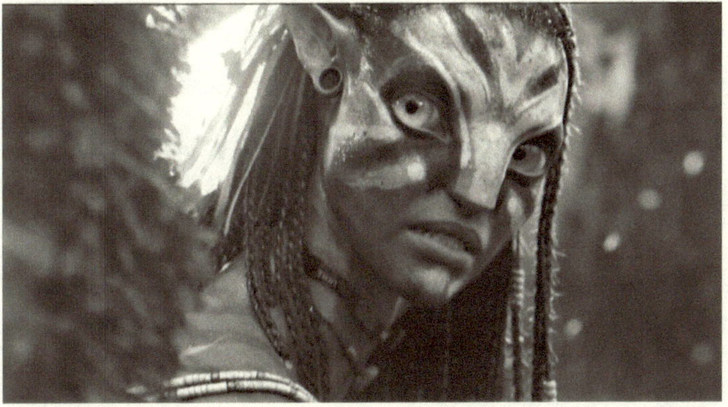

Image 13. The use of long lenses in virtual cinematography lends a veracity to images of the Na'vi in *Avatar* (Cameron 2009).

Even before he won the Academy Award for his work on *Avatar*, Mauro Fiore ASC had amassed an impressive track record as a cinematographer of genre pictures of surpassing beauty. His use of natural light on *Tears of the Sun*, the dynamic camera moves of *Training Day*, and the gritty allure of *The Kingdom* are testaments to his significant gifts as a visual craftsman. Even when lensing with film lights, Fiore's work is notable for its ability to exist in the middle range; he adopts a medium-contrast style. A notable example is *Southpaw*, which captured the emotional struggles of its boxer protagonist through an image that was sharp—befitting the fact that it was digitally captured—yet allowing for subtle gradations of color and an image that flirted with murkiness without ever succumbing. Fiore is similarly adept at carefully calibrating his lighting to evoke the passage of time, the subliminal passage of a day a major contributing factor to the sense of temporal continuity in *Training*

Day, and a major factor in its narrative power, the sense that all of the action takes place over a twenty-four-hour period. His work on *Avatar* is equally intriguing for technical and technological reasons. It was the first major 3D film in many generations and was arguably the largest effects film in history. Where Dean Cundey provided the lighting and camerawork that created the real world *Roger Rabbit* occupied, on *Avatar*, Fiore's cinematography was integrating with the far wider digital world of Pandora.

The following interview was conducted between Lindsay Coleman and Mauro Fiore in October 2012.

> **Lindsay Coleman:** To be selected as Janusz Kamiński's cinematographer on *Lost Souls* must have been quite flattering. It was your first time as a full-fledged DP, his first film as director.
>
> **Mauro Fiore:** I think, looking back, that I was the only cinematographer who could have possibly shot that film because of the history we shared. We went to film school together and then he moved to Los Angeles and called me out to Los Angeles to help him on projects. Eventually, I became his gaffer, then shot second unit for him. We were roommates for around ten years. We have a major history together. What's great about Janusz is that he's an instinctual cinematographer. He's not at all afraid to feel a particular way and really go off on it. He's not at all theoretical in his approach, he goes off feeling. He's able to really do amazing things that way. Sometimes it's the most amazing thing you've ever seen, sometimes it works, sometimes it doesn't work. He's a courageous cinematographer. Working with him instilled great confidence in me, that I could be a cinematographer.
>
> **LC:** In my previous interview with him, he discussed looking for images of unconventional beauty. Is this an approach you follow yourself?
>
> **MF:** I think in shooting a movie you look for those very specific images which will help tell that specific story. What's most interesting about a project is to try to find what is most specific to that particular story. You need to find a specific image for a specific story. That's when it's incredible! I don't know if I agree with that approach you described him referencing

because, at times, that romantic image, or that typical image, may be the best way to express that moment. I also feel that sometimes, by leaving out certain clichés, you're not availing yourself of the complete vocabulary of film. You're putting a stop to certain expressions. I don't feel that way.

LC: Do you feel each of your films has such an image as what you just described?

MF: I would say that my attempt is to always try to find that singular image. I'm not quite sure if all of my films have that singular image, but during the process I'd say yes, I'd say maybe. The long form is to find a specific image to a particular scene. So, you have to break it apart, scene by scene. There's a development in the long form. It's not just one image. Let's put it that way.

LC: So, is it many images that add up to a singular image?

MF: I would say, what is it, that a given scene is specifically saying visually? That's where you can look at what you've contributed to a scene to make it that much more interesting, or that much more special.

LC: Do you feel a series of images sum up a film like *Avatar*?

MF: *Avatar* was more like a technical challenge. I think there are so many images. Also, the fact that there is so much CG connected to it, and the fact that I had a reference to that CG, but didn't really know it. I think that was more of a technical challenge, per se.

LC: How do you feel about the influence on filmmaking in general with your choosing to shoot Avatar in 3D?

MF: Everybody seemed to feel, distribution-wise, that they had to do the next action film, following *Avatar*, in 3D. Once the theaters were prepared for 3D, it all of a sudden became about having product, having enough product that was 3D. 3D has become less of an aesthetic choice, and more of a distribution choice.

LC: Do you feel proprietary of 3D? Do you feel ownership of the format?

MF: I don't really look at it that way. For me it was an experience, at the time. It was certainly very interesting, lighting wise. It's much more sculptural lighting, because it is not any more a two-dimensional plane that you are lighting. You are actually able to see three-dimensionally. That was a huge breakthrough for me, to lighting for a three-dimensional effect. That normal silhouette that you would go to for dramatic purpose doesn't show the same effect in 3D. That same image would just look like a cardboard cutout on paper. Now, you can see all of the way around a person's head. Usually, you're lighting a 2D image to make it seem more three-dimensional. You're lighting a face from one source to seem more dimensional, or pushing in lightness or darkness into your backgrounds or separating your heads from the background to enhance the illusion of three-dimensionality. In 3D it already has that depth, so you have to adjust your lighting approach. You can't just rely on what you did before. Usually, you'd fog out a background, or throw it out of focus. That would create less depth, or isolate a person's face with a long lens. Now you can see that background in three dimensions. So, do you want to throw it out of focus? At times you may want to, but at other times you may want to see because what's behind you may be even more interesting than what is in front of you. Those aspects of 3D were really challenging and interesting. I feel like now it's becoming a much more approachable medium. You're able to see what the 3D image looks like now on a monitor, as opposed to having to having to go to a theater to watch your work, having to put on goggles. Now you're able to have a playback monitor that is three dimensional. Now it *really is* an aesthetic choice.

LC: Beyond the question of 3D, *Avatar* was also shot digitally. Do you feel that we would only be in what would be classified as the infancy of digital? I ask because there seems to still be uncertainty as to the exact phase we are presently in of the new digital cinematography era.

(Context must be given here. This interview occurred almost nine years ago, and in the intervening period a huge amount has changed in terms of the technology involved in digital capture, and digital cinematography generally. Fiore's response must be seen in this context. His remarks are specific to that period of digital cinematography.)

MF: I feel that digital at its present stage is constantly mimicking film. It's trying very desperately to be film, but it's not. It hasn't really had a chance yet to develop its own aesthetics. There are certain experimental projects which could only be done on digital, or only could be done on a portable camera, but when it comes to theatrical filmmaking and classical storytelling, digital is just not there yet. I think it eventually will happen. A lot of projects, in terms of having a lot of visual effects, it just becomes easier to shoot digitally. One film I shot, *Real Steel*, suited a digital storytelling approach. It's not just about my view as the cinematographer, it is also about complementing the needs of everyone on the production. If I am told that the film could be better rendered digitally, then it's up to me as the cinematographer to move the project along, even if I know that we could get better visuals if we shot on film. As a part of the collaborative process I must try to make digital work.

LC: When in conversations with cinematographers I have found there is criticism of the economic imperatives behind the switch to digital. What are your thoughts of this undercurrent of cynicism directed at digital?

MF: I think a lot of that is to do with the fact that it is a new medium. There is a fear built into the response to that new medium. There's still a lot of room left to explore in digital, and I feel the minute digital separates from film will be the moment it has a life of its own. I don't feel one way or another about a project. I feel that it is great to have that digital medium at your disposal. There are certain projects that lend themselves better to digital, there are certain projects that lend themselves better to film.

LC: Some cinematographers point out that all of the tricks involved in cinematography are the same as they have ever been. With the smoke you used in shooting *Avatar* to enhance the 3D effect and assist with the highlights, that is really a use of a technique as old as film itself.

MF: I would say that the tools we have at our disposal, that we have to work with, are the same tools as we've ever had. The use of long lenses,[1] throwing things out of focus, using wide lenses for dramatic purposes.[2] One thing people forget, when the question is raised as to the place of cinematographers in cinema's future, is all of that leftover cinematic vocabulary that we have at our fingertips, that visual vocabulary we've developed over the years. I would agree that the approach hasn't changed. It's a matter of applying that certain vocabulary to a different medium.

LC: On a technical level, it is worth noting that a lot of cinematographers complain that digital cameras ruin the skin tone of actors.

(Again, it is worth noting that, through the circumstances of this book having a long gestation, a significant amount of time has passed since this interview was conducted. Given this fact Fiore's response must be contextualized as being based around existing digital cameras at the time of the interview.)

MF: I think I agree with that. The one thing we are missing in the digital image is a whole dynamic range, like four stops of dynamic range. That has to do with a whole bunch of things like color, and any kind of definition, and brightness. That, inherently, gives you a whole lot more detail in faces. Whereas digital may throw skin tone to a particular parameter, or LUT,[3] film interprets it much more instantly with a much smoother curve.[4] At times it may seem like digital is interpreting very strange skin tones, but that's all about the fact that it's not able to handle a huge dynamic range, quite the color range that film is capable of. Along with the assembling of thousands of lines to create an image digital is definitely harsher in its interpretation of an image.

LC: Lighting in a digitally generated environment, when shooting *Avatar*, did you feel liberated or constrained by certain CGI parameters?

MF: I feel like, for me, on any project, once I get through the technology is when I can really do my work. The minute I accept that it was 3D, or digital, the minute I can experiment in a much more flexible way and not look at as a technical experience, the more I'm able to express myself in my work. There's a lot of things I went into learning and experimenting with on 3D and digital, but once I have those things worked out for myself, I was still able to make it much more an artistic experience for myself.

LC: John Seale, the famed Australian cinematographer, speaks of himself as a technician, as opposed to an artist. What would you classify yourself as?

MF: It's a difficult question. There's definitely a craft involved in our trade with what we're doing as cinematographers. To call myself an artist, I feel it's erring a bit on the side of pretentiousness, so I try to be a little bit more modest. I try to approach projects from an artistic standpoint, in other words to tell a story visually and use the tools of a visual artform to tell that story. I think it is definitely an artistic approach, to a certain extent. Even though it may be technical, and though some people are very interested in the technical aspects of it, the moment I can separate myself from the technology is when I feel that I am doing something really interesting.

LC: When have you felt that you've had those moments?

MF: I try to have those moments as much as I can on a film. There's definitely moments where the technology took over and it became very much about satisfying the filmmaker. There's a lot of emotional support that you offer the director in your role as a cinematographer. A lot of the time you get involved in that aspect of it. Being involved in a long project, hanging in with the director, I think those are the things you struggle with in actually doing your work.

LC: Looking at *Avatar*, James Cameron loves blue—blue light, blue characters. That goes back to *The Abyss*, to *Terminator 2*. How much do you feel his penchant for blue is stamping your visual approach?

MF: Yes, he does definitely love blue. (*Laughs*) With Jim the approach is different from any other director because he's so

> involved in the technical aspects. With other directors, they would leave the technical aspects with me as a cinematographer. But Jim has a lot to do with the technical approach. Jim is an engineer at heart. All the technical aspects of the film he's involved with. Whether it's a matter of developing that specific camera, or developing a particular technique, he's involved with it. You're sort of on a voyage of exploration with him. With him you're trying to discover things, rather than going in with your expertise. There's influences you can try. You're discovering things together. And that's what's great is that he's so open to exploring new paths and pioneering new approaches that he has the time to experiment with while you're making the film. I'd say that was really what I took from *Avatar*.

~

In the context of what was discussed in the introduction to this volume, Fiore's remarks take on a particular relevance. It is worth considering that Fiore on one hand exemplifies the necessity of broad expertise on the part of the cameraman, and an attendant mastery of the language of film, as well as the requirement to service a vision as potentially expansive as the likes of James Cameron. The neutral position on 3D he mentions speaks to the fact that a given film's cinematography is unique and specific to the film and script that originate it. To attempt to replicate this is often a folly. Yet the paradox of film as a commercial medium means that cinematography, like any other element from a successful film, will be imitated until it becomes clear that imitation cannot replicate the success of the original. *Avatar* was conceived, designed, shot, plotted, rendered with effects in mind, and projected in a 3D format by exhibitors cognizant of the fact that it would be consumed by the majority of audience in said format. Fiore's job—the techniques he brought to his lighting and the movement of the camera—was constantly accounting for this fact and how he might integrate with the combined venture the film ended up being, even down to the advances it promoted in the exhibition of a 3D film. In this respect, 3D cinematography, and the somewhat derided phenomena of 3D post-conversion (shooting a film in 2D and converting it to 3D after the fact), became a fad based on the misinformed notion that projecting any film in 3D, or creating a film in the 3D format in postproduction, was enough to guarantee a film's success.

Notes

1. Long lenses refers to cinema lenses commonly called telephoto. For 35mm imaging (film or digital) they are generally those above 75mm.

2. Wide lenses refers to cinema lenses commonly called wide angle. For 35mm imaging (film or digital) they are generally those up to 28mm.

3. LUT is an acronym for look up table. This term is used to describe the procedure of applying various looks to digital footage. Usually done before production, or often on set, the digital imaging technician works with the cinematographer to design varying looks that can be applied to the footage to get the desired look for the movie. These are nondestructive digital recipes that are put into the metadata of the image files to allow the cinematographer to have the dailies look as close to the desired final look as possible.

4. Curve refers to an X-Y axis graphic representation of the tonal qualities of the image. The bottom of the curve, or toe, is the shadow or lowest area of luminance. The upper area, or shoulder, is the highest area luminance. The amount of steepness in the curve indicates how much tonal range is in the image.

Peter Deming

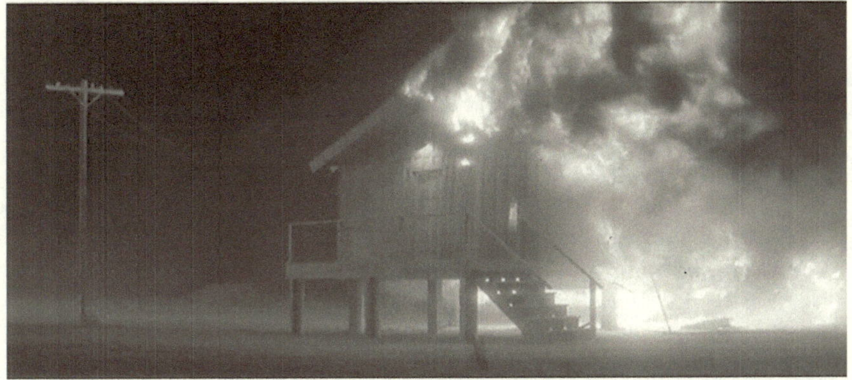

Image 14. A building explodes into flames in *Lost Highway* (Lynch 1997).

With close relationships with filmmakers such as David Lynch and Sam Raimi, the career of Peter Deming ASC has spanned from low-budget horror and teen films in the 1980s through Lynch arthouse triumphs such as *Mulholland Drive*, and Disney blockbusters such as *Oz the Great and Powerful*. Interestingly, even Deming's more esoteric projects have focused on modern twists on familiar genres. *Lost Highway*, for instance, has strong noir elements. *Drag Me to Hell* is a half-serious, half-hilarious exploration of that great horror trope, the Gypsy's curse. As much as Deming has worked in the horror and thriller genres, he is equally adept at comedy pastiche in the form of two of the three *Austin Powers* films, the original and *Austin Powers: Goldmember*. His affinity for genre has borne considerable fruits. His 3D cinematography on *Oz the Great and Powerful* allowed him to explicitly evoke the original *Wizard of Oz* cinematography, this time working from a digital camera.

His collaborations with Lynch are full of experimental cinematography and surreal, unforgettable imagery. Beyond these obvious successes, it is worth recalling his presence on historically significant works in the past forty or so years of U.S. genre cinema. Before the early 1990s explosion of African American crime dramas and their strong box office, there was a fun little film called *House Party*, a hit comedy with an all-Black cast. Years earlier he shot the pioneering slapstick horror *Evil Dead II*. Then of course there is the *Scream* series, all at least partially shot by Deming.

The following interview was conducted between Lindsay Coleman and Peter Deming in June 2015.

Lindsay Coleman: At the start of your career, you were working in some intriguing genre films. One which is often underrated is *House Party*, not least for the quality of its cinematography. All of the night exteriors in suburbia must have been tricky on *House Party*?

Peter Deming: Yes, it was tough for me to expose, especially when shooting an African American cast at night. We shot that in '89. It was the first time I didn't really have film dailies. Postproduction on the film was done on a system from Lucasfilm called Montage, which was basically a wall of VHS machines, literally fifty, sixty of them. The dailies would go right to tape. They would cut on tape, so I got to print a reel here, a reel there. I couldn't pull takes because they had to print full camera rolls. They couldn't cut the negative until they went to "conform" it,[1] so I didn't really see the movie until we did the first answer print. Then I was gauging overexposure, underexposure based on the rolls I printed and got to see in the lab. So it was really nerve-wracking, to say the least. Once we did the first answer print, I got to see what we had on the emulsion and how it was going to print. To say I played it safe in exposing the film is probably fair. We were able to print stuff down to where we wanted. That ended up being a good thing.

LC: It would've been tricky, in terms of the difference of the complexions of the actors Kid and Play. Especially when they were in two-shots.

PD: We looked at the early reels we printed and determined that Play needed an extra half stop, or 3/4 stop, in terms of exposure.[2] There were times I let that drop in the car when they're driving around. In those scenes, I had enough back light, or edge light, not to lose them. He was sort of tough to overexpose. In a way, I was sort of safe. There was never going to be an issue of burning him out. It's definitely something we keyed in on early on.

LC: There are some extended dance sequences toward the end of the party in the film. Could you talk about blocking them? They are very effective in terms of the coverage you got, as well as the camerawork you achieved.

PD: It was choreographed really well. We had to shoot the dancers head to toe and that was tricky. It was the middle of a party, but we have to film in that way without it seeming artificial. At one point Reggie Hudlin, the director, just said, "Let's get the Steadicam." Let's just get in there, let's just keep the camera moving. So that's what we did. We dropped what we were doing. We then covered the dialogue also with the Steadicam. Credit to the operator, Kirk, he had a good feeling for the music. There was enough dynamic movement in the shots. Once I saw it cut it together, I saw that really worked. It really felt fluid.

LC: On *Scream 3* you went with a high-contrast, saturated look for the night scenes. That was distinct from *House Party*, and maybe represented an evolution for you. What led to that approach?

PD: I don't know. Maybe because I had done two already. I felt on some of the first film, and then on the second film, the blue that we were using for the nights didn't really agree with some of our cast. I kind of felt, also, that I didn't want to repeat the same approach as on the first two.

LC: Were you also thinking about how the blood would show up? The attacks happen at night, so it is a relevant consideration.

PD: Always! That was always one of director Wes Craven's major concerns. We had half a dozen different bloods, as far as redness, lightness, darkness, depending on what we were shooting, daytime, nighttime. That was definitely a concern. I liked playing with skip light, or glint light, off the blood.

LC: What I like is the black of blood near the central coagulation, and the red near the edges.

PD: We actually did a lot of tests just on the viscosity of it, how it would flow. If it was blood on a person, or blood on the floor, we had different things we would use.

LC: How do you feel about sticking key lights near blood?

PD: If it's good blood, I have no problem with it. If it is not good blood, you have to rethink it.

LC: Your stars have to look good, even if they're injured.

PD: Yes. (*Laughs*) That's true. In those movies the blood technology was good, so I wasn't worried.

LC: With Ghostface, the killer in the films, you have a character wearing a white mask against the black costume. But at the same time, you have to get a sense of the violence and force being exerted by the individual inside of the costume. I would guess this can be tricky with a black costume, against a dark background, or an attack orchestrated at night. You also have to deal with motion blur because the character is moving quite fast. How do you deal with all of these challenges?

PD: Ghostface . . . I loved the mask. Sometimes you did not want to see the body, just the mask. If the body sunk into the shadows, I thought that was cool! (*Laughs*) On the second and third film, we tested fabric such that it would have a sheen to it, or some element to it, that would pick up light. Obviously, it is a very high-contrast situation with the white mask against the black hood and robe. We needed something going for it so you could have the sense of movement. The costume had a silkiness to it so that it could pick up enough light. I don't mind the ghost face floating around in the dark, but I do understand, on a narrative level, that you do need to see the action which is occurring, what the character is doing. I think working on the edge of that, in terms of the contrast, the light on the costume, is really a lot of fun.

LC: Neve Campbell, the heroine of the films, is a former ballet dancer and has an intense physicality. How do you navigate the camera around her, calibrate your camera to her explosive movement? I notice you often keep her at the center of the frame.

PD: She definitely is those things. But she is also very savvy to where the camera is, what it can capture, how fast she can go. In that way, she's very knowledgeable about the technical aspects of it. We found a comfort zone very quickly.

LC: Were you operating?

PD: Yes, I was.

LC: As much as you can focus on things which are practical and physical in your cinematography, you equally can be completely abstract. The spider crawling up the wall in *Lost Highway*. What the hell is that about!?

PD: I think the spider was just something which happened there. It was a long lens. It was difficult. Working with David Lynch sometimes, you just grab stuff like that. You don't know if it is going to be in the movie, you don't know what it is for. That, combined with the flies in the light, buzzing around, it's just mood stuff.

LC: Were you a student of his films before you started working with him?

PD: Oh definitely! I remember seeing *Eraserhead* in 35mm when it first came out. I went to see it with my college roommate at the time. (*Laughs*) I remember we walked out of the movie and just went and had a drink and really talked about it for quite a while. After that I saw everything of his. When we worked together, I felt like I knew him from his movies. I felt I knew what he liked in front of the camera. What his tastes were in terms of lighting and camera movement. For better or worse, you catalog his movies. That doesn't mean the film you're working on with him will be a direct reflection of his previous works, but at the very least it is a point of departure.

LC: Looking at his visual motifs, the fan representing that evil is nearby, or his use of a bare lightbulb, were you drawing on these motifs, or were you consciously constructing new motifs?

PD: I would say we were constructing new motifs. Whether it's conscious or unconscious. There is a certain ambience on the set which permeates the crew. The interesting thing about working with David Lynch is that the screenplay doesn't give anything away. You go into a scene without know the back-story of characters, whether characters have tension with each other, whether it is a happy or a sad scene. Yet when he gets in the room with the actors it becomes obvious whether this is a happy scene or a sad scene. It is given away in the body language and it all becomes more clear.

LC: The love scene between [Bill] Pullman and [Patricia] Arquette is shot in slow motion. It is quite unusual. How would you go about determining the frame rate on something like that?

PD: That is something which David Lynch really specified. We had shot the bulk of the scene. Then he said, "I want to do this shot over here at 120 frames." So we said, "Okay."

LC: Would you say you were printing down a lot on *Lost Highway*?

PD: I wouldn't say I was printing down a lot. I would say I was really riding the edge. David Lynch really likes things murky. If he had his way, I'd be underexposing a lot of the movie. There were some early shots I wanted to do over because I felt they were underexposed. He said, "No, I love that." The whole movie was spent riding the edge of properly unexposed versus unexposed. The shot where Bill Pullman is looking for his wife, and walks down the corridor and disappears into black, that was an effect which we spoke about. I think if you rely on printing down to get that effect you are setting yourself up to fail. We were working with such low light levels that the light really did drop off that much. To your eye, he would almost go into black, but not quite. I would call the lab and say, "He's got to go into black at the end of the hallway!" (*Laughs*)

LC: What was your stock?

PD: It was 500 of the day, which I think was 5293.

LC: What about crazy overexposure in the scene in front of the car in the desert, before the Bill Pullman character returns?

PD: Again, David Lynch and I discussed that. He knew enough to know that I would have to do some testing to get that effect.

LC: I would say so. Patricia Arquette could have ended up a white blob!

PD: Yes. We did some tests. He wanted to lose some detail, but not for it to totally white out. He wanted the audience to see that it is a face, and eyes, and her blonde hair, but that it would be so glowy that it just became this ethereal image.

LC: Was the exposure the same where Balthazar Getty is looking up to her?

PD: I think that the way it was blocked, them in front of the car, the headlights were sort of from the back of him. So instead of six stops overexposed, he was more like four stops overexposed.[3] You saw him a little more.

LC: Cinematographers talk about moments which scare them. Being that overexposed, was it scary?

PD: It wasn't because we had tested it. It's always a little scary, yeah. There was a period of shooting for two weeks in Death Valley. The film would go back to the editor in LA and we'd have to call up and say "how does it look?" We didn't see that stuff until we got back. They were loving it. We knew it was working. The scary stuff, for me, was around the cabin. You're supposed to be in the desert in the middle of the night. You've got the light on the cabin. You've got the headlight on the car that turns off. Those are your only sources. It's scary, first of all; to expose it, second of all; to make it look natural, which is sort of impossible. You don't want it to look lit, or silly.

LC: I always love the scene in which Arquette points at a photo of herself and her doppelgänger and says, "That's me." I can never, never tell exactly who she is pointing at!

PD: Yes. And I think that's on purpose. (*Laughs*)

LC: The shot of Robert Loggia on the phone to Getty is really a classic bit of horror cinematography.

PD: We had a soft toplight on Loggia. We didn't want to know where the characters were, so we made sure to not give away much of the background. It helped create a really creepy mood. On the shot of Balthazar on the other end, he was on the phone in a hallway, and then he comes and stands in a doorway. There's a dining room behind him, but you can't see that because it's all in black. Normally, you'd put a little bit of backlight on him to separate him from that blackness, but I liked playing around with not doing that. He had the frontlight, but he sort of melded into that black. To me that's much creepier. It's sort of like "what's going to come out of that black?" What's back there is sort of a subtext to the shot.

LC: It must be interesting in utilizing horror aesthetics, but then not delivering on the scare.

PD: Yes, the scare is in the characters and the dialogue, it's not in the physical expression of a scare.

LC: I'm always fascinated by emotional violence on screen. There is a lot of emotional violence in both of your Lynch films. How do you determine a visual strategy to express emotional violence?

PD: There was some stuff with Loggia in the tailgater scene. I think it is one of things where you set up a powerful composition. To me it's in close, on a medium focal length, and maybe the camera is a little low to give that person power. It depends on the block as well. I think sometimes scenes are just blocked that way anyway. He's over that guy, he's pistol-whipping him, we are shooting up at him. To me it's a focal length thing. You want to be in a 35–40. If a character is moving at you, you want to feel that movement, you don't want to compress that shot.

LC: The shot of the explosion of the cabin in the desert in *Lost Highway* was quite beautiful. Did you design it that way, or did you just get lucky?

PD: It wasn't actually designed to explode at all. We were done shooting. We were getting ready to pack up. The producer was saying that the art department would come out and dismantle the cabin once we had the negative report.[4] We starting thinking, can't we just blow it up? We asked the effects guy if he could blow it up. He said, "Sure, I can blow it up, give me twenty minutes." I think we had three cameras. One was normal, one was overcranked, one shot in reverse. We didn't know if the footage would ever be used. David Lynch found a place to put it.

LC: Don McAlpine talked in *American Cinematographer* about adjusting the exposure as the explosion progresses.[5] How did you go about achieving that?

PD: Well, it's tough, especially when it's an explosion taking place at night. I think with the initial explosion you're sort of screwed. Unless you're shooting in the day you're always going to lose a certain amount of that. Once that initial burst is gone, whatever fire and smoke follows, you sort of have to gauge. Having done some fire work prior to that, having done some tests, you know that at an eight—or whatever—fire is correctly exposed,[6] you sort of judge that on the spot and adjust accordingly. The film stocks are quite good, so they could handle a lot of the high end.[7] So you approach it from that direction. We were fortunate that there was a lot of black smoke mixed with the fire,[8] which really helped with the exposure a great deal.

LC: The film *Lost Highway* has so many visual gracenotes in it. It's tough to know where to begin. How about the extensive highlights on the chrome surfaces in *Lost Highway*?

PD: We were using nets on the back of the lens,[9] so any highlights were accentuated. It sort of had that halo effect.

LC: How about your use of overexposed toplight on the jail scenes?

PD: (*Laughs*) I think that I had that light coming in when he was let in from the stairway. I wanted it to feel like a dungeon. He was coming from a place of light to a very moody place. Some of it was stylized stuff David Lynch wanted to try. There were some shots which were extremely out of focus. We couldn't get the lens out of focus enough, so we'd unseat it and physically pull it out of the camera so we could defocus it even more. That became a motif in the second half of the movie. The scene where he is looking at the ceiling light with the flies around it we were booming up toward it with the camera, and pulling the lens out at the same time.

LC: Do you worry about damaging the lens?

PD: Oh yes, for *sure*! The personalities of most first assistants won't let that happen.

LC: So, they're going to stop you? (*Laughs*)

PD: We'll they're the ones who are doing it, so they make sure everything is safe. You're basically changing a lens as the camera is running. There is nothing abusive about it. It is just unusual.

LC: When Pullman transforms into Getty, and Getty becomes the protagonist, there is a feeling in the film that both day shots and night shots have this dreamlike quality. How do you maintain a continuity in creating that particular mood?

PD: Right. Well, the images are only about half of it. Color palette, the speed of camera movement, and so on is certainly very slow and pleasant. There is also the sound design David Lynch chooses, which is such a huge part of everything he does.

LC: Did you ever disagree with David Lynch during the shooting of the film?

PD: I don't think so. There is a great amount of freedom working with David Lynch. You can really interpret things, lighting-wise. He talks about the mood of the scene and then just lets you go and create it as you see fit. There was a scene in *Lost Highway* where we lit it and David Lynch came out and said it was not what he wanted. So we chatted. Then it basically came down to us shutting off every light except the key light. We then shot it with just one light. I'd heard stories from *Twin Peaks*, the series, where he'd done the same thing. There would be a night exterior in the woods and then he'd just turn off one light after another until it was just lit by a flashlight!

LC: Let's move to your second collaboration with Lynch, *Mulholland Drive*. I have to ask about a very specific shot in *Mulholland Drive*. Lee Grant really gets horror lighting when she appears at the door of Naomi Watts. She basically plays a creepy old lady who mysteriously appears.

PD: Yes. It's funny, because the whole effect came out of the screen door. And she set up that effect herself. The light was set up, and when she opened the screen door it created that shadow that crossed over her head. I never really talked to her about finding that shadow, and I'm not really sure if she was conscious of it. She seemed to be playing into, finding her light, or lack of, in a great way. We wanted it to have a mood, but it excelled in a way which was just organic.

LC: It's quite organic because it looks as though the character is blind.

PD: Yes, I agree. It's very strange. She has this faraway look. Because you can't see her eyes well, I can see how you would think that.

LC: In *Mulholland Drive* the camera feels like it is a person in the room. In the infamous scene where Naomi Watts is crying and masturbating, the camera is slightly above her but there is also slight movement to it?

PD: Yes, there was.

LC: It's very intimate, but it also gives the experience of the camera standing and watching.

PD: In that scene the camera is like her partner. It is a love scene and the camera is the partner in the love scene. I think there was a lot of aggression in that scene for a sex scene. It goes back to your question about shooting motion, shooting people who are angry. Getting in there on a 35 or 40 [mm]—focal length is such an important part of capturing the emotion in a scene. I hope the audience is not conscious of it, but it translates so much emotion, particularly when an audience watches in a movie theater. I think when she's on the couch and she's moving left or right or forward you really feel that proximity. It makes the audience feel uncomfortable. If you're watching that scene and that action on a longer lens, it's almost like you're spying. You still feel uncomfortable, but less than you would if you were right up close to her and that action is happening right in front of you. That really lends to the anxiety of the scene.

LC: Naomi Watts was apparently very upset shooting the scene, so would you say there is a documentary element to the scene?

PD: I know it was difficult for her. Any discomfort she felt she channeled into the character. If that was being thrown back at David Lynch, it worked for the movie.

LC: When there is the reveal of the alternate Watts, and her alternate storyline, in the flashback toward the end of *Mulholland Drive*, there is a very fast camera POV shot from Watts's perspective, which moves over the top of her couch to reveal Laura Harring. It is not just the narrative reveal, which is significant, but also speed of the camera move which punctuates it.

PD: That was something which David Lynch concocted. It was that same thing of the lens choice in being able to feel with the move that you are right next to Laura Harring.

LC: What do you feel the story of *Mulholland Drive* is about?

PD: You have the Watts character reflecting on what she thought would be an idealized version of Hollywood. But that then devolves toward the end of the film with her trying to get the upper hand in a cat fight.

LC: Do you think it is fair to call Justin Theroux the film's villain?

PD: No, I wouldn't call him the villain. Maybe a little bit. He's the prize these two women were fighting for. In the dinner scene, he is fully aware of Watts's sadness and bitterness, and rubs salt in the wound a little bit by announcing his engagement to Laura Harring. It's very Billy Wilder via David Lynch.

LC: In both versions of the story, he is the smartest character in the film.

PD: Yes, though I think the cowboy is maybe *the* smartest character.

LC: Theroux's scene with the cowboy features the Lynch motif of a bare bulb.

PD: There's a lot of bare bulbs, that is true.

LC: Are you consciously aware of adding to the Lynch canon, adding to his bank of indelible images?

PD: No. Sometimes David Lynch will lay out a scene. It will be a night scene.

Can I have a light here?

You can have one bulb, that's it. One bare bulb.

Okay, I'll take it.

LC: What about all the fuss over the meaning of *Mulholland Drive*, people asking what is its true narrative? Do you feel there is too much fuss?

PD: There is too much fuss. But it is also understandable. What it requires from the viewer is much more challenging than the average film, in which everything is tied up neatly. This really requires some effort and some participation. But it is infinitely more solvable than *Lost Highway*, which I am still trying to figure out!

LC: Maybe the point of that film is when Patricia Arquette whispers to Getty, "You'll never have me."

PD: David Lynch started as a painter. He's still a painter. Like a painter, he arrives on the set with a general idea of what he's going to create, then he allows his interaction with others, the inspirations of the day, to contribute to his final output. I think that there are parts of films which are about a certain amount of experimentation. It's about, with the final product, looking at the canvas in a museum. Ten people will have ten different impressions of the canvas. David Lynch loves having people look at the film he produces, be entertained, but also wonder and speculate as to its meaning.

LC: I'd like, at the end of this interview, to talk about some of your recent forays into digital cinematography, specifically *Oz the Great and Powerful.* This was a huge production, not least in the lengths you went to to create the lighting effect of the sun in a studio for the film. The artificial sun for *Oz the Great and Powerful* seemed incredibly difficult to achieve.

PD: That was a tough one. We had very big sets on very big stages. We needed a sun source to carry 250 feet and have enough exposure to shoot 3D. We built a very large unit which we felt coped very well with day exteriors.

LC: Did you try to think of other alternatives?

PD: We sat around in prep and discussed. We knew nothing existed which could meet our needs, and that we'd have to create it. We had to make a group of lighting units together to accomplish this. We settled on the idea we came up with. We had a smaller version of it, then a bigger one. We built two, and then a mini.

LC: It's incredible.

PD: Yeah, it's nuts.

LC: Looking at the beginning segment of the film, do you feel there is much of a future for digital black and white, given that they now have a special Alexa that shoots black and white.[10]

PD: Absolutely! There's the Red Monochrome as well.[11] Obviously, on that we shot color then converted to black and white, just drained it of color, and also worked with the contrast and brightness. The quality of the black and white was somewhat soft in terms of contrast. *The Wizard of Oz*, in the early section, was almost gray and white, it wasn't a very punchy, contrasty black and white. Modern black and white is much more contrasty. I think people are used to that more modern look.

LC: The depth and resolution of digital black and white is exciting.

PD: Yes. Black and white photochemical was great, but it was slow. I think with the old film, your whites were never white white. But with digital you get a really clean and pure white. In any case, what you can get from digital in the end really comes across just like film.

LC: So perhaps the debate will subside if the end result is so close.

PD: I think it is very close, and I believe it will subside. The debate between film and video is really one of texture. Video has a texture that film doesn't have, and people are just adjusting to this new texture. Now you have digital trying to move back to the texture of film. Will it be exactly the same? No, but it will be pretty close.

~

The specific relationship that emerges from Deming's descriptions of his collaborations with David Lynch is one of clear chapters. As a college student, Deming came under the Lynch's influence when the director's distinctive style was just emerging. Produced over several years, the film *Eraserhead* was not only a notable "midnight movie" of the 1970s, but also a visual treasure trove of nightmare motifs. Deming became a student of the film. In the following two decades, Lynch's style evolved and influenced Deming as a cinematographer. In this interval, Deming's artistic and technical evolution as a practitioner has enabled him to effectively accept the aesthetic baton in his collaboration with Lynch, being placed in a position of trust to elaborate and extrapolate on Lynch's aesthetic. Two decades later, this relationship, along with Deming's acumen in the realm of digital cinematography, has only grown. In the eighteen-hour series of *Twin Peaks: The Return* Deming not only shot every episode, he made exceptional contributions to the distinctive digital look of that series.

Lynch shot *Inland Empire* using a small prosumer camera and established an affinity for smaller, less high-powered cameras. He and Deming discussed the use of digital SLRs as the major camera to use on the series. A compromise was arrived at. Deming was able to negotiate, in conjunction with Lynch, with the Showtime Channel to ensure that the series would be shot at a lower-than-typical resolution. Although it is typically network policy to capture a series in 4K, the series was shot using the Arri Amira camera, which uses essentially the same sensor as the Arri Alexa, but records at 3.2K, which could be up-resolutioned to 4K. In turn they rented 1960 ultra-speed lenses from Panavision to soften the sharpness of the digital image. Some of the results, particularly in the wintery day exteriors, are unnerving and striking. Most significant to their developing collaboration in the era of digital capture was Deming's ongoing exploration of LUTs. Typically around sixteen LUTs could be stored in the Amira. This was not sufficient for Deming's requirements. Rather than endlessly storing and importing LUTs to the camera, Deming devised four basic LUTs: day interior, day exterior, night interior, night exterior. He built on them in terms of green/magenta shifts for mixed-light stations, as well as differing levels of saturation and contrast. For these four categories, Deming was to develop a total of 120 LUTs. Rather than lighting, then shooting, and then creating a LUT, he would pass on to the DIT requests with respect to contrast and green suppression and have a wide range of LUTs to sample before shooting a scene. These new LUTs were placed in the four general categories he had devised. This facility with LUTs enabled Deming and Lynch an even more condensed creative process as they might easily see an assortment of different possible aesthetics for a scene. Thus, more than two decades since the start of their collaborative relationship, the director and cinematographer persisted in evolving their shorthand with the new possibilities of digital capture.

Notes

1. Conforming is the process of matching and replacing the completed final edit (after the picture is locked) with the original camera negative or digital files. Editing was normally done on a workprint (struck directly from the film negative), or now in the digital age, with smaller proxy files such as QuickTime ProRes or DNxHD. Lucasfilm's Montage system was an intermediate system where the film neg was transferred to VHS tape, the material was edited on tape, and the film neg was conformed to match the tape edit.

2. Film (and digital) does not have the same dynamic range our eyes do. It cannot "see" as wide an exposure range. One result of this is that dark or shadow areas that look fine in life, on set may look too dark when the scene is recorded. Dark costumes, night scenes, or darker-skinned people may require the lens aperture to be opened more—letting more light on to the film—so

that shadow areas will reproduce as they appear in life. One stop of increased exposure results in twice the amount of light getting to the sensor. The increased dynamic range and better noise management have made this less problematic in newer digital sensors.

3. At four stops overexposed, we are allowing sixteen times more light on to the negative than a normal or correct exposure. At six stops over we have sixty-four times more light. Given that some areas of the image are already brighter than mid-gray and that no one can see the image on film until it is processed and printed, it pays to know the point at which a very bright scene becomes a white scene before you shoot.

4. A negative report (neg report) is sent from the lab after processing to the set at the start of the working day, detailing the physical condition (any scratches, hairs in gate, dust spots, etc.) and usually remarks on focus and exposure. Sleepless nights and early morning calls to the lab contact are not unheard of.

5. As an explosion progresses, the amount of light generated rapidly increases and then dies away. It is sometimes possible to "ride the exposure" by manually adjusting the aperture of the lens as these lighting changes occur to keep the exposure within the range of the film/sensor.

6. Experience or testing will provide a general exposure guide, and in many cases the more violent part of the explosion may fit quite well into the top end of the dynamic range without aperture adjustment.

7. One of the attractive characteristics of film stock as opposed to digital sensors is its capacity to "roll off" highlights rather than cut them off suddenly (clip the highlights) as the exposure approaches its upper limit.

8. By mixing dark and black tones with the highlights of the fire, we get some contrast, and the spread of smoke may have reduced the intensity of the brighter areas.

9. Nets—often made of fine weave silk or nylon stocking material—can be fixed over the front or rear element of a lens to provide a slight diffusion and to make highlights bloom or buzz. Cinematographers can occasionally be seen browsing the aisles of lingerie stores in search of the perfect net.

10. Arri Alexa XT B+W, ISO 2000 shoots only monochrome (and infrared)

11. Red Epic-M Dragon Monochrome Camera, ISO 2000 shoots only monochrome (and infrared).

Bibliography

Williams, David E. "Twin Peaks: Dreams, Doubles and Dopplegangers." *American Cinematographer*, July 11, 2018. https://ascmag.com/articles/twin-peaks-dreams-doubles-and-dopplegangers.

Dion Beebe

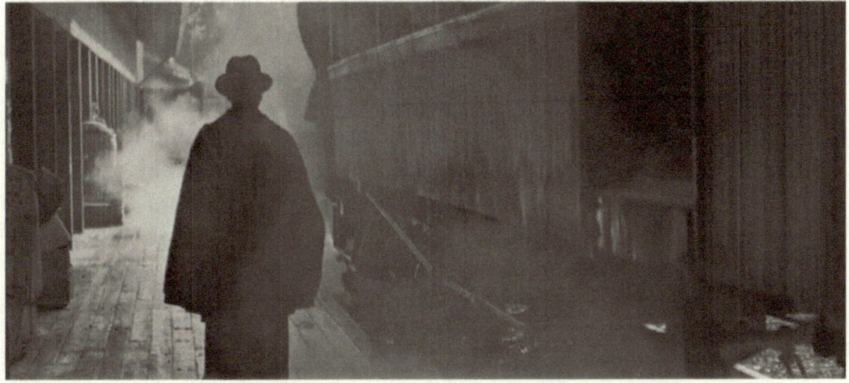

Image 15. The winter light produced above illustrates the silking required for the set in *Memoirs of a Geisha* (Marshall 2005).

FOLLOWING A DECADE OF QUIRKY Australian dramas, Dion Beebe ACS ASC experienced his major North American breakthrough with the musical *Chicago*, followed quickly by the digital cinematography breakthrough *Collateral*. An Academy Award in 2005 for *Memoirs of a Geisha* was followed by work in the smart blockbuster *The Edge of Tomorrow* and the musical *Into the Woods*.

Beebe has a talent for embracing logistically complicated projects. On *Memoirs of a Geisha* he had to determine how to create a wintery look in the harsh California summer sun. On *The Edge of Tomorrow* he needed to establishing continuity in his lighting for a battle scene shot on a huge beach, and then repeat the sequence several times throughout that film. *13 Hours* saw him dealing with a similar challenge, this time helping Michael Bay with blocking and shooting of a battle sequence spread out over a square quarter mile. On a level of pure aesthetics, Beebe frequently accepts major challenges. On *Green Lantern*, with digital costumes being mapped onto actors in postproduction, Beebe had to devise a lighting system wherein the light from the suits would help illuminate the actors. On that film, a similar challenge was stepping into an aesthetic paradigm where the color green dominated throughout. Thus, an actor being self-lit from below in a world full of green was Beebe's challenging brief.

The following interview was conducted between Lindsay Coleman and Dion Beebe in January 2013.

> **Lindsay Coleman:** Let's look at one of your earlier films, shot in Australia, *Praise*. When I spoke with John Curran, the director, about *Praise*, he talked about the challenge of showing Sacha Horler, the female lead, as the hero saw her, and as she appeared in everyday life. How did you go about achieving this? It was a tricky brief. Horler is a beautiful actress, but the character was overweight and had a lot of eczema in the film.
>
> **Dion Beebe:** It was. That film is such a credit to John, in terms of the tone, and to Sacha, in terms of how she portrayed that character, revealing this ballsy, confronting, yet sexual woman; I don't think I can take any credit for that. Certainly, in terms of photographing it, it's challenging. The choices we made, in terms of color and tone, how we photographed her, we would certainly hope that that assisted what she was bringing to the story as an actor. It's very much a collaboration. Often, in movie-making, you're taking an actor and creating a character. Sometimes people just walk on screen and that character is just who they are. Very often you're also trying to make them feel smaller and less significant. You're making coverage choices to undermine that character. Other times you're making choices to heighten the impact of the character. That becomes a choice of angles and lighting. You can either exaggerate or diminish a character's presence on screen and I will use the techniques, in consultation with the actors and the director, which best achieve that.
>
> **LC:** I always like the end section of the film, where you feature a lot of greens and browns in the men's shelter the hero finds

himself in, and then in the last shots you switch your lighting such that everything becomes much more clean and crisp.

DB: When John and I started working on it, we knew we wanted to create a world that had its own particular beauty. But it was a sort of tobacco-stained, dirt-under-the-fingernails look and sensibility. It had its own aesthetic and comfort within that world. When you come out of that world into a more sterile world, you really feel that transition. At the same time, you miss the world you've departed, even though we know that this is the kind of world which we, in mainstream society, shy away from.

LC: If you look at *Praise* and *Holy Smoke* coming so close together, in the late 1990s, they are pretty rough on Australian society.

DB: I don't really see it that way. I think with *Praise*, it's rough, the characters are rough, but there is a sensitivity, a sensibility there, there's a strength in the characters which is more of a celebration than a dismissal or a criticism. I think Sacha's character in *Praise* is incredible. I mean she's in not attractive in a classical way, but the strength of the character is phenomenal.

LC: I always enjoyed the line where she asked why she was kicked out of home as a teen and she says, "I used to bring boys home and fuck them." (*Laughs*) She just says it matter-of-fact.

DB: Exactly. And the same thing is there with Kate Winslet's character in *Holy Smoke*. When the film came out in Australia, people there felt that the film was mocking Australia. There is humor there, but the main character is a very strong female character. She comes through the story and finds the strength through this crisis. Both films pose questions of national identity and the popular persona of Australia. Yet both films show a strength in the Australian personality. Really there is much more in both films to be celebrated than criticized.

LC: Looking at the films, do you feel that cinematographers help Australians, in terms of how they see their own country?

DB: I would certainly hope so. As an Australian cinematographer, having made a number of films in Australia, we are presenting a vision of Australia to not only the Australian public but also the world. We're making particular choices, crafting particular kinds of images, and if you look back in the history of Australian cinema, you'll see this steady progression of really iconic imagery. I think these movies become a part of the fiber of the country. In an odd way, they become a part of the mythology of the country. If you look at *Picnic at Hanging Rock*, there is something mysteriously Australian about that film. *Breaker Morant* is not set in Australia but it just somehow feels like an Australian story. It feels Australian. How you identify that feels debatable . . . it's something to do with the characterization, the scale of the land . . .

LC: I think that Dean Semler's work on *Dances with Wolves* work owes a lot to his Australian background.

DB: Exactly. If you experience that sense of standing in the Australian Outback, or standing under a sky that is that large, it's hard to be an arsehole.

LC: When I spoke with cinematographer/director Warwick Thornton, who of course won the Caméra d'Or at Cannes for his film *Samson and Delilah*, he discussed the huge limitations in terms of equipment and stock Australian cinematographers must deal with. For someone like you, once you get to Hollywood, you can make even more of the amazing resources you are granted.

DB: There is some truth in the idea that to make films in Australia you are working with the bare essentials. It'll often be one truck, with all the grip and lighting equipment thrown in, and a van for your camera gear. I remember shooting the documentary *Eternity*, and it was just myself, my assistant Sion Michel, and the director making the film. It was just us, with a couple of lamps, and a 5K generator tucked in with the camera gear. I think you do figure out how to be resourceful and how to make decisions that are made because of the resources. Making that move to Hollywood those sort of skills do help you. You do have to learn how to spend the money. When you do have to the resources you get on blockbusters, I must admit that when I came over here I found myself still veering more to the approach of a camera in a van. You quickly realize the complexity and scale which is possible on these larger films, and yet you can also see how the resourcefulness you acquired working on low-budget Australian films will only serve you well.

LC: Which Australian cinematographers did you look up to? Was Geoff Burton's work a big influence on you?

DB: Oh definitely, I was always a big admirer of Geoff Burton's work. Geoffrey Simpson also I considered, and consider, a fine cinematographer. John Seale, I was also a big fan of, and he actually presented me with my diploma when I graduated. He has always been extremely encouraging. We certainly look to our heroes, the work being done by the cinematographers around us, and I know for myself that I always felt encouraged and inspired by the work they were doing, by the possibilities.

LC: My research indicates you were considered a star student at AFTRS [Australian Film Television and Radio School].

DB: I don't think so. I think that's fine in retrospect. People look back and think that. When I was there, you were just a student. You were there making student movies. I don't think there was special treatment. There was the special Kodak student filmmaking award. I didn't get that in my graduation year. That went to another student. I don't think I was a star student. I was fortunate. I shot a lot of short films while I was at AFTRS. Some of those films went on to win awards at ACS and at the Australian Film Institute. That sort of recognition and those accolades really do give you a big boost. I certainly felt the recognition I got from the ACS went a long way to give me confidence in the work I was doing.

LC: Warwick Thornton spoke with me about the constant anxiety cinematographers feel in their perfectionism. Do you still feel that way?

DB: If you take on the job, the responsibility, you take on the pressure. You figure out a way to handle people questioning you . . . the format you want, the number of cameras you choose, the lenses, film stock. Some of the questions relate to budget, some are aesthetic. It's a constant, let say politely, conversation, between you and producers, directors, first ADs, and so on. And that pressure only increases as budgets get bigger, movie stars get more famous, that is not going to go away. You have to be prepared to answer questions, to work with people. You have to listen to those questions, not just feel like you're defending a position.

LC: Let's talk about the camera you shot one of your most famous films on, the Thomson Viper, which you used on *Collateral*, followed by *Miami Vice*. Jeff Cronenweth, when I spoke with him, talked about the Thomson Viper being buried by the industry. Your thoughts?

DB: It might be more of a conspiracy theory that I don't really know about. I also think that Thomson faced a very established motion picture machine in Arri, and Sony, and Panavision systems and cameras. My experience with the Vipers was that it was very pioneering days with *Collateral* and *Miami Vice*. But between *Collateral* and *Miami Vice*, with requests that we made to Thomson to work on their cameras, nothing really happened. There was no real participation on their part in terms of working on the motion picture side of the technology or the business. My feeling is that they were dabbling in motion pictures, they weren't really committed. Their involvement was more on the side of their still cameras, as well as television broadcast cameras.

LC: Do you feel that *Collateral* and *Miami Vice* will be the signature Thomson Viper films in cinema history?

DB: I think that they are both very different films. I think, and this is a big credit to Michael Mann, that *Collateral* put digital filmmaking, in a motion picture sense, on the map. It was a bold move on Michael's part to do it, and he proved that you could make a big, commercial picture on the medium. Not only that, but you could also use the medium in a particular way. It was clearly its own format with its own quirks, its own signature.

LC: *Collateral* is very significant in the history of cinematography, it's significant to your career. All of that aside, how do you feel about it as a film?

DB: I'm proud of *Collateral*. It was a hard film to make. Michael Mann is a very demanding director. I think it pushed some boundaries in terms of the technical achievements of the film. I think it does have a place in terms of the history of digital cinematography.

LC: I saw *Miami Vice* twice at the movies, even bought the DVD twice! Despite the rabid fandom of people such as myself, it was perhaps not the success some had hoped. Do you feel it is misunderstood?

DB: In some ways. It got caught at the classic Hollywood juncture. Michael wanted to make a film that was much more cerebral. Hollywood wanted to make a deep cover cop film, a commercial action picture. The film found itself sitting somewhere between the two in the audience's mind. I don't think there was a question in Michael's mind. In his mind, he was making a love story, a story of forbidden love. A cop in love with a sophisticated criminal. In some ways, maybe it *is* misunderstood or misinterpreted. Maybe the expectations placed on the film were different to what was actually created. You don't control that. You make a movie. Out it goes. Then people love it or hate it.

LC: Your work on *Memoirs of a Geisha* was remarkable in that you argued for the need to cover in silk a massive set, thus breaking up the harsh California light. Given that the film was set in winter, this certainly made sense. Your use of silks on *Memoirs of a Geisha*—do you feel that was an aesthetic achievement or a logistical achievement?

DB: (*Laughs*) It was an aesthetic and a logistical achievement. It was an important decision. When we set about to make the film in California, and 85 to 90 percent of it was shot in California, we faced the struggle of how are we going to capture seasons in a city, and a state, where the sun shines three hundred days of the year. To do that, we needed to control the sunlight. This is something cinematographers have done since they first started shooting films. So the decision came up to silk the town, the set of ***hanamachi***. Then, of course, the first conversations are aesthetic, what can we achieve? We can control the season if we can control the light. Then the conversation turns to logistics and cost. I remember being pulled into a meeting in Sony to talk about the silk. It was going to cost the production a million just to do the silk. They wanted some guarantees. If we're going to spend this money, is this the right call? Can we do this in post, can we do this on a smaller scale, and so on. It was, of course, all the questions you would expect. To their great credit, they went with it. It's one thing where the idea is one thing, "let's silk the town." And then the reality is that it is a set the size of two football fields, and we're going to throw a big cloth over the whole thing! That all sounds great in theory, but to pull that off, to get people to believe in that, to then make it a reality, is really something. There were a lot of great people involved, one of them being my great key grip, Scott Robinson, who has since passed away, and my gaffer who I still work with, John Buckley. It was a huge undertaking, but it paid off. It paid off for the movie and it paid off for me too, quite nicely.

LC: Given the present state of DI technology, could it have been achieved in the DI?

DB: The same effect could not have been achieved in the DI. Not even today could it have been done in the DI. If you have a character standing in full sunlight, there is nothing which you can do with that other than to embrace the full sunlight. Either we broke up that sunlight with the silking, or we had to deal with that harsher look. It is a good question though. Sony was certainly asking similar questions at the time, what with what they knew a DI was capable of. They wondered if it could not be used to create, in post, light appropriate to the various seasons. But you know, the possibility of us creating the light that would be found when it might be snowing in the story on a hot, bright California day, it's just not possible unless we can control and canopy the sky like we did. To their credit, they could have said, "We're not doing it." It was risky. The chance of that just up and blowing away, the potential for that was always there. But we were lucky. There were safeguards built into its design. It hadn't been done on that scale before that time, and it hasn't been done on that scale since.

LC: I spoke with Jost Vacano, the cinematographer of *RoboCop* and *Total Recall*, and he said he shoots for the audience first, the director second. Do you feel that way?

DB: I feel I am always working with the director. Each film experience brings with it a unique view of whatever the subject and content is. It is important to respect that and to try and identify that. That is what makes so many movies which deal with the same subject, and yet deal with it in so many different ways. There is always a unique approach specific to a unique vision. Audiences will like it, or they won't like it. But, if you are trying to cater to the audience, it's tricky. That's the studio's job. As a cinematographer, my feeling is "let's look at the scripts, let's talk to the director, let's try to find the unique voice of the movie."

LC: Do you feel that you are serving your own muse?

DB: No. Somehow, we all do, in some ways. I try to consciously stay aware of the director's vision. When queried and questioned about stuff I do try to listen, to walk around the problem and see it from some other perspective. If I come in and am trying to serve my own purpose on a project, I am just going to keep repeating myself. It's much more interesting to find other ways to do it. It keeps the whole process more fresh and interesting. Every time I start a new project I am very excited to be, on the one hand, dealing with a very similar subject, yet in a very different way thanks to the collaboration.

LC: Do you feel attached to the work you do, or do you feel more like a craftsperson for hire, unattached emotionally?

DB: I definitely feel attached to the projects I work on. When things don't work I feel as devastated as the director. I set out to do the best work on any project I take on. When that doesn't work out, it is disappointing. When things don't work out, the cinematographer is less in the spotlight than the directors and the producers. I still see it as a reflection of my work. It still hurts.

LC: What about success? It is incredible the individuals you beat that year for the Oscar, in 2005. That must give you a feeling of incredible pride.

DB: It is something I am extremely proud of. That whole journey is such a surreal experience. To go through that whole Oscar race is. I'd had the advantage of going through it once before on *Chicago*, and that was totally weird. *Geisha* came around, I wouldn't say I was a seasoned Hollywood player, but I would say I was more prepared emotionally for that journey. It is odd, there is such a spotlight thrown on you. It is flattering, but also confusing. It's very easy to get a little lost in that whole process. I was definitely proud of the work. So much blood and sweat went into that movie, from so many people, that you walk away with an Oscar feeling guilty. So many people helped contribute to that aesthetic and yet *I* ended up with the Oscar.

~

This interview was conducted during production for *Edge of Tomorrow*. This particular film involved (as would Beebe's later film shot with Michael Bay) maintaining controlled lighting conditions over a vast physical space where a battle was waged throughout the course of both films. *Edge of Tomorrow* involved lighting conditions being somewhat controlled during a daytime beach invasion. *13 Hours*, a depiction of the Benghazi incident, involved a night assault by combatants on a US government compound in Libya. The scope and logistical challenges for both films were considerable and seem to suggest Beebe enjoys working on a large canvas. In terms of his personal aesthetic, scope seems to be a consistent theme in Beebe's Hollywood career, be it the theatrical lighting on stages for the musical numbers of *Chicago*, the comprehensive transformation of the lighting environment on the set of the *hanamachi* in *Memoirs of Geisha*, or the evocation of a gaslit, 1930s London in *Mary Poppins Returns*. Scope aside, Beebe, true to his statements on working with directors, appears to have a genuine knack for serving the specifics needs of his directors, who are usually at crucial technical junctures in their own developing aesthetics. Production on *Collateral* was impeded by a fractious relationship between cinematographer Paul Cameron and director Michael Mann. Beebe was able to step in and deliver on the specific technical and visual demands Mann was placing on him. *Edge of Tomorrow* was the biggest film yet of Doug Liman's career (even more so than *Mr. and Mrs. Smith*) with its complicated visual effects, major battle scenes, and complicated script. Beebe's willingness and ability to serve such specific requirements of script and director speak strongly to how a cinematographer may collaborate in the most elaborate, challenging visions.

Christopher Doyle

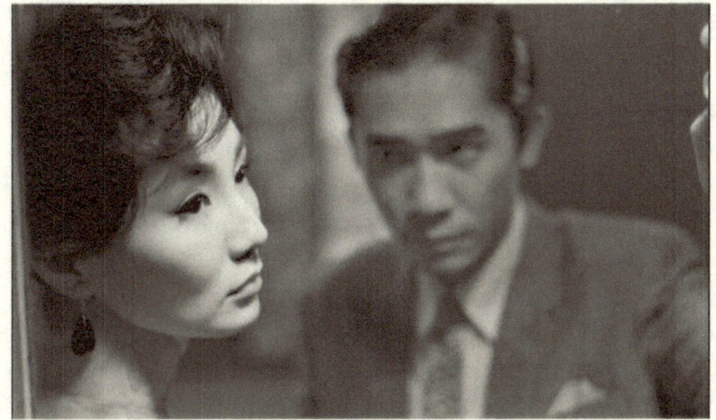

Image 16. A woman (Maggie Cheung) in *In the Mood for Love* (Kar-Wai 2000).

One of the most celebrated cinematographers of the 1990s, Christopher Doyle HKSC began his career in Hong Kong cinema, making his reputation with films such as *Chungking Express*, *Ashes of Time*, and *In the Mood for Love*. He went on to work in Hollywood and independent American films such as *Paranoid Park*. Doyle is also a director. While many cinematographers are respected, revered, and studied, it is very rare that a cinematographer achieves a level of fame/notoriety akin to their director or perhaps the film they are working on. Doyle has certainly achieved this, his work often so striking, so memorable, as to nearly eclipse the narrative, performances, and quirks of his director. Remarkably this has never been a point of complaint against Doyle; rather, his work, even in its eye-catching bravado, complements narratives that often focus on the mysteries of love, time, and the beauties of the world.

Doyle has often worked on rapturously romantic films such as *Happy Together*, *2046*, *In the Mood for Love*, and *Chungking Express* and he has equally invested in serving the sometimes clinical visions of auteurs. He was cinematographer for Gus Van Sant's shot-for-shot remake of *Psycho*, Van Sant's documentary-influenced *Paranoid Park*, and Jim Jarmusch's hypnotically paced *The Limits of Control*, and Neil Jordan's modern-day fairy tale *Ondine*. In all instances, he proved stylistically adept, opting for a strong emphasis on composition in Jarmusch's film, a rigorous appropriation of the original Hitchcock film in his remake with Van Sant, and the evocation of a particular, mystical flavor in the Jordan film.

Doyle made some controversial remarks on the Academy Award for cinematography being awarded to Claudio Miranda for *Life of Pi*, challenging whether the visuals on the film, a blend of live-action cinematography and digital effects, could even be considered cinematography in conventional terms. This was the major subject of the following interview.

Lindsay Coleman interviewed Christopher Doyle in April 2013, at the time his comments on Claudio Miranda's cinematography on *The Life of Pi* were attracting online controversy.

Lindsay Coleman: Let's start first with what is most topical. Do you see yourself as a leader in the cinematography community, in light of your recent comments?

Christopher Doyle: (*Laughs*) It's called going viral, is that what you said? I have been surprised that people of genuine status in the cinematography community have been extremely supportive. Most of them said, "Thank God you said it, because everybody wanted to say it!" I could modify it, I'd love to modify it, I'd love there to be more dialogue about what I said, because it's important. We are at a turning point between cinematography, and the whole package of what a film starts with and ends with that has to be addressed, and it's not being addressed traditionally. What needs to be addressed is what is our role is, as cinematographers. Why don't you just get some kid out of high school, or film school, because that is what the impetus is toward. If you want people like us, if you think we have something to give, let us give it to you. Don't clip our wings. If it includes a great number of other people involved, then you should acknowledge them. I think that the structure of filmmaking and the approach to cinematography has changed so much in the past five or six years and people have to address it. They have to address it not just by making 3D, not just by remaking all of these other films. We have to go into a new sphere of collaborative, or constructive, or economic, engagement. That is the thing that is happening. That is what I was pissed off about. I have no ax to grind against anybody whatsoever, except against the system, which has to be punched in the face to realize that they should take their glasses off. They should take their 3D glasses off and take part in something which is engaging, apropos [of] which is engaging with the changes which are happening in visual experience. I think, and I think Anthony Dod Mantle would also think, and those of us who care would think, "Why the hell would people pay us to do a job if it wasn't better than what someone could capture with their iPhone, or had something explicit to say, or had some resonance, or had some personality?" Everybody has a phone, everybody is a cameraperson now! We would dare to say, "I have something to say!" But if you don't want to hear us say it, then go and get everyone with their iPhone and make it, which is okay, which is more Dogme 95 style, which is a different kind of filmmaking. Which is great, which is fine. I am not a protectionist about my role in the history of cinema. I'm there! You can't get rid of me, fuckers! We have to engage with the times, we have to adapt and engage with a new perspective. It is like the New Wave, it is like what happened in Brazil in the '60s, it is what happened in China in the late '80s. This is great! But let's engage, not just keep on remaking fucking *Internal Affairs* number sixty-five! *The Departed* didn't even acknowledge that it was a remake of a Chinese film. Yes, that's what I am talking about, all of this kind of shit, you know. Let's move on, let's have an engagement. The accountants can't do it. The sixty-two-year-olds which make up the Academy of Motion Picture Arts and Sciences can't do it. The people who determine awards don't know what they are fucking looking at. Let's get the young people, and the real people, engaged in a dialogue and really get things going. We're ready, I'm ready!

LC: Are things so dire for cinematography? Many of the interviews I have conducted have had cinematographers expressing some pessimism. You sound hopeful to me.

CD: Oh, I have hope, great hope! As I have said, if we have something to say, it comes from who we are. It doesn't come from the fact that I have a camera. Everyone has a camera these days in that you have phone, I have a phone, we all have phones. Everybody knows now the technical terms of cinematography, which nobody knew ten years ago. Nobody knew what a clapper loader meant. People now are extremely "cinema savvy." But being cinema savvy is not what it is about. It's life savvy, which is what it is about. I know so many kids who want to be Christopher Doyle. Good luck! I don't want to be Christopher Doyle! I've had enough of him! (*Laughs*) And, second, why would you want to be Christopher Doyle if you can't be yourself firs? As with any education system you have this situation where people come out and think they are God's gift to cinematography, or to literature, or to marketing. That's what's happened, education has become a business. They know my films from just looking at them. They don't know my films from coming on set and working a twenty-hour day, being exhausted, working in 122-degree Fahrenheit conditions, humidity, and trying to work out every shot as you go. They don't know this stuff. They don't have any life experience. They haven't lived. They haven't been in jail—I have—they haven't been in a complicated love relationship, they haven't lost their parents, or their most loved person, at the age of ten. What are you going to give to the world but another fucking reproduction of the film experience? The best version of it is the Coen brothers, who actually have a life, and then reinterpret works, with the help of Roger Deakins. That's astonishing, but that's just 1 percent of the solution. Ninety-nine percent of people are reproducing films without any life experience, without any irony, and without any of the technical expertise that Roger has. So what are you going to do? I am very positive though. Kids come up and say, "I am going to do this." That is very interesting technically but what do you really have to say that to me? What do you have to share? That pushes us to be more exigent for ourselves. The most astonishing thing about getting older is you know there are no answers. But the questions are so important. As you get older, the kids think there's answers, but there's no answer . . . whether it's about life, or religion, or what you eat, or how you eat, or the ecology of the environment, there's no answer. But the questions are important. When you get older, the questions get really important. I want the kids to give me the questions.

LC: Is cinema a great way to ask questions?

CD: Any art has to be. It has to be an affront to the status quo. It has to be an engagement with things that really matter. If it's just entertainment then give them an Academy Award. Ha, ha, ha!

LC: *Slumdog Millionaire* is a film shot by Anthony Dod Mantle which is mainstream, won many Academy Awards, yet still engages powerfully with themes of loneliness and poverty. Is that an example of asking the right questions?

CD: Personally, and again who am I to criticize my best friend, personally, and again I am not a film critic, if you look at it from the point of view of my experience, it is structured in more of a conventional Western cinematic way. In terms of structure. But in terms of the dynamic of the cinematography, it jumps into the stratosphere of engagement, of intent. That is why I love Anthony! And that's why I love Roger Deakins. There are a few of these great people out there who are using the guts, the physicality, of cinema, of the camera, of light, of textures, to go beyond what is written on the page. I call it "a way with words." It has to be about a way to work with words, but also to go beyond them, and that is what we should be doing. We should be engaging in this synesthetic, this very physical way, and that is what *Slumdog Millionaire* is extraordinary for. Not for the happy ending, not for the structure, which is really very conventional if you look at it. On the level of cinematography, it is a work of compassion, of engagement, using the tools of our trade with compassion, with feeling, to create a texture to the space which wouldn't have worked in a David Lean kind of way. Or in a Coppola kind of way. Certainly, not in a Michael Mann kind of way. It would have been too slick.

LC: Roger does come from a very extensive documentary background.

CD: Exactly. Roger comes from documentary, and shooting a film like *Sid and Nancy*, and look at Anthony and I, we are both camera operators. Neither of us have been to film school. I think that that's important. Our engagement with the camera is physical. We all operate. I think that that's important, the physical relationship between the person in front of the camera and the audience is mediated by us. Rodrigo Prieto is the same. I say that there [are] only three people in cinema. There is the person in front of the camera; the person closest to them who is the operator, us; and the director. All the real cinematographers are closest to the actors. Therefore, the bridge exists, the energy is transmitted directly, there's no corruption . . . when people say it looks cinematic, our lighting looks like cinema lighting, I know it's an insult, that means what we have done isn't engaging enough. We've made it too formalistic, or we've made it too artificial. Of course it has to convey a sense of beauty, or a sense of the meaning of the scene, or engage in some way, and that's why it has to come back to those three people. It is about us filming the person, or animal, or object in front of the camera such that they have a visceral experience of what is happening in front of the camera.

LC: You said before you don't want to be Christopher Doyle. If you don't want to be Christopher Doyle, then who do you want to be?

CD: I've only rarely been Christopher Doyle. I am Du Ke Feng, my Chinese name. He is much more interesting. He is a softer, more gentle person. Sixty to seventy percent of the films I've made are by Du Ke Feng, my Chinese name. He's quite a different person, believe it or not. It is quite important to me that you have this distance. I think that the objectivity one has as an artist is very important. You paint, paint, paint, and then step back. You have to be engaged, you have to be subjective, you have to be totally involved, you have to be in there sweating with the actors and the crew, yet you also need to have some kind of remove. I'm lucky enough to have both of those attributes. I was born in Australia, but most of my films are made in Asian environments, so I have a distance which is very useful for an artist. There is the balance between knowing what you are doing well enough, yet also being objective enough to disregard it sometimes, or to be supercritical, or at least seeing it from another angle. I think that, to me, is the most useful aspect of my two personalities, and certainly my role in Chinese cinema, has been enhanced by the fact that I am not Chinese. In that vein, have you noticed how all of the best American films are made by non-American cinematographers? All the great cinematographers have that distance. Unfortunately, up until now, American culture was so dominant that we all know enough about it to engage, and yet we're all from somewhere else, so our engagement has a distance, has a reflective element to it, has an objectivity, that an American cinematographer couldn't have. The balance between objectivity and subjectivity is what it is about! I have an added advantage in that I'm not even Chinese.

LC: When I spoke with Emmanuel Lubezki, he observed that he feels he fails often in his work, in his cinematography. Is this a sentiment you identify with?

CD: We can't sleep at night when we're shooting. It's impossible! There is not a fucking image that doesn't go through your head all night. You cannot sleep! It's best if you are not with someone at that time because they end up asking you to move to the sofa. There's images in films that I shot twenty years ago that still come back to me every two or three weeks. I can't tell you what they are. They fucking haunt you forever. You tried so hard, and for one second, literally one second, you may have lost concentration, or you may have been distracted by something, or you may have given in to the whims of an actor, or been subject to some technical failure, and then you regret it forever, for the whole of your life, especially the night it happened. But I think that's great. It's exhausting, of course. That is why I am so positive about the kids, because we are more exigent than they ever could be, because we've gone through it for so long, and because we're used to it, because we do want them to push it, to demand stuff of us, to push us, otherwise why would we dare to say to the audience, "Hey, come and see my film," if we didn't think it was something of honor, something which we have put all of ourselves into. Anytime you are one percent short of everything, it keeps coming back to haunt you.

LC: A number of films you made with Wong Kar-wai are explicitly concerned with love and passion. However, I would put that the actual lover in *2046* and *In the Mood for Love* is you and your camera.

CD: Of course! Don't tell my girlfriends about this. Of course, I love Maggie Cheung! We don't need to consummate it because I have told her so many times with the camera. Isn't that an incredible pleasure? It doesn't need to be consummated. That would be superfluous! We've already made love with the image, with the light, with the proximity that you experience, with the way that you feel at the end of the take, I mean it's so much more intense, it's so much more intimate than sex.

LC: True. But you have also made films which are more clinical in their visuals. Do you feel *The Limits of Control* is about watching human beings, rather than any specific action or story?

CD: Yeah, yeah. But that's Jim Jarmusch. That to me was quite difficult. I had just done a film of my own in Poland which we did in twenty days and to me Jim's rhythm . . . again in deference to the friendship that we have . . . I wonder sometimes if the rhythm I have is too hasty for Jim. Jim needs a certain rhythm, and I don't know if I engaged with it well enough. Personally, I am very proud of the film, but I wonder if I hadn't just come off a film shot in twenty days, or I hadn't, for example, been working for the previous five years, if I might have found a rhythm more appropriate to Jim's taste. Jim is an observant person. He thinks things through much more than I do. I have to act things through. So I'm not sure how people see the film, or how it relates to his other films. I just did it as best I could.

LC: How conscious were you on that film of following in the footsteps of someone such as Robby Müller, who of course shot many of Jim Jarmusch's previous films?

CD: Nobody can follow in the footsteps of Robby Müller! Robby Müller is walking on the moon, and we're on planet Earth. I regard him as a friend, though I've only seen him perhaps ten times in our lifetimes.

LC: He is very sick. [*Note:* Robby Müller passed away on 3 July 2018.]

CD: I know, he's been sick for two years now. And we all know, and we care. Steve McQueen and others, we all know, and we all care, and we speak of him often, the same we did as with Harris Savides. Again, it's a situation in which, despite how few times Harris and I saw each other, there is still some link, some sense of community, that is quite astonishingly intimate. The same is true with Ed Lachman, Roger, or Rodrigo. What, we've seen each other ten times in our whole lives? And yet it's there! The community, and the sense of intent is so basic to how we work, and the films we make that you just sense it. It's always there. Robby is always there. He may leave this world soon, but he is there in all that we do and . . . what more can you say? What more can you hope for? I think the great thing about what we do is that it resonates. You mentioned in an earlier conversation that other cinematographers admired my work on *Paranoid Park*. I didn't know that. Or *Rabbit-Proof Fence*. I have no idea who's seen it, yet somebody like yourself mentions its impact. What greater pleasure could you have in life? To know that the work you have done has reached people that you've never seen, never met, or never expected would respond to your work. Because

> of this we have a great responsibility to do the best work we can, to be true to who we are, to hopefully engage in the questions that are relevant. It isn't about the money, or the fame, or any of those other things. It is about engagement.

~

The interview articulates the basic challenges with which contemporary filmmakers are presented. In an era of democratized photography and cinematography, most individuals being able to produce footage, edit it, and then distribute it to ever-widening audiences, the specific exclusivity which existed for filmmakers is certainly diminished. Doyle's perspective is that genuine artistry is rarer than technical skill, the ability to produce "slick" cinematic imagery. Arguably, per Doyle's description, the club of those who may demonstrate said artistry is small. Doyle's perspective is essential in that it's so specifically that of a cinematographer, in turn championing what cinematographers contribute. It helps elucidate the tension between the creators and distributors of film and television. Peter Doyle, to a degree, is on the flip side of the conundrum that Christopher Doyle describes. His finishing work on films represents the needs of many groups, including producers and distributors. Yet it is well worth noting that he in turn champions (from a pragmatic and technical standpoint) the necessity to defer to the kind of experienced and artistically gifted cinematographer Christopher Doyle represents. Even in the years since this interview has taken place, there have been no simple solutions offered to the issues raised. As the cinematographer himself points out, there are no easy answers.

John Mathieson

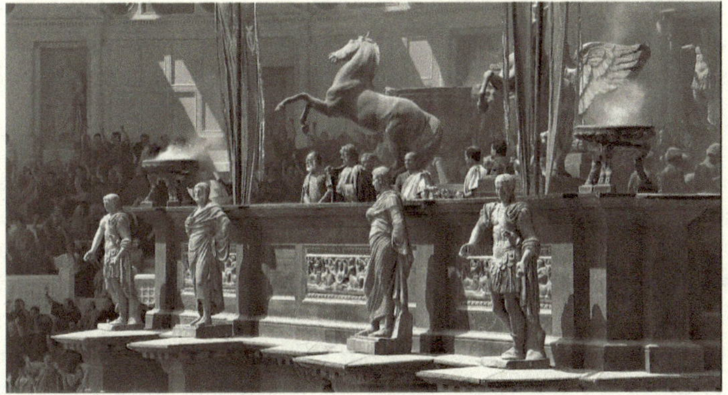

Image 17. A wide shot of nobles in the Colosseum illustrates the lighting of the set in *Gladiator* (Scott 2000).

John Mathieson BSC is a British cinematographer whose innovative work on music videos and independent films in the 1990s led to working with the likes of Ridley Scott and Joel Schumacher. He is known for his work on the films *Gladiator*, *The Phantom of the Opera*, and *Kingdom of Heaven*. Mathieson has been nominated for an Academy Award twice for his cinematography and is a vocal advocate for celluloid over digital cameras. Mathieson apprenticed under Gabriel Beristáin on Derek Jarman's *Caravaggio*, expanded his skill range with experimental videos for Siouxsie and the Banshees, then committed to the eye-popping vision of director John Maybury on the Francis Bacon fictional biopic *Love Is the Devil*. He adopted a surprisingly anachronistic shooting and lighting style on the period film *Plunkett and Macleane*, then proceeded to vivid, epic cinematography in his collaboration with Ridley Scott on

Gladiator. Mathieson has maintained his commitment to vastly differing textures, visual environments, lighting approaches. One need only look to his collaboration with Scott on *The Kingdom of Heaven*, a film whose visuals evoke the wide desert spaces of David Lean and a version of medieval France seemingly shrouded in permanent half-light. Equally, Mathieson may be a disciplined adherent to genre photography, his visual pastiche of the cool 1960s on evidence in his photography for the Guy Ritchie adaptation of *The Man From U.N.C.L.E.*

The following interview was conducted between Lindsay Coleman and John Mathieson in October 2013.

Lindsay Coleman: Let's go back to the very start of your career working as a cinematographer. Tell me something of what your experience was like working with Derek Jarman?

John Mathieson: Back then, the British film industry was very stodgy. You had to be someone's son, or nephew, to get into the industry. It took you years to work your way up to being a cameraman, or a production designer, or whatever. Derek, he was outside of the union and wanted everyone to run around and really have a go. We didn't really realize that his life was going to be so short then, but it doesn't matter. You should always run around like your life's going to end tomorrow and do the right thing.

LC: Jarman would operate cameras himself sometimes, and of course Ridley Scott has discussed doing that also. What's that like working with directors who are so technically capable?

JM: I don't think Derek was technically capable at all. I don't think it was anything to do with being a mad fussy queen or anything, but he used to like to really to catch things with Super 8. I remember one time he bought the film, for a pound, off the production and kept shooting the next day in Super 8. Rid could never, and would never, work on a budget of that size. He did one shot on *Gladiator*. I can't remember his operating on another shot really in all the years after that. I know he used to operate a lot more. I think what was happening was he would shoot with a lot more cameras. His knee used to give him terrible trouble, and we are always on location with Rid, so once he got himself plonked up he didn't see himself humping up a ladder to direct a camera, he would watch on his video monitor. He would also draw you a picture. Most people draw storyboards and it might be rough, just a few lines, or it might even be very nicely drawn, but Rid can draw what it will look like on a 75 or 80mm lens, which is quite an odd thing to do, to understand, when you are drawing a picture. Most people draw on a 24mm, or maybe a 35mm, lens. We're supposed to perceive things at 50mm but we don't actually see at 50mm. People's drawings of a frame will be kind of flat. He can draw even on a 300mm lens, it will have depth, it will have specific placement. He can draw a quick scribble and say, "Go and do that," and you're walking up a mountain, or up a hill, and you look up and see, ah that's what he drew! He remembers things, not photographically, but he remembers the essence of a frame, and the feeling of it, and says, "Go and do that." Ridley was making great films when I was wet behind the ears, so I wouldn't tell him how to frame things. On a Rid film, you find yourself doing things that he might like. You offer up an idea and he likes it or doesn't like it.

LC: If I may, I'd like to address an observation I made a few years back. Looking at *Robin Hood*, another film with Ridley Scott, how do you feel about your work on the film? You seemed, in the *American Cinematographer* article, to have been frustrated by the process.

JM: It took a long time to get going. We were on it, more or less, two years. We kept missing the seasons. We had two really beautiful winters. The reference was an old Bruegel painting, I can see it now, I'm not sure what it was called. It's a painting looking down on a village from a hill and there's some very dark trees in the foreground. Then there's two hunting dogs coming down to the village which has got thatched roofs, smoke from their chimneys. It was very much a barren, hard time, a hard, medieval winter of famine. And that's what we wanted to do on film. We had these two fantastic, really hard winters with hoarfrost, the trees were gnarled and twisted. And the woods themselves, it might sound obvious to say, but in the winter, you see far more because you see great distance. Beechwood in midsummer, the blanket of leaves is incredible. You can't see anything. You don't get the depth, and even if you do get depth, the trunks have this dusting of green algae on them, so everything is green, on green, on green, which is a bit of a tricky color when it starts to fill in everything. Everyone starts looking a little magenta by default so it's hard to make anyone look good. I don't really light exteriors that much, I just try to use what's there. I used a couple of huge things called soft cells tied together, but you can only penetrate so deep because, as I say, the leaf coverage is so deep. We ended up shooting in high summer due to circumstances, so the woods were not as beautiful as I had hoped at all. There was nothing much that could be done about that though. You bring in a lot of lights, but it doesn't do the job you want them to do. During the short days of winter there were some dull, Tupperware skies, but really wonderful dark trees without leaves, and there would have been these sorts of figures darting around. It also would have made the feeling of the film—Rid wanted this country in famine, everything has gone to rack and ruin—difficult to convey that really when everything is lush, and green, and beautiful (*laughs*). We did a digital grade, I wasn't actually sitting in on the grade. It was the first film I didn't have enough time to grade it. I was starting something else. My instructions were not followed correctly. I don't like it when I look at the film. It wasn't as I'd wished it to be. I wish we did it in England, finished the grade there. We did it over here in LA. The timer, has he been to English woods in the middle of winter? No. Or the middle of summer? You are trying to explain stuff to people. This desaturated, cool look. I don't want that. Things don't look like that. It's not a commercial. It's a story. It's a real story, with real people, in a real time. And that's not the way it ended up.

LC: Okay, let's look at the issue from the perspective of technology. Do you feel the Alexa might have made things better on that film? It has been heralded as one of the major cameras of our era.

JM: No, not really. I believe it would have made things worse. I think the problem with digital images, everyone is talking about crispness and resolution. I mean we've got enough sharpness, we always had enough sharpness. Ironically everyone is starting to put on crappy old lenses and softer anamorphics in front of the Alexa or the Epic to try to soften them down, to try to get the image to look less crisp and weird. There's the crispness, the resolution everyone goes on about, but how much more resolution do you want? I mean are we supposed to be like hawks or night predator animals? Our eyes are good, but not quite like that. My criticism of these cameras is that their colors are no good. They can't seem to reproduce the colors that you see in everyday life, or the colors that Kodak film have been giving us for years, or that they have been able to process at laboratories like Technicolor. The colors tend to polarize, they go toward their primaries. And you can see that a little even in *Robin Hood*. The arrival of the DI [digital intermediate] was the beginning of the end for the great film cameramen, where you could really pull out these colors. Everything screams toward their primaries with digital cameras. It's like when you watch sport in [high definition], the grass is not that bright green. The shirts they are playing in are not that bright red! Yet to watch a game it kind of helps because you can see where everything is. You can see whether the ball is moving or not. If we'd shot *Robin Hood* on the Alexa, the woods would have been super green and the tunics would have been super red. Everything would have polarized toward their primaries. The problem, as you see, is that when you hit something complex like a flesh tone, they do no reproduce them very well. I was just doing a low-budget thing, very like Jarman, a film on the composer Benjamin Britten, Margaret Williams directing. We ended up shooting on the Red One. I went into the grade with this guy where we were trying to get a teaser ready for Cannes. Everything we shot we had to put a window over.[1] You wanted detail in the sky, you had to put a window over it. The flesh tones looked like Plasticine [modeling clay]. They looked like that base that you have to put on your car after you've had a scrape, just before you put the proper color back on. They spray that gray, then they make you up again all pink to try to get that flesh color. It looked absolutely flat and awful. The guy doing the grade said, "This is a good camera." I couldn't believe it! But it's conditioning. People are watching things shot on these cameras, they're getting used to it. This guy, he was in charge of grading, he was talented, he knew his machine, he knew what he was doing. But he just couldn't put his image up and say bang, there it is. That's the grayscale, that's how we want it to look.

LC: Would you retime *Robin Hood* if you could?

JM: Oh yeah! Oh God, yeah. I was really disappointed. They said they did what Ridley wanted. Is that really what he wanted? Did he spend time with you? I do think it is very much a part of the job today. If you shoot an Arri raw,[2] and Arri raw looks ghastly, it's difficult to get authorship because basically, people can go off with these images and grade them any way they want. With film you would have much more control as a cinematographer in terms of the final image.[3] A good grader, timer, would always find the image. You always knew they would find that. They would find what you were trying to do. Now it's very difficult. There is no form, there's no mid-space, no 18 percent gray Macbeth chart you work off.[4] If you hold up a Macbeth chart with a grayscale in front of a digital camera they say, do you want what the grayscale looks like or do you want to grade the picture? You used to be able to hold the grayscale up if you wanted to swing the light this way or that way. Sometimes you'd cut a bit of lighting gel over the lens to give it a blue look, hot grayscale normal, then put a little gel over it, or green, or something, and that would give an idea to the graders. "Ah that's what he wants to try and do! Somewhere there, or bang on there, or somewhere in between the two." But a digital camera won't do that, it simply won't do that. You can either grade for the grayscale, and if you grade for that grayscale on the Macbeth it looks like fucking hell! Or you grade to the image, and what to your eye looks good, then you look back at the Macbeth and that makes no sense at all either so you don't see that anymore. You don't hold those things up because they don't make any sense. There is no norm, there is no center point.

There wasn't exactly a center point on film either, but you could find this point which contained your hue, your normalization, your exposure, that you were trying to convey to the grader, and they would get hold of that. That's just gone now. Yes, with a film like *Robin Hood* you've got to, as a DP, see your images all the way through, otherwise someone will, along the line, even if they've never been to a fucking wood in the home counties of England, they will interpret what they think is cool, or whatever, and do what they think is right for the image. It's difficult to have influence on that.

LC: Some cinematographers I have spoken with feel strongly about a sense of their own authorship, others say that once they are paid, the images belong to their employers. Where do you fall on that spectrum?

JM: I've never made a film for the money. If you're making a film for the money, good luck to you, keep everyone happy. Keep the studio happy. People won't actually remember your work. Did we get into it so someone could do it for us? No, we wanted to do our thing. I've fought with Ridley, I've been toe-to-toe with him a few times about ideas for *Gladiator*, and other ones since then. I've fought for what I thought was right. I didn't do what he said. I was one of the first DPs that wasn't his assistant. I didn't know what the form was. I just did what I thought was good. You trust your eye and do what you think is good. You're not being devious, or trying to go against the director. You're doing what you think is best for the scene. If they don't understand you, or want to walk hand in hand with you to that image, then you do it yourself. And you fight to defend it. Against producers, against directors. It's better if the director works with you. It's surprising though how many directors are not concerned with imagery, who are not concerned with colors. They want to focus on performance, my God, there is enough to do there anyway. You are left to your own devices. I don't think that is a particularly good thing because you do do it by yourself. I think it's much better to have a conspiracy, and a collaboration, and do your thing with them. The difficult thing sometimes is that everyone wants everything to be seen from every angle. Well a film isn't about that. Clint Eastwood says, "They know what I look like at this stage in the film. I can start in the dark and walk into the light." That's what film's about. It's about playing with light. It's about playing with those things and not seeing everything all the time. I've fought with Ridley a few times, and a few other people, only to be told after, "Ah that's one of our best scenes." I thought, "You didn't fucking say so at the time!" It works because it's got rhythm, it's got a different look to things. The film is not about every picture being absolutely exposed all the time. With this Arri raw situation at present, and all these other damn things, that is the danger, that everyone's work will look the same because everyone has seen everything from every angle. So whoever the cinematographers are which say, "Oh well, I'll do it for the money and just give them the images," well you're not really a cinematographer. You're not doing what you got into this work for. You're just being some kind of consultant. Everyone's going digital, digital, digital. Well, if you look back a few years from now, you'll see that some of their best work was done when they were doing it by themselves on film. Someone in *Side by Side*, the documentary, said, "DPs just want to make it complicated with their lenses and exposures," and I thought, "You fucking bastard, do you know how difficult it is to stick your neck out front and really do this?" It's a *lonely* process, and sometimes there is no one with you. Your technicians are smiling like a member of your family would, but they can't really help you. You're out there on your own, you're doing the best you can, what you think is best for the movie, best for the story, the direction, best for the situation and the lighting, and it's a *lonely* process. Sometimes you get your head bitten off. I've gotten my head bitten off a few times and ended up on podiums giving lectures about how wonderful this film was. It is about your eye. That is what you are being paid for. For your eye, your opinion. They may not always like that. But you are shaping it. It is, after all, a film.

LC: Which, do you feel, of the films you have shot really contain your own authorial stamp?

JM: You mentioned to me, in our correspondence, that you like *Plunkett and Macleane*. Everyone seems to like it in Australia.

That was what bagged me *Gladiator*. I did the eighteenth century, with the candle light, with a bit of punky kind of attitude to it, not sort of "let's put lots of golden light everywhere." I kind of played with color difference there.

LC: It wasn't *Barry Lyndon*.

JM: No, no. Fuck *Barry Lyndon*. Everyone loves *Barry Lyndon*, but no I didn't want to just show "I can do *Barry Lyndon*." It wasn't that sort of movie anyway. Much as Jake [Scott] loves *Barry Lyndon*. The film I shot a few years before, *Love Is the Devil*, directed by John Maybury, had a dirty, hollow look to it. It's become very fashionable now to use green gels, but we did it at a time when it wasn't fashionable. I did it to hollow out, to kill . . . there is something about death in Francis Bacon, all that bone white, and this sort of liver darkness in the shadows, the sort of blood colors, everyone looks like they've been slightly dead for twenty-four hours, with this greenish hotness, and this nasty sort of presence of cigarettes and canned bully beef and the whole Bacon's world of postwar Britain that he seemed to be locked into.

LC: How did you achieve the distortions in the images? That was probably one of the most remarked-on aspects of the film's cinematography.

JM: Alan MacDonald, John Maybury, and I made lots of music videos over the years. Around the time, I remember doing an Absolut Vodka ad and said, "Let's shoot the whole thing from the bottom of a bottle of vodka." I thought to do it in a very kind of drunken way. So we shot it though ashtrays, through old glasses, funny bits of blown glass that I'd collected along the way. We weren't trying to make a Bacon painting and go, "Oh, aren't we clever!," we were hinting at—or we were moving the actors into—that drunken space. He was an incredible soak, old Bacon. Quite a lot of his interviews, he is absolutely soused in them. He did a famous one with Melvyn Bragg, that Bragg is quite proud of, in which they both got wasted. They were both drunk, but Bragg actually got to the quick of the man. Yes, he was a drunk, and he was off his chump, but he also had this kind of existentialist, trippy way about him, he liked the chaos and brutality of this drunken world. You find out these things about him, having made these music videos, having been off your face a few times, some pretty interesting images at the end of a shoot can manifest. I wouldn't recommend it as a way to go about things, but there is a way of getting into that space and thinking differently about things. In *Love Is the Devil* I instinctively did something that's raw and obvious. I think with images, and filmmaking, that you've got to be obvious. You don't want to be subtle. You've really got to ram the ideas down people's throats. It's really about getting empathy or communication with an audience and to do that just be obvious! Let the images, the style in which they are constructed, directly complement the ideas of the story. A lot of those ideas will fall by the wayside because people don't get what you were trying to do, or don't know what you knew already. By not being very subtle, you can create a look which is strong and unique, without stamping on the director's or the actors' thing. You can bring things to a scene which will move it into another space.

LC: Emmanuel Lubezki says the images he creates will be around at least for the next couple of years, in the minds of those who saw the film. Do you work on a similar basis?

JM: No, but I will do from now [on]. I think that's a really great idea. He's made some better films than I have, so the memories from his might be around a lot longer. I think that's true, I think that's right. I should treat things with a bit more reverence. But going back to what I said, you should be obvious. Just fucking say something. Don't go with "Oh let's go with that but maybe a little bit less." There's enough television out there. There's enough average filmmaking going on. So why not just be bold and have a go?

LC: There are some risky images in *Plunkett and Macleane*. You really underexpose some of your images. Do you ever feel you've gone too far?

JM: There are times. There was a film I did recently where the shot was a rough and then they kept it in. Basically, I ran out of light. The thing with *Plunkett*—I do like the way that film looks. I do like the murkiness of it all. You could call it underexposure if you like. Actually, I didn't shoot on very fast film. We only shot 200 ASA. Because it was Super 35 optical blow-up. This was before you could work on the DI. Now you just take Super 35 and go straight to DI. This was optical blow-up, so you have to go through another stage. And it's an optical print, it's not a contact print. It is a step down. So what we found was that the high speed film, the 400 ASA at the time, 5293 or 5298, it was giving us good rushes, but by the time you took it through to the optical squeeze to make an anamorphic print, the grain came up on it. The grain came up at this later stage so it wasn't there when you were seeing flat rushes, so that obliged me to go down to the next slowest stock, which did hold up, which was a stock called 5274. That was a wonderful, wonderful film! It was tungsten balanced, which I didn't try to correct. It created a lot of funny hues which I did try to pull back halfway during the grade and you'd get some very funny things. That was probably part of it. And we were shooting in Prague in the middle of winter! I didn't mind that we couldn't really light the whole frame. It wasn't a big budget. But what do you do, chuck in your hand? Or have a go at a minty, underexposed image? And that was the time. These guys were living in a dark, old, underlit slums of London.

LC: Do you feel all great cinematographers must be brave? It seems to be that is what you are really championing.

JM: A lot of the great cinematographers are playing with things right on the edge of exposure. Or, they're doing some chemical, genius thing like Harris Savides used to do. He didn't make the biggest films, but all of the other cinematographers would sit up and watch the things that he used to do. He was a real photochemical wizard. He was very comfortable doing some crazy things that a lot of us don't have the balls to do. Darius Khondji, [Vittorio] Storaro, Gordon Willis, Douglas Slocombe, Freddie Francis, Alex Thomson, these guys they dick with things . . . they play with things right down to the edge. They play with dark and shadow, not like the pussification which is going on with the business now. They say, I want a doorway over there, and a light over there, and everything else is black. You look at *The Third Man*, shot by the Australian Robert Krasker, the light goes on in a window, then you see Harry Lime in the corner. He is seemingly being lit by a lightbulb going a hundred yards across the square. Impossible of course! But the cinema, and the drama, and the lighting of that is extraordinary. You don't see that stuff anymore. People just don't do it. They just don't have the nuts for it. You stick your neck out, and that's when you feel lonely. You've been shooting nights for three days and you go into dailies and think, Christ, I hope they're going to like this. I've done this right on the edge. I have had Ridley drag on my elbow and say, "You didn't do it *all* like this did you?!" You think, "Oh God, yes I *did*." But to see it afterward you think, that was a great thing to do. So yes, it is a lonely process, it is for the brave. Cinematographers do attempt the summits by themselves sometimes. The ones that run around and please everyone. Well you carry on doing that, making unremarkable images.

LC: There's a great moment in *Kingdom of Heaven* where Orlando Bloom's character goes to Golgotha. It's very darkly lit, that shot, but it is also the major turning point for that character in the movie. It's almost completely dark. What guides you in a moment like that in terms of your lighting?

JM: Well, I always like to take it to the wire (*laughs*). And, yeah, he is looking for an epiphany, and absolution for his sins in that scene, and he ain't gonna get it. So it seemed logical to go lonely and dark on that weird little hill. We probably shot a bit later than we should have done. (*Laughs*) Rid wanted to keep going. Sometimes you have to say, "I'm sorry, that's it, I can't go any more." Difficult thing to say sometimes when the actor finds the rhythm. If we'd done that film digitally it would have been brighter, it would have been pulled up. There's something about film stocks at that level of light, it's so intolerant, and weird, and it gives it a kind of magic. *Brighton Rock*, which I shot, there's actually moments where you can see the light dying on a beach, and all the colors go brilliantly vivid before the sun sets. And it's a brilliant moment in the story where the characters are at their closest. Yes, we should have started an hour earlier, but it wouldn't have been as magical.

LC: You seem unique in that, of the cinematographers I have interviewed, you are one of the very few to admit an influence of painting on your work.

JM: Rid always did that. We had one painting by a nineteenth-century French romantic painter, on which has this rather overweight gladiator with his foot on his victim, in an arena with his head raised up to the imperial box. That was one of the visual references for *Gladiator*. There were strips of light in the painting. That what made me put up the most expensive shadow in cinema history, the fabric to cover the arena so we had light and shadow. The whole *Gladiator* thing became more like theater, so we had a big spotlight over whatever Russell Crowe was doing. We didn't have a script. I had just that one painting on the wall. That was it. I sat in my office, which is a portacabin in Shepperton Studios, thinking, "Screw this! I'm going to go off and shoot a commercial." Which I did, and then that was a bit of a misadventure. Then, I wondered, "Who's going to shoot that film *Gladiator*?" There I was, moonlighting, and thinking they'd probably be pissed off with me. But that's all I had. I looked at Georges de La Tour, Joseph Wright of Derby, Caravaggio, yeah, you look at those pictures. Rid looked at those pictures, Jake Scott and I looked at those pictures. We can't paint . . . a lot of cinematographers can draw, like David Tattersall, some are good draftsman, but what did people do before cinema? They looked at paintings. You'd go and listen to a play. You didn't go and watch a play, interestingly enough. Until the eighteenth century, theaters started lighting plays, but until then where did the imagery come from? From paintings. On films you don't go off and do what you want every day. You simply don't do that, it's a collaborative process. Painting, they didn't have any of that stuff. They'd just start with their canvas. They just started doing what they were doing. And why they did what they did, and what made them see that light, or try to bring it to life, to get depth into paintings . . . when you go to galleries it's interesting how patrons are fascinated about how the illusion of depth is created with a 2D medium . . . So we don't really need 3D cinema (*laughs*) . . . that actually creating depth in a frame, when you see it done well in a painting, they are fascinating. Everyone should experience them firsthand. Some of them can be shocking, really shockingly brilliant. Don't look at them in some coffee table book!

LC: The color, most of the time, is off anyway in those reproductions.

JM: They fuck up the color, but also there is this whole 3D effect which occurs when you are exposed to the actual painting, which you are aware of as you lean on one foot, and then switch to another, you actually see that paintings do something strange as well. People will queue around the block at Trafalgar Square to see some Vermeer! There is something going on there. It's the punters, Joe Blow. You ask them, "Why are you seeing this painting?" They probably won't be able to tell you. But they know it is having an extremely powerful effect on them visually. It is important to me for sure, a real influence. And it helps with your shorthand. If a director says to you a shot is a de Chirico, early Chagall, early Picasso, then you know exactly what they mean. You can pinpoint something because it was one person, in a room, doing exactly what they want. It wasn't someone on a film doing a collaborative thing. It was absolutely a flavor. In cinematography, it is very difficult to talk about color. You can't actually talk about color because it is just *color*. If you talk about a painting, and the colors they used, then you can say you know what a director, or whoever, means exactly.

LC: Do you feel you're adding to the visual history of humanity?

JM: I don't know. I feel a part of it. The power of the cinematographer has become more and more diminished, particularly from what it was in the late '70s, early '80s. One of my gaffers, Bill O'Leary, he's worked for a long time in the industry and he's seen the power of the cinematographer diminish. It's diminished because these days you've got these monitors and everyone is pointing and poking and saying what's wrong with them before you even started really lighting, or framing, or anything. You get a great movie, shot by a great cinematographer, and he's probably been battered by the studio, been Judas-ed by the director, and yet they've stayed solid and true to their original vision. That does become a part of our visual culture, our visual makeup, I suppose.

~

The issues that plagued the filming and postproduction of *Robin Hood* occurred during what could be argued was the "mainstreaming" period of digital capture for cinematography, with many of the biggest productions making a sweeping shift to digital. Naturally, a cinematographer working on projects of the scale Mathieson does would need to determine how to engage with the DI suite in postproduction and acquiesce to the possibility of using digital cameras during production. In his more recent films, this has happened for Mathieson. He opted to shoot *Mary Queen of Scots* using the Panavision DXL, fitted with Sphero 65 lenses, shooting in 1.89:1 but framing for a 2.40:1 extraction. The vintage Sphero 65 lenses were well aligned to the typical types of characteristics in an image Mathieson is attracted to, including moderate focus roll-off, subtle aberrations, and perhaps most notably, pleasing flesh tones. Last, they were fast enough as lenses (all the way down to T2) to allow Mathieson to comfortably film in dimly lit period interiors, very much akin to some of his work on *Plunkett and Macleane*.

The adventurous spirit described in the interview that Mathieson hoped to invest in his cinematography continues, now with the active collaboration of his DIT. His DIT in *Mary Queen of Scots* assisted him in protecting the image from overexposed blocks of clipped white. This advice spurred Mathieson's creativity. Rather than stopping down to avoid clipping, he placed elements to alleviate what would otherwise be a blown-out highlight, thus not needing to adjust his exposure. This digital camera, the DXL, was capable, according to Mathieson, of capturing an exciting level of detail in highlights. Working with a collaborator in his DIT thus enabled Mathieson's inventiveness to persist, without having to compromise to a limited array of options that he seems to have previously believed a digital capture system would offer him.

Notes

1. A window is actually a visual window placed over any area on the image to do controlled adjustment to that area alone, or to everything around it without affecting the image in the window. On modern post systems, there are an infinite number of windows available to use.

2. Arri raw is an image capture system available on modern Arriflex digital cameras, considered the highest quality due to its expanded latitude and widely adjustable final image. The ISO or ASA sensitivity of the camera when shooting is only a metadata reference and can be changed to anywhere in the available range of the camera when finishing the images. Most other camera manufacturers have their version of raw, a name taken from digital still cameras. They are not uncompressed, but much less so than most other systems like ProRes, Rec. 709, and so on, which have the sensitivity "baked in" to the digital files.

3. This might be read as misleading because shooting on film is not what gives the cinematographer more control. It keeps others in postproduction from greatly altering the captured image if the work is done photochemically in the traditional film sense, and not in a digital intermediate where the film negative is converted to digital files. At that point in the DI, there is almost as much control to alter the imagery as there is in material originated digitally, especially in so-called raw. If the film is transferred to a digital file, you have as much control in the DI suite as you do on an Alexa raw file, unless the negative is highly over- or underexposed.

4. The Macbeth chart was developed for the print industry and worked well with photochemical timing but not so well with digital because the colors are in a different color space than the RGB or P3 of video and therefore reproduce differently. I believe that Mathieson is actually combining two different chart references here. There is the 18 percent gray card, which is the value used by light meters for judging exposure. If you expose a grey card correctly at the value where the lens T-stop is set then the way you want the scene to look should fall in place. If you put a color over the lens or light when you expose the gray card, the timer will then adjust to remove that color, bringing the gray back to neutral, which will effectively color the scene opposite of the color you used. For example, if you put blue on the card the timer will remove the blue, effectively adding red-orange to the scene. In reality there are charts for digital gray and color reference that use colors that exist in the digital video realm. DSC makes one of the best, and the old standby Kodak gray card is still applicable.

Luciano Tovoli

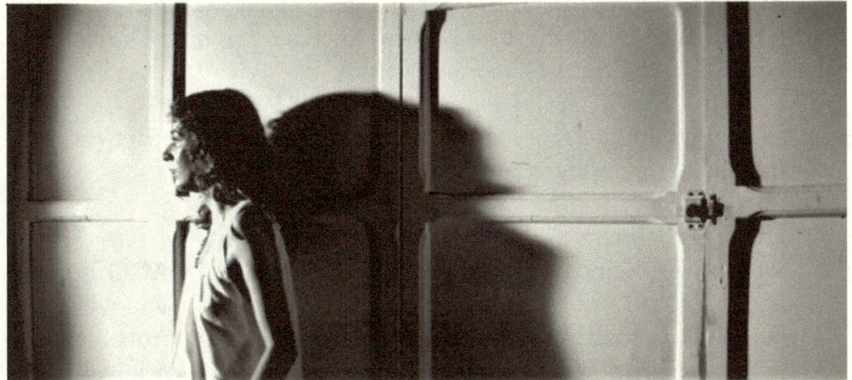

Image 18. An illustration of contrast in *Suspiria* (Argento 1977).

SINCE THE MID-1970S, LUCIANO TOVOLI ASC, AIC, FSF has alternated between hyperstylized European genre films such as *Suspiria* and naturalistic Hollywood family dramas such as *Before and After*, or the visually low-key cinematic oeuvres of Maurice Pialat and Francis Veber. Mixing in with these are the gangster picture *Kiss of Death* and early experiments in video filmmaking in *The Mystery of Oberwald*. A key figure in the establishment of IMAGO (the International Federation of Cinematographers), Tovoli has persistently experimented with a variety of formats, including his foray into 3D with his longtime collaborator Dario Argento and color, frequently creating vivid color "symphonies," to use his expression. What is remarkable about Tovoli's legacy as a cinematographer has been his ability to imbue a style entirely specific to the picture, whether hyperreal or realist, colorful or monochromatic. Each stylistic approach is bolstered by a highly attuned conceptualization on

Tovoli's part, a trait somewhat rare in cinematographers, who are often more prone to claim there is little design in their work.

Lindsay Coleman spoke with Luciano Tovoli several times in 2013 and 2014.

Lindsay Coleman: In your time as a mentor of younger cinematographers, which have impressed you the most from the outset?

Luciano Tovoli: There are not many young cinematographers that I've followed from the start of their careers. However, I do greatly admire the two French cinematographers Darius Khondji and Bruno Delbonnel.

LC: How do you feel IMAGO has changed in its impact on the cinematography community since its inception?

LT: A true, international, cinematography community *did not exist* between cinematographers before I founded IMAGO in Rome in 1992. Today, it is making a huge difference and will continue to make even more in the future. I will probably be known in film history less for my films (some of which are gorgeous and I am known for my modesty!) than that I, with my friend Gabriele Lucci, began the first international festival dedicated to cinematographers. It was in L'Aquila, Italy in 1981, well before Camerimage in Poland. I will also be known for my idea to create IMAGO, the European Federation of Cinematographers, which today has become a worldwide organization.

LC: How much do you identify as an academic in the field of cinematography and film? Or do you see yourself more as a practitioner? I ask because you clearly pride yourself on your knowledge on the history of cinematography.

LT: I absolutely refuse to be considered an academic. That doesn't interest me at all, even though I have always taught at universities and film schools around the world and most recently at the Louvre Museum in Paris. My role there is to be a witness to what it means to be a working cinematographer in possible ways, both artistically and physically, and impart this knowledge to the "students," whoever they may be.

LC: Why do you feel the importance of the work of cinematographers does not always translate to the filmgoing public?

LT: The film directors would like to have the cinematographer's knowledge of filmmaking, but don't. During the prep and shoot time they desperately seek out collaboration with the cinematographers. When the film is finished, they seem to immediately forget that collaboration and truly believe that they were the sole creator, author, of the film, which they are not. Yet the press indulges them and their unjust belief.

LC: How would you describe the camaraderie and competition found among cinematographers? I have certainly noticed it in my conversations with them over the years, this unusual blend of attitudes they possess toward one another.

LT: At our first international meeting at L'Aquila in 1981, we broke through the individualism that had until then dominated the cinematographers' way. Since then, at the festival and through IMAGO, we gave the opportunity for cinematographers to exchange their experiences to a degree that before then had been considered impossible to do. As to the competition you refer to, I prefer to say that cinematographers compete with themselves, not with their colleagues. I consider competition between colleagues to be a manifestation of childish weaknesses that should be treated by professional doctors.

LC: Let's look at one of your most celebrated early films. *The Passenger* features the integration of the footage of a genuine execution. How did you feel about the addition of this imagery to your own?

LT: I think that the scene of the real execution gives to the film a necessary link to the crude reality hidden in the history of Jack Nicholson's character's quest, the trafficking of arms. I know, also, that since my first viewing I have been unable to watch this scene without a sense of desperation at the cruelty and incredible violence of which human beings are capable. The director, Michelangelo Antonioni, played with this provocative element of the included execution footage in a dramatically efficient way. In a certain way this intolerable, realistic moment became the core of the film.

LC: In contrast, your cinematography in *Titus* blends elements which are intensely cinematic with obviously theatrical techniques. How did you and the director Julie Taymor come to determine the balance?

LT: Making a film means to wake up very early in the morning, go to the set, and be assaulted immediately by hundreds of decisions you must make. Every day they must be made immediately. Then you go back home (usually a hotel) very late in the night, dead with fatigue and without time for too many refined consultations on the set! We have to shoot and move on, every day! And I like this pressure enormously! With the director, we cinematographers run a marathon, elbow to elbow, and if one of us accelerates the other one has to keep pace or is dead! You must look at things as they are and not like they are falsely depicted! Personally, I do not like very much to make films where you have plenty of time because you become immediately lazy and less creative! I like a director with whom I speak at the beginning and I meet at the end with the same amazed smile shouting: "Ah, you survived, too! Congratulations! Let's go have a beer!" I probably related more to each director as a person, and possibly focus less on the film we are doing! I can affirm that this is the simple truth, valid for every colleague. But my pals do not want to declare this simple truth because otherwise they fear to not appear serious enough, and not be called again by the directors and producers who hire them.

LC: A ha, so I imagine that is probably the more pertinent approach you took in many of your collaborations. Even so, there are definitely changes, film to film, in your ongoing collaborations. You collaborated with Dario Argento on a number of horror films. Of these, *Tenebrae*, made in the '80s, is much more muted visually than *Suspiria*, made in the '70s. What prompted this change?

LT: Being that the two stories of *Suspiria* and *Tenebrae* are totally different, I do not see how I could have thought to utilize for *Tenebrae* the same style as *Suspiria*. This is really an elementary thought, and as a normal cinematographer you do not need to be an Oscarized genius to understand this point. In other films I have had the temptation to steal from *Suspiria*, and in some cases I did, but certainly not on *Tenebrae*! In *Tenebrae* my idea, and I have to say that it was a very good idea, was to light the night scenes in a way that neither the victim nor the assassin could have a single shadow to hide in. It is the story of a killer, so this was very effective. So *Tenebrae*'s night scenes are more lit up than you would find in footage from the sunniest day. Also, in the day, you have shadows. In *Tenebrae*'s nights, the shadows do not exist, causing extreme desperation for the terrified fugitive, and prompting the furious pursuit of the killer. The light grew to have the role of co-protagonist in the film's creation.

LC: You have spoken of a "color symphony" being achieved in certain scenes of *Suspiria*. Do you feel the club scenes in *Kiss of Death* achieved similar expressionistic heights? They certainly seem to!

LT: *Kiss of Death* is a film which has to do with very savage human behaviors. It is a noir film, full of criminals. The expressionistic side of my lighting in *Kiss of Death* was aggravated by the knots of inexorable fear and consequent aggression which the characters experienced. In *Suspiria*, the human beings are not allowed to change. Thus, I chose for *Suspiria* the absolutely pure and virginal colors, and for *Kiss of Death* I mixed impure colors. The ontological myths of *Suspiria* did not have the contaminations that were found in the damned Hell occupied by the characters of *Kiss of Death*!

What I intended was that in *Kiss of Death* the actions of humans come from a knot of human contradictions, feelings, and very primitive compulsions, and in an uneducated form for that, I needed contaminated and impure colors. In *Suspiria*, that for me reached the plane of a Greek tragedy, everything in the story is classical, and in a certain way superhuman, coming from the myths that ruled the human mind since the beginning of time. For that I needed primary colors.

LC: The way you shoot nights differs greatly film to film. In *Murder by Numbers*, the nights are warm, umber-colored. In *Single White Female*, they are bluish. What is your color philosophy for shooting nights?

LT: Apart [from] the fact that I refuse the idea of being aware of a preconceived or precooked philosophy for shooting night scenes, being myself a total improviser abandoned to my sensations of the moment whenever I shoot, I recognize afterward, sometimes as much as two years later, what my intent might have been in taking a particular approach. I recognize having chosen the warm, amber color for the night scenes in *Murder by Numbers*, that the use of color was commenting on the underlying romantic story between the two protagonists, and the bluish tone in night scenes of *Single White Female* conversely represents the absence of any loving feelings between the two protagonists of that film. It is always a matter of the characters and how they play their role. This reveals to me how they should be lit. I have always been very interested in actors. I can change the light of a close-up according to changes an actor might make, take to take, and then consequently I can alter the lighting for the entire set. This kind of confession normally terrorizes producers, but who cares!

LC: As a final question, how much do you believe lighting and cinematography mimic and stimulate aspects of human physiology and the nervous system?

LT: When I set up the extreme contrasts in my color palette in *Suspiria*, I consciously forced the minds of the audience to process this extreme visual information. In a vain attempt to normalize these colors, provoking a kind of internal fight inside the spectators, in harmony with the film's narrative intent, I can definitely say I consciously influenced the nervous system of my audience. Beyond this we enter the territory of science,

> and I am as far from science as the peaks of the Himalayas are from the sand of an Australian beach! The little technique that allowed me to be a cinematographer my thirteen-year-old grandson Filippo could apprehend and master in three days. I am speaking of the technique, and not of the creative process, that has the unattainable depths and mystery, and not only in the field of cinematography of course.

~

What Tovoli discusses is not just the creative and expressionistic use of color, but the unexpected use of color. To color his night exteriors warmer and later cooler colors suggests a creative approach unbounded by "standard" cinematography for day and night interiors and exteriors. However, what Tovoli describes goes beyond such unconventional approaches. An amber-colored night is unexpected, given the trend toward bluer nights, or cobalt-colored nights. But it can find some subliminal precedent. Amber can, with a sufficiently careful rationale, be placed in the same color space as sodium vapor–lit street scenes shot at night. Even if these sources cannot be seen, there is enough of a precedent for warmish night scenes such that the specific umber described can be rationalized by an audience. However, in relation to his "color symphonies," Tovoli and the filmmakers he works with avoid anything that might be construed as a clear narrative or practical motivation for a scene heavily featuring a striking color look. For instance, in the nightclub scenes in *Kiss of Death*, there is extensive use of colored light coming from below and above the stage, creating a kind of aquatic wash of color. In itself this might seem typical of a garish night club, yet in many of these scenes the nightclub is empty except for the film's villain, the club's owner, played by Nicolas Cage, various exotic dancers, and a handful of the villain's goons. In short, the nightclub is closed, yet lit as evocatively and luridly as though it were packed on a Saturday night! There is no specific motivation for the film's lighting in this instance other than to create an interesting blend of colored lights to highlight the major resonating themes of the film: paranoia, violence, and decadence. In the case of *Suspiria*, the narrative is set in a ballet school, yet Tovoli lights through silks to create an intensely red set, in both the foreground and the background, the young dancers bathed in saturated red light. Red is not a subliminal color presence in these scenes. Rather, the relationship is somewhat inverted, with the sets and actors effectively subsumed by this saturated color and the scenes' dominant impression being the redness. The visual impact of this color is so intense that it transforms the scenes into sequences whose primary effect is psychological. The visual message of the film's themes of death, horror, and cruelty becomes transformatively clear.

Rajiv Menon

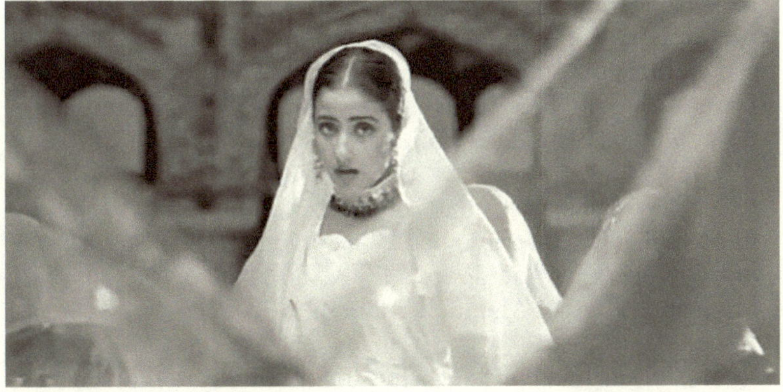

Image 19. Shaila Banu (Manisha Koirala) in an early musical number from *Bombay* (Ratnam 1995).

RAJIV MENON ISC HAS ENJOYED a successful Bollywood career and a long collaboration with Indian auteur Mani Ratnam. His films include *Bombay* and *Guru*. Primarily based in advertising, Menon is one of the most successful ad men of the subcontinent. A mentee of the noted Indian cinematographer Ashok Mehta, his greatest film achievement is doubtless *Bombay*, one of the finest films in India's cinematic history. Menon's style features a sensitive blend of naturalism and romanticism on that film, certainly apt for what was arguably a political parable-*cum*-family musical.

The following interview was conducted between Lindsay Coleman and Rajiv Menon in November 2012.

Lindsay Coleman: First if we could address your influences, in particular Ashok Mehta, your mentor, who shot both *Bandit Queen* and *Kahl Nayak*. What do you make of his working on such contradictory material? One is a fairly naturalistic biopic, the other an ultrastylized piece of Bollywood escapism.

Rajiv Menon: I think in some ways Ashok Mehta is an enigma. In some ways Ashok was born and brought up in the Bollywood, commercial industry so he yearned for commercial recognition and success. His eye was that of a realistic cameraman, but in some ways he had this cowboy fetish, which can of course be seen in *Kahl Nayak*. On the one hand, he wanted to be part of Bollywood, and on the other hand he wanted to shoot something interesting. His interesting work was something like *Utsav*, but he achieved his money, and his recognition, and his commercial stardom while doing *Kahl Nayak*.

LC: I have to take advantage of this rare opportunity to speak to an Indian cinematographer. What do you make of the work of your peers? What do you think, for instance, about the cinematography of Manmohan Singh?

RM: I think he continues in the commercial film genre where it is largely soft light and about trying to make the actors look good. I think the Bollywood film industry was struggling when it moved from the film noir black and white to the color era. They couldn't get their contrast right. They were softening a lot of light, using a lot of fill. Neither was source lighting ever there because they were always shooting in unrealistic sets, or they were shooting in the meadows of Switzerland or New Zealand. You can't take that work very seriously as photography.

LC: This is interesting, because there are certain masala elements to *Bombay*, a film you shot for Mani Ratnam. How do you reconcile that?

RM: The masala element of *Bombay* is the use of songs in a larger, serious narrative. That is the way we Indians use melody in order to narrate something. If you have a song like "Tu Hi Re," it condenses the love story by the third reel, and by the fourth reel she's run and come to Bombay. By the fifth reel she has a child. The story is essentially about losing your children, and coming back, so there is an allegorical reference to Sita searching for her children from the *Ramayana*. In that sense, it weakens the narrative, but really it is a case of not only having drama, but also melody plus drama . . . it is melodramatic in that sense. Something which is uniquely Indian.

LC: "Kehina Hi Kya" is very sensual and evocative as a song, the first major song of *Bombay*. Did you storyboard it?

RM: No. You go to a location and, in a sense, you have an idea, and the idea is that you need to climax the song two or three times. In those moments you have to visually capture the energy of the sufi singer, or the glory of the composition. You learn how to pull off a song. How do you use the long shot? How do you achieve the big close-up? How do you communicate that? This balance must be struck in a song between great close-ups, great location, great song, great choreography—which is largely midshots—how do you get that sense of energy where camera and composition come together? The song is taking place in a real palace designed for royal interaction by an Italian architect, but what we are trying to communicate it is a Muslim wedding, and we are trying to use the pillars to communicate that it is an Islamic meeting place. In a Tamil Islamic weddings—and of course *Bombay* is a Tamil film set in Tamil Nadu—there is no role for women to sing and dance, but that idea of women dancing is from a tradition in Malayalam Muslim weddings called Oppana. And such weddings are of course held in the state of Kerala. Mixing Oppana, putting it in a Hindu palace, portraying a Muslim wedding, it's a strange potpourri!

LC: Manisha Koirala, the female lead, is not an obvious singing-and-dancing entertainer like, say, Madhuri Dixit, another actress of the period. What was your role in *Bombay*, in terms of lighting her?

RM: At that point she had just come off shooting *1942: A Love Story*. I remember we were doing twenty-hour days on *Bombay*. Mani Ratnam really likes to push things to the edge. He's had three heart attacks already! He likes to think he is going to battle. Her mother came to me and said, "In the last film she looked so good." It was shot by Binod Prahban. Every time she would get to look slightly tired, he'd tell her to go and sleep and everybody would wait for two hours! I said, "I know I have a reputation to worry about, but that is impossible!" In the end, we sorted it out and we didn't have to have the two-hour breaks so Manisha could get her beauty sleep. After that her mother never came to me again with such requests. It was really a matter of capturing her beauty in the first three reels though. After that she is a mother, you have the childbirth, and then the riot, you know you're going to shoot her through tire smoke in riots, so in the first two or three reels you have to really showcase her beauty. So you have the rain-soaked, pristine environment in Kerala and the way she looks, wet and moist, in the monsoon. The monsoon kind of lends itself to bluish light, and when she lost weight she looked pale and yellowish. Her skin kept on changing, so sometimes I would use a Cosmetic Peach filter,[1] sometimes I would fill in an older, kind of muslin cloth to deal with the fact that she was prone to this kind of Parsi skin tone. She had great skin! But she could look pale at times.

LC: The monsoon scenes at the start of the film, how much of that was exposure or grads, how much the actual conditions?

RM: "Tu Hi Re" was shot over four days through the rain. We'd come home at the end of the day and our hands would look as though we had been in the swimming pool all day! Just wrinkled up because we were in the rain most of the time. A lot of the sequence is under real cloud cover. At that time I had read an article by a British cinematographer in which he wrote that in Britain they don't use the 85 filter so much.[2] I would just pull off the 85 filter and let the cool light come through. Sometimes, when you use the 85 filter, the image can just look gray and muddy! The greens get screwed up. But when you are in the rain and you pull off the 85 filter, the greens look really radiant! I was looking at the green and having that sense of coolness you associate with monsoons. Monsoon is the coolest time that you can get in south India. It is not only the rainiest time, but also to communicate that sense of cool that you don't get in summer. Summer is dry and terrible, so for us rain is the equivalent of a life-giving spring in south India.

LC: One thing I have noticed during times in the Middle East and south India was that when rain comes, the atmosphere becomes much clearer. You can see things, colors pop out, all of a sudden.

RM: All the dust settles down.

LC: Was the rain and monsoon a part of the script then?

RM: We knew we would be shooting the riot sections with a lot of dust and smoke. If the riot section is gray and dusty, the early love section should be pristine and green, it was that kind of logic.

LC: *Bombay* is considered by many a masterpiece. But do you feel it could be argued it is a propaganda film?

RM: I have heard it argued by some that it shows the Muslims in the film as the aggressors, but I know that Mani Ratnam is an atheist. He doesn't allow *puja* on set. In general, he has a left-of-center views on things. The popular narrative in *Bombay* is that the political party called the Shiv Sena and the police took on the riot together, but there was in some ways a simmering tension that was existing at that time. The mafia, which was made up of Muslims and Shiv Sena, were both involved in supporting the riots. To some degree, it was like the Los Angeles riots in that it was a situation that had been brewing for a long time. I think the film is simplistic in that it imagines that everybody can hold hands and that everything will be fine. It's not in that sense a very serious political statement.

LC: In *Bombay* you also shoot the Tamil landscape in a memorable way, even using a crane for a number of very high shots of the landscape. How would you describe your vision of the south Indian landscape?

RM: One of the things which happens when you shoot rain—most people think you can just put a rain machine and shoot—but what happens in monsoon, especially in Kerala . . . I used to travel by train from Chennai to Kerala. There is no monsoon in Chennai and then in the morning when you cross over into Kerala it's just *green*! You can see next to the train tracks where wood is stored, and moss is growing from it, and I used to see the moss on the rooftops in between the terra cotta, and in every little small place and crevice there would be greenery! To capture that greenery, it's not going to be possible through filming a long shot. I mean, you can get that green from shooting a paddy field. But to get that green where it is right in the middle of the monsoon, where day after day it rains, that sense you get in Kerala. In the "Tu Hi Re" song, for the first three days we tried to wait out the rain because it was so hard. Then we started shooting in the rain. So it was something like seven days of nonstop rain. I was lucky that I got a good song in there! But to capture the latrite walls and the little green plants that grow between that, the sense of the landscape without trees and just the fort wall, it was incredible. You know if you look at that sequence I was very influenced by Grigori Kozintsev's *Hamlet*, where the windswept quality of the fort in that Danish area comes through in "Tu Hi Re" very well. I very much admire the way that film demonstrated how to shoot the sea and a fort!

LC: Do you feel Tamil Nadu is cinematic as a state? It is quite flat and brown in parts.

RM: A lot of the popular shooting destinations in Tamil Nadu are invariably next to the mountains. Pollachi, Tirunelveli, and so on. Very few films are set in the center of Tamil culture because it is absolutely flat. Flat landscapes, in which there is growing paddy, are very difficult to compose unless you have a foreground, a middle ground, and background, or you choose to go high up, which is what we did. And one of the reasons we used Tirunelveli in *Roja*, or in *Guru* where we used Pollachi, they are all right next to the mountain, and you get that picture postcard quality of mountain with a sigmoid curve. I think in some ways it is a primal way of us looking to Ansel Adams ideas of landscape,[3] or seeing mountains in the distance and creating a strong line. The foothills are really a beautiful area.

LC: Do you feel Tamil cinema is one of the more sentimental forms of cinema in India?

RM: It is very strongly emotional, but it is also a state that is very rich in visual culture. If you watch a Tamil film, it is the only film where if the cinematographer's name comes up people clap in the theater. People clap when they see your name. After *Bombay* had been out for fifty days, I walked into a theater where it was playing and when my name came on people were whistling! What is that? When Manisha Koirala left her house, and was running out of her home, people were clapping. I have seen that happening in *Titanic* and the ship is sailing and dolphins are jumping near the prow, and people clapped in the theater when the dolphins jumped. Tamil Nadu is a sentimental culture, but it is also a culture that is very receptive to the visual and to visual metaphors. I think that is what makes the Tamil people very bold in the way that they use color. If you look at Tamil literature, it is divided by geography. There is *thurindi*, which is the mountains, *neydil* is the area around the sea coast; so there's a very strong sense of geography in Tamil literature.

LC: A scene which is interesting in *Bombay* is when Arvind Swamy pours petrol on himself. To a degree, it is melodramatic, but the emotional power of the scene is undeniable. When is a scene too over-the-top? I would argue in *Roja* where Arvind Swamy puts out the Indian flag which has been torched with his body, that is too much, too melodramatic.

RM: In the scene Arvind Swamy is not succeeding in reasoning with the rioters, so he is just saying, you can kill me, in that sense. His standpoint is taking on the Hindu fundamentalists, thus saying you can burn me now instead of burning somebody else. Setting fire to oneself is a very normal form of suicide in Tamil Nadu for some strange reason, self-immolation. It is seen as a Shavite metaphor for burning oneself up. The great devotional saints of Nandana and others have always burned themselves up. I think it is seen as some kind of ultimate sacrifice that you can do. You can see this happening in Buddhism. You very rarely see people setting themselves on fire in the Western countries. You see it often in China. You see it often in Tibet. It is something to do with the culture which has cremation in it. It is very much a part of the Indian ethos of altruistic suicide.

LC: Do you think that is why the film didn't translate so well to Western audiences?

RM: I think so. I think the film came across as too melodramatic, too simplistic. It really did well for some strange reason in Japan! I think that the Japanese have a very strange way with dealing with why they like Rajnikanth, the famed Tamil actor. They like manga comics and there is some strange similar connection with why they like *Bombay*.

LC: But you don't know what it is?

RM: No, I'm not a sociologist. Neither am I a film student. I make movies but I am not an academic in that sense.

LC: Flame in *Bombay* is something nightmarish, and is very important as a visual motif. How did you go about filming flame?

RM: I think for a lot of the flame sequences, I would pull the 85 [filter] off and put in a red enhancer when the light goes down. One of the crucial things about shooting flame is that you shouldn't shoot it at midday or 3 pm. The ambient light at around 5 or 6 pm is the best time for shooting fire. Most of our flame scenes were shot in late evenings or near twilight. The flame looks brighter. If you shoot at midday it looks pale, it looks like a kitchen flame. But if you want to see the flame it needs to be at least two times brighter than the ambient light.[4] We shot the taxi burning scene at around 5 pm.

LC: Did the fluorescent lighting which is found so much in India pollute any of your lighting?

RM: It does in the background to a certain extent. Sometimes, when you are trying to communicate that it is that sort of a space, like a bathroom, or bus station late at night, you have to use fluorescent as such places are lit by fluorescent. I don't mind it so long as it is a part of the scene. Sometimes, I will use fluorescent as fluorescent, just use a color correction filter on it.[5] These days we use so many Kino Flos we don't find it that objectionable. Sometimes that bluish light actually adds to the scene. The scene where the boys are returning from Keertan and the men are coming out of the mosque you have that fluoro light present.

LC: How do you feel about sodium lights?[6]

RM: I used them in *Guru*. Fluorescent light tends toward blue-green, and sodium vapor tends towards yellow. In between this you had neon light, which was more blue. I did some research when preparing for *Guru* and found that Marine Drive in Mumbai was one of the first places to use neon lighting. Before Tokyo, before Singapore. But Marine Drive is this long stretch which uses neon lighting. Colaba was lit at that time by gas lights, then they were shifted to electric lights in that period. It does change the way the light looks.

LC: Bombay is famous for its pollution. How did that effect how you went about shooting *Bombay*?

RM: Every time there is a riot in India, you find there are always a lot of slippers [flip-flops] left behind. People are running around and their slipper gets left behind. So when we would shoot those scenes, I'd bring out a sack of old slippers and spread them around the road. Also, when there are strikes people tend to burn truck tires to block the road. For the riot scenes, I would use these truck tires for the background, and burn them, and smaller tires for the front to make what was a set in Chennai look like Mumbai during the riots.

LC: A very powerful scene in the film is when one of the main couple's twins awakes from a nightmare. He has just survived nearly being burned by some of the rioters. How did you go about lighting that?

RM: If you look at it, there is a bluish light on his face, and behind him there is a yellowish table lamp. I shot it with a macro zoom, two ways.[7] So you have on the boy a light which is cold and soft on top, so you can't really see his eyes, you can see his forehead. When somebody is getting up from a nightmare and you see the eyes completely, it doesn't really lend itself. But if you see the forehead, a little of the upper lid, it somehow looks more terrible. So toplight, soft light, not hard light, so the skin of the child, of the young person who is so troubled, comes through. That was how I hoped to capture the child's nightmare.

~

It is tempting to think of *Bombay*, and in turn its cinematography, as being transcendent of the conventions surrounding Bollywood cinema. It was dubbed from its original Tamil into Hindi, the language of Bollywood films, and was produced as a regional Tamil film. It attempts to dramatically re-create a traumatic moment of urban strife from a mere two years before the film's release. Its cinematography focuses on monsoonal south India, and alternately a riot-blighted Mumbai. In short, it is not traditional escapist fare in the Bollywood mold, and it does not focus on typical visual tropes and settings consistent with the mainstream Hindi film industry. It was meant to be accessible and engaging to the whole subcontinent, an important work designed to aid in national healing following the Mumbai riots of 1992–1993. Its score and musical numbers were incredibly popular at the time, and the film was a commercial hit. In short, although the film's subject matter may have been unconventional, much of what was required of Menon was his aptitude at translating the material into a visual potpourri, to use his own words. This would in turn translate the films disparate influences—religious strife, interfaith marriage, conventional romance, secular humanism—into a visual feast easily recognizable to Indian audiences. Remarkably, this meant establishing a shorthand inclusive of numerous other influences—such as Kozintsev's *Hamlet*—while recognizing the necessarily specific nature of the film's narrative, rooted in the geography of Tamil Nadu and Kerala. In conjunction with the more conventional elements Menon described is his cinematography for some of the film's musical numbers, which suggests a fluid approach to the film's cinematography. This allowed for myriad influences—commercial, artistic, cultural, geographic and climatic—to determine how the film's eventual complex aesthetic materialized.

Notes

1. The Cosmetic Peach filter is a warm and diffused gel for lights made by Rosco especially for smoothing and complementing skin tones. There exist several variations of the cosmetic gel filters which are basically a colored gel combined with a light frosted diffusion in one gel filter.

2. An 85 filter, more specifically a Kodak Wratten 85 filter, is a color temperature correction filter to adjust the shooting light to the color response of the film being used. An 85 is orange and is commonly used with tungsten-balanced film in a daylight shooting situation, when the film is balanced for 3200° Kelvin and the daylight is closer to 5600° or 6000° K. It helps balance the skin tones and other warmer colors to match the film's response. Without the use of the 85 or a similar warm filter, the film will be very cool, or blue, when developed and printed. In the photochemical process, it was not easy to fully correct in the printing, whereas in the digital finish it is almost completely correctable if desired.

3. Ansel Adams was among the most famous black and white landscape still photographers in history. He worked principally with large-format box cameras and is most famous for his landscapes of Yosemite National Park and his "Moonrise, Hernandez, Mexico."

4. The term "ambient light" refers to the light that is present in the ambience at the time of day. When the ambience is bright, it is more difficult to see things like flames, whereas when the ambience is low, low at night, it is easy to see even a small flame, like a cigarette tip or lighter.

5. Color correction gels are used for various types of lighting adjustments. If the lamps that need correction are part of the set, or scene, then usually they are in the form of gel filters that are applied to the lamps. If the entire scene is lit by sources needing the same correction, an equal filter can be put on the camera lens. This is less commonly done. Typically for cool white fluorescent lamps, a "minus green" of varying strengths will be used: 1/8, 1/4, 1/2, or full depending on how far you want to neutralize the green spike. A minus green gel appears magenta to the eye.

6. Sodium lights are more correctly called sodium vapor lights. They are a predominantly industrial lighting source with a metal halide discharge source that appears very burned orange to the eye and on most film and video sensors. They were developed and used for lighting industrial parks and city streets because of their relatively low energy consumption for the lumen output and long life.

7. A macro zoom is a lens that has the multifocal length properties of a zoom lens while also being able to focus at macro close distances, often on the front element itself. They are more common to find in 16mm lenses than 35mm motion picture. Some exist for 35mm still photography but are not true macro lenses, which should be able to record a life size, or 1:1 image on the film.

Russell Carpenter

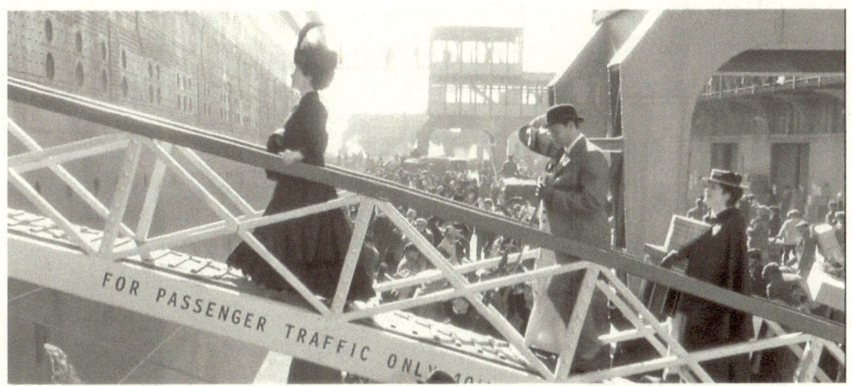

Image 20. Rose (Kate Winslet) and Cal (Billy Zane) enter the ship in *Titanic* (Cameron 1997).

Russell Carpenter ASC began his career working on Jean-Claude Van Damme pictures. His distinct flair and ability to transform generic scenarios into visual feasts, caught the eye of James Cameron, and they collaborated on *True Lies* and *Titanic*. Carpenter proudly represents a cameraman from the classical Hollywood tradition, dedicated to making actors look beautiful and settings appear romantic and vivid, and using the technology at his disposal to achieve that. Since winning an Academy Award for *Titanic*, he has shot films such as *Charlie's Angels* and *Ant-Man*. It might be argued, since his early genre days, followed by his period with Cameron, he has specialized in romantic comedies and light action comedies. Some of his films, such as *Shallow Hal*, engage explicitly with the politics of beauty, and interestingly, sometimes the images Carpenter has helped create have come under criticism for being sexist or dated in their outlook. He has been responsible for the composition and lighting of some of the more memorable representations of love and romance; *Titanic* is a treasure trove of unforgettable images.

The following interview was conducted between Lindsay Coleman and Russell Carpenter in February 2013.

> **Lindsay Coleman:** Let's go back to your early career as a DP, when you were shooting what were arguably B films, but each possessed a distinctive visual flair. Previous to his major stardom, the production values and respective looks of Jean-Claude Van Damme films varied, yet *Death Warrant* has a memorable "brimstone" look. How did you arrive upon such a look and go about achieving it?
>
> **Russell Carpenter:** I'm not sure how we got to that look, but Deran Sarafian, the director, and I were probably going for a "prison is the bowels of hell" motif. It's pure fantasy for sure. I used a lot of warm light in that movie, but the overall effect was heightened by the use of coral filters,[1] which have a very particular way of warming the image. One has to be careful not to go too far with these filters because they affect the overall image and will start to contaminate the shadows with a warmth that looks very unnatural.[2] A lot of these strong filters have fallen out of favor in the world where most color correction is now done in the Digital Intermediate stage, and so many filters can be replicated in this process. I contrasted the brimstone look with a surrealistic choice of color for other scenes, as in a sequence in which I wanted an extremely saturated blue-violet. I think I used Rosco Congo Blue in one scene. It photographs beautifully but lets so little light through that a cinematographer has to use an enormous amount of light to get an exposure.
>
> **LC:** Just before what was arguably your major breakthrough, shooting James Cameron's *True Lies*, you shot *The Lawnmower Man*. It was an adaptation of a Stephen King short story and starred a pre-Bond Pierce Brosnan. *The Lawnmower Man* represented a blend of old genres and new: sci-fi thriller, virtual reality scenario, horror. What challenges did this represent?

How do you feel the effects, early CGI, integrated with your cinematography?

RC: The main challenges at the time were: what can I do to earn a living? After that, everything was cake. Luckily at the time, the effects really didn't have to integrate with the cinematography in the same way they do now, which is coexisting in the same film frame as part of the same cinematic reality. The "virtual reality" was rather innovative at the time, but just a first tiny step in the CGI path. There was a challenge, however, in lighting the costumes that Jeff Fahey and Pierce Brosnan wore, which were accentuated with a material that only illuminated when hit with immense amounts of black light.[3] It was pretty much impossible to take either incident or spot readings under black light, so we made several tests. If we were helped by black and white Polaroid photography, we could make decent assessments of how the black light would photograph. I don't think it was too conscious, but somewhere in my mind, I wanted the world of the lab, in which many of the film's major scenes occur, to be quite different from a world in which the viewer felt the effect of natural light in the world outside.

LC: Your next major film, *Hard Target*, was the Hollywood debut of John Woo. It must have been exciting to work with such a visual director, and also one who puts so much thought into technique.

RC: John designs his shooting sequences quite intricately and can routinely shoot with six cameras—each placed at such an angle and frame rate to contribute a specific "slice" of the action. John's method is not to just set several cameras up and later cut the action conventionally. He has very much cut, recut, and assembled the scene in his mind. Each camera's shot provides a piece of the action which propels the kinetic energy along into the next shot, and that shot does the same for the next shot. I found it to be an exciting way to work, and quite different from what I was used to at the time. The challenge for me was that once all the angles were set up the cameras are "seeing" each other since they are often surrounding the fight sequence. It takes a while to hide the cameras from each other. However, the greater challenge is on the lighting end of things, because a lighting motif has to be created to support shooting the action in a 360-degree circle. On *Hard Target*, I used fire effects and harsh beams of light coming from up above to support the action when we were shooting in a large warehouse where Mardi Gras floats were stored. This motif supported a variety of shooting angles in which we didn't have to relight for each angle.

LC: Now we come to the films which really were the foundation of the reputation you now enjoy, your two collaborations with James Cameron. James Cameron's love of the color blue is well known. How much did his fondness for the color influence your approach on *True Lies* and *Titanic*?

RC: Jim loves a very special, and very specific, blue palette in the lighting from which he can create a unique sense of what nighttime reality is. It is contrasty, and luminous, and the skin tones are usually much hotter than might be found in "nonfilmic" nights. As you've noticed, the blueness of *True Lies* and *Titanic* is very much in the lineage of *Terminator 2* and *The Abyss*. It is a blue that is edged, and broken, with white light in some circumstances, as when I lit Jamie Lee Curtis in her famous stripping scene in *True Lies*, will augment the blue.

This is a highly stylized nighttime reality, but it's a clever way to stage large action sequences at night and light a bit hot. Technically, we'd start by shooting daylight balanced sources,[4] but use a tungsten-balanced film,[5] but that alone would only get about halfway to the saturated blue that Jim loves. Later in post, Jim would work very closely with the color timer to bake in a more intense blue, and they would take care to make sure the actor's skin would not go magenta.

We both knew that playing the tragic night scene in *Titanic* in Cameron's luminous piercing blue light was not historically in line with the moonless night of the tragedy. However, the "playing field" of the sinking ship, and the enormous territory of sea around it, meant using very large lighting sources. The two sources used for this broad area were large Musco lights, and also HMI helium balloons.[6] The balloons provided a more satisfactory, softer and less directional light, but the Muscos were far more efficient at pushing light over long distances, which was of course important given the space we were lighting.

With the Muscos, however, I had to give up nuance and control. Having said that, they were sturdier and more practical to use at long distances in the sometimes considerable winds that came up on the coast of Mexico where the studio was.

The other issue was that the amount of light that provided a proper exposure on the actor's faces for the wide shots made the sides of the ship too bright. In 1996, digital grading, and the ability to use windows to control specific portions of the frame, as far as exposure and color, was not available. It really made things a problem when lighting for wide and tight shots at the same time, as was often done in the massive action scenes in the last third of *Titanic*.

LC: In conversation with another cinematographer, around the time of *Titanic*, he remarked to me that your work on *Titanic* was more on the side of conventional cinematography and involved taking fewer risks. What are your thoughts on such remarks?

RC: *Titanic* was definitely a visually conventional film, in the sense that I tried to adhere to some of the style and conventions of what is considered the Hollywood period style. In fact, in my initial talks with James Cameron about the visual style of *Titanic* he just said, "Hey, you know what these films look like? *Howards End*." So I definitely referenced the work of Tony Pierce-Roberts on the Merchant Ivory films. Now, within those visual parameters I did not do so much risk taking in the shadows of the tonal range, but I did have fun with overexposure in several scenes, just gracenotes here and there that look like mistakes. For instance, when Cal Hockley and Rose walk up the boarding ramp into the ship at Southampton there is a shot from inside the ship looking out just as they enter. I had two large xenon lamps pointed down at them,[7] and overexposed them massively for a few moments. It was a nice little gracenote. I also strayed a bit from the norm in using bounced light from unusual directions, such as the scene in which Rose's mother tightens Rose's corset in their stateroom. In one of the angles there is a Degas painting, and I used that as a bit of an inspiration. I bounced a 4K HMI PAR into a four-by-four bead board card,[8] and keyed them from the direction of the floor (using a bit of soft side light to wrap the effect around their faces a bit). If there was any risk-taking in the film, it was more on the technical side because of the degree of difficulty shooting for up to twelve or thirteen cameras, at the same time, working in an environment of fast-moving water. That really tested me.

LC: *Titanic* was a cathartic film. You have voiced your love of the spiritual cinema of Andrei Tarkovsky. Do you feel *Titanic*, in moments, achieves similar spiritual resonance?

RC: That's a question more for Cameron. The effects in *Titanic* were not just in the service of spectacle. Cameron's genius is that he pulls the viewer into an immersive experience. I feel some of the very simple effects, the morphs from 1914 to 1997, were extremely powerful. People poke at the dialogue of the film, and that is a portion which is more susceptible to criticism, but in terms of structure, and the language of the camera, Cameron is a genius.

LC: The *Charlie's Angels* films were about making beautiful women appear as glamorous as possible, while maintaining a playful tone, very much in the brief of classic Hollywood films. How much do you see your work as a continuation of that tradition?

RC: I would place myself very much in the heart of the Hollywood tradition of keeping the leading ladies in as glamorous and beautiful light as I can, unless the script and director call for something otherwise. It's in my blood and marrow, and I can't really apologize for it.

LC: The *Charlie's Angels* films tread an interesting line. On the one hand, they are about "girl power," and on the other they arguably objectify women (even though this can be analyzed in postfeminist terms). How do you go about determining the manner in which the camera "looks" at women?

RC: Honestly, the film was made for fun and was a kind of a slightly more grown-up version of the *Powerpuff Girls* cartoons. The director, McG, wanted to keep the film light and airy, and the girls' visual sexuality owed more to the aesthetic of the Gil Elvgren pinup art and try to be "audaciously goofy" and innocent at the same time. I suppose the line the director walked was to objectify and empower the women at the same time. . . . I think the movie existed in its own giddy little world, the same way Wes Anderson creates a world in his movies that the audience is invited to play along in. That said, there were times that the camera contributed to lighthearted cheesecake by being placed at an angle that drew attention to the actress's figures.

LC: Do you feel your aesthetic of what constitutes beauty has evolved?

RC: Oh definitely. It's a part of my journey now. I'm in my sixties now. I really hope I have twenty more years to go, because I am just now hitting where I want to go. There's part of me that's very old school. I love the dream of the old Hollywood picture. I love glamour, but I really want to move away from that. I think I'm done with romantic comedies, where everyone looks so great. Over the last few years I've been doing a lot of street photography. I love the beauty of natural light now much more than I did. I really admire someone who can make images that look very natural but also beautiful, like Chris Menges.

LC: *21* was shot digitally, and was one of the earlier films to be shot digitally. How does a given story ideally lend itself to digital?

RC: *21* was a movie ideally suited to digital capture. I used the Panavision Genesis with Panavision glass. Up to the point of time I shot *21*, image capture in casinos meant building up the lighting on the casino floor to levels high-speed film stocks could handle, and this often meant that the light energy emitted from built-in lighting took a bit of a backseat to exposure needs and the character of a casino environment was altered in small or large measure. I really wanted to capture the beautiful and unnatural colors of the Las Vegas casino interiors and using the Genesis was a major help, not only because it has an inherently fast ASA of 640/800,[9] but because we could use the 360-degree shutter option and get even more stop.[10] This allowed us to use the Panavision 24–275mm, and Hubble zooms,[11] for our very dark interiors. Also, the built-in illumination on the casino floor became a major character. The Genesis also saw into the shadows in greater detail, and I did not have to spend unnecessary time pushing fill light into different spaces.

LC: Cinematographers can be very complimentary of one another's work, but also very critical.

RC: Yes, that is true. Sometimes people have made comments about my work and I can say, yes, fair enough. Or I can say, well, that is what the director wanted. McG wanted a very pop sensibility on *Charlie's Angels* and *This Means War*. I've taken some licks for that. But at the end of the day, I think he seemed happy. I could turn around and do something very different from someone else. Then you might see something like Ellen Kuras's work on *Eternal Sunshine of the Spotless Mind*. Then I would say, "Oh, I could never conceive of such an approach. It is brilliant!" The vision still comes through.

LC: Finally, lets discuss a film which I feel to be significant in your career. *Shallow Hal* is a film about the hero's need for beauty and glamour. Was this, or any of your other films, particularly autobiographical or personal to you?

RC: Good question. I do think that for a long time I was very attracted to the iconic film images and beautiful close-ups that I saw in the movies. I liked that world for a very, very long time and I still love a wonderfully composed and lit close-up, and I admire the work of the great fashion photographers. The downside of this is that one can easily succumb unconsciously to a notion of "beautiful" as the media defines and redefines it perpetually. Our culture rewards people who possess physical beauty with a celebrity, and a status, out of proportion to their actual achievements. I work in a profession in which I'm mostly asked to make beautiful people even more so, or as flawless as is possible. There does not seem to be much in mainstream entertainment cinema that reflects the world as it actually is, or human beings as they actually are. I thought the Farrelly brothers tried something really different for them at the time. They took a chance and deviated from the expected. I loved what they were trying to do with *Shallow Hal*, which was challenge this notion of only accepting "the clinically beautiful woman." I think that what is constantly changing for me now is where I find the "beautiful." Today, I find the beautiful in what others might consider dull, ugly or not worthy of attention. I really love the little poem by Emily Dickinson. "'Tis not revelation that waits, / But our unfurnished eyes." I suppose that kind of intense seeing takes a lifetime to develop.

~

Carpenter's particular philosophy on lighting may still be seen in his present output. His work on Marvel's *Ant-Man* is significant in its use of specifically glamorous lighting achieved on-set, rather than in post-production tweaking. His choice to light lead actor Paul Rudd's torso from the side emphasizes not only that his star is fighting fit but also conforms to certain masculine ideals of physical beauty. The look Carpenter created for *This Means War*, along with its director, McG, came under criticism, but it was very much in line with Carpenter's pop sensibility honed on the earlier *Charlie's Angels* films—an often stylish and meticulous approach to studio lighting—with McG, and thus consistent with an aesthetic they developed and clearly believe in. Perhaps similar to Dean Cundey, Carpenter is an avowed lover of the kinds of visuals the Hollywood dream machine has always been so expert at creating. In the present era of dying movie palaces, audiences flocking to the likes of Netflix, and a preponderance of superhero films, it is worth acknowledging that such an approach represents the continuation of a visual tradition now in its second century. Old-style glamour lighting and photography are not in vogue as they once were. In an era of Instagram accessibility, the notion of stars as gods and goddesses has been hijacked by the same stars becoming their own cinematographers, shooting footage of themselves at birthday parties, at film premieres, walking their dogs. Visually, audiences are being conditioned more and more to perceive their favorite stars as ordinary humans as we scroll through an Instagram feed at the end of the day. The remove of old-style glamour has become a rarer commodity. Carpenter's ongoing championing of such a style ironically ensures diversity in the imagery we encounter of stars, and allows for the continuance of the notion that glamour has a vital place in the visual language of film.

Notes

1. Coral filters are made in varying grades from very light to what equals a full Wratten 85 color correction filter. They are a warming filter that can be used to balance the light back to 3200° K when shooting tungsten film in daylight as the ambient color temperature shifts. They are often used to add some amount of warmth to a scene in film and digital capture.

2. Carpenter is referring to color shifts that can occur in the normally black or neutral shadow areas of an image. This contamination can be warm due to the effect of filters like the corals, but it can also be cool if blue filters are used. This is now even more adjustable in the digital age, where one can affect the shadow tone separately using many of the color correction tools either built into the cameras or the grading tools as part of the post process.

3. Black light is an ultra violet light source of a wavelength that is barely visible to the naked eye. When it illuminates objects that have specific colorants in them, they glow very brightly. White will glow an unnatural bluish white. Many people have experienced the black light effect in night clubs and shops that use black light fixtures to illuminate brightly colored posters, clothing, and makeup.

4. Daylight balanced sources include HMI lamps as well as certain Kino Flo lamps (5600° K) and many new lighting fixtures including LED and plasma phosphor.

5. Color motion picture film was produced in two types: daylight balanced (5600° K) and tungsten balanced (3200° K). The tungsten film reads bluer than natural when exposed with daylight sources. See *McCabe and Mrs. Miller* for a very creative use of this method, as well as the inverse method.

6. Balloons were filled with helium and contained varying types of light fixtures in then to provide a floating, large soft light for interior locations where there was no place to rig or it was to big for conventional mounting, and for large mostly night exteriors simulating moonlight or sometimes daylight.

7. Xenon lamps are a very powerful and concentrated discharge light source that give off a lot of heat. Almost exclusively found in fixtures with a parabolic

mirror, they are known for their parallel projection with little or no spread, so they are often used to simulate sun rays. The fixtures use a flat protective glass where color gels can be placed. When placed any distance from the lens, the gels will burn up very quickly. For this reason, the xenon rays are often bounced into a mirror with heat-absorbing gel and then aimed in the desired direction so as not to injure anyone or burn up the set.

8. Light can be considered to be either directional or bounced (indirect]. One can bounce light from large rags or small show cards or mirrors, almost anything including the Earth. HMI PAR lights come in many sizes from 200 W to 24 KW. They are a metal halide discharge lamp that uses a ballast to energize them, are generally daylight (5600° K) balanced and very efficient compared to tungsten fixtures.

9. High speed is normally accepted as a film stock over 250 ASA. The highest ever produced commercially was 800 ASA, though the most common high-speed stock was 500 ASA. The supposedly high ASA rating of the Genesis and many other digital cameras is equal to the highest film speed sold. It has been shown that the ratings claimed by most manufacturers are often exaggerated.

10. In the history of motion picture mechanics the shutter angle of the cameras has been nominally between 144 and 180 degrees. The most that was possible due to frame rate and pull down time was 210 degrees, which was available on Panavision cameras. Only since electronic cameras were developed has any shutter angle greater than 210 degrees been possible. That option basically leaves the shutter open for twice the exposure time of normal shooting. That translates to effectively one extra stop of exposure without changing anything else. The downsides of the 360-degree shutter is that the image has more intraframe motion blur and oddly makes the image to appear more like live video, often referred to as the soap opera look.

11. These are the big, heavy long focal-length zoom lenses that have a lot of glass and aren't nearly as light transmissive as prime lenses can be. The Hubble reference is to the space telescope that magnifies images of celestial bodies millions of light years away.

Martin Ruhe

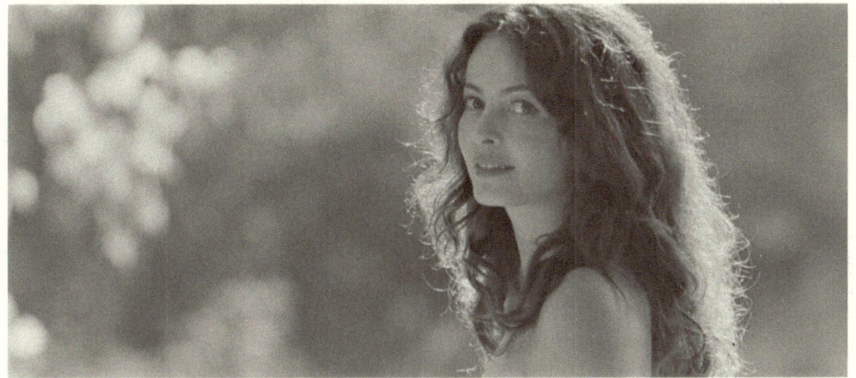

Image 21. Clara (Violante Placido) in *The American* (Corbijn 2010).

Martin Ruhe ASC is a German cinematographer who has come to particular prominence in the early 2000s. He is known for his work on the films *Harry Brown*, *Control*, and *The American*. Working in black and white and then color, on *Control* and *The American*, Ruhe enjoyed a fruitful collaboration with photographer-turned-director Anton Corbijn. These films are notable, aside from their assured narrative execution, for exemplifying the relative potentials of either approach. *Control* features a sensitivity to the potential of the negative for subtlety in black and white cinematography of the twenty-first century. Characters are still crisp, even in shadows, the texture of the actors' skin ably captured even devoid of the richness that skin tones bring to color cinematography. Equally, Ruhe uses the natural palette of locations on *The American*, be it the soft white of a snowscape or the fluorescent wash of an Italian café late at night. Ruhe has also worked on commercials and music videos for bands such as Coldplay and Depeche Mode.

The following interview was conducted between Lindsay Coleman and Martin Ruhe in March 2013.

Lindsay Coleman: If we may, I'd like to start with a general conversation I had with Darius Khondji. He observed that in his work with Danny Boyle on *The Beach*, Boyle would favor lighting for the scene, the overall set, and blocking from there. In contrast, in his working with Roman Polanski on *The Ninth Gate*, Polanski had adjusted the light with each new setup, effectively lighting for a specific shot. Cinematographers talk about lighting for the shot or lighting for the scene. *Harry Brown* seems a mixture of these. How did you determine the balance?

Martin Ruhe: I think I would rather light for the scene rather than the shot, and then find the shots within the scene. Lighting shot by shot, sometimes you lose the context. If you light the room, then you get to see what's in the room. If you light shot by shot sometimes everything gets more perfect. You lose a sense of reality. I once spoke with Harris Savides about this. He lights rooms, then he sees what happens in the room. That's his philosophy.

LC: I was watching *Reds* the other day, shot by Vittorio Storaro. That style of Storaro's is very expressionistic, very striking.

MR: Well, Storaro, he's another story. Color has overtaken him in the end. I think that is always the danger. If you go shot by shot, then you do things which seem right for the shot but destroy for the viewer their sense of orientation, and that can take you out of the scene. I think, if you are lighting shot by shot, you end up more focused on lighting faces.

LC: There are very warm-looking nights for *Harry Brown*, in terms of color temperature. How did you arrive at that approach?

MR: *Harry Brown* was special. We had a lot of location pictures taken at night. There was so much beauty in these shots. It's really an ugly place. A nasty place. But if you see them at night, it's very beautiful. The colors are wrong. It's very orange. Sometimes it's lit by mercury vapor,[1] sometimes sodium vapor.[2] I loved these location pictures, I loved how a single practical light source would give so much ambiance. So I tried to minimize my lights. We didn't use a lot of film lights, but instead went much more in the way of industrial lights, light sodium vapors, which you can't control very much. But I like that. That's what we did there. On *The American* we shot in a village, and they also have similar lights. Of course, you can shut them off, but it didn't feel appropriate. It should feel like it would if you went out there at night to take pictures, to walk around.

LC: There was an interesting effect, in the night scenes, where the street lights pool to create this seeming network of pathways. Was that deliberate?

MR: It was a route we went into. I went to the location and started scouting months before we started shooting because we kept getting pushed back. I live in Berlin, but I went over to shoot commercials in London. I stayed a few days longer to do some location scouting with the director. I could start to see how it looked there. There was another thing. It became clear that we needed to shoot digital on *Harry Brown*. It was my first feature in digital so I said, "Let's take it to the limit." So we did. We went to 1000 ASA. We shot with minimum lighting. We shot with Master Primes with very minimal depth of field.[3] I think that what we gained from it was that sometimes when you see film sets at night, when you see films, you can see where the production ends when you see the edge of the lit area. I didn't want that. I didn't want this to feel like a film. I wanted it to feel like you're there at night, that the setting of the story is a real place. It's what it feels like at night. It's also the world Harry lives in. By going there, using minimal lights, our sets don't end, it blends in. If you see wide shots at night, you don't see the edge because we used a lot of practical lights.

LC: Please tell me more about that freedom you have described which practical lights afford you?

MR: In *Harry Brown* he tortures the young man he captures. He takes him to a burned-out flat where his friend used to live. I thought it should be dark, it should be really dark. It should not be nice. A couple of scenes we lit with bare light bulbs. That's one of those, where we actually only used one bare light bulb. I thought, "That's what it would be." Also, that scene was shot in the studio but it did not want to feel like a studio. It's a nasty scene, so it shouldn't be nicely lit.

LC: You shot the "Talk" video for Coldplay. That's the opposite—as stylish as it can get. You used a blurred 3D effect in the video t was quite influential on adverts which came after it.

MR: That was actually a reference. Chris Martin is a big fan of Kraftwerk. They wanted to wear glasses, like on the album cover for Kraftwerk. It was the director Anton Corbijn's idea to add the effect, which is basically how a 3D image looks if you are not wearing the special glasses. If that was influential, it's nice, but it was actually looking backward rather than starting something new. Music videos used to be very influential. I'm not sure how influential they can be these days. I never watch them anymore. I did hundreds in the '90s. I wish they got more notice, but a lot of them have gotten so cheap that it's hard to watch them.

LC: Do you see your work on commercials and cinema as distinct? What is the relationship of what you are learning on one in respect to the other?

MR: You're still the same person, so you do things in a similar way, you experience things in a similar way, but of course if you do a commercial to sell a car, and you shoot the car in a studio, so it becomes quite technical. It's not about philosophies of light. It's about showcasing something. But I met Anton Corbijn on music videos, and I met some other people on commercials. It allows me to work in the States or Europe. I get a lot of experience. I get to try things; it takes away a little bit the fear. I learn about digital cameras which I can use in work with film. I know both worlds.

LC: Given that you have started shooting features in the era of digital cinema do you have a particular film which you feel is a very fine example of what digital can do?

MR: *Harry Brown* (*both laugh*). No, but I think *Harry Brown* was good because people didn't realize that it was shot digitally. I think I like *Harry Brown.* I did *Page Eight* and I won an ASC award for that,[4] but that was for TV. Speaking of orange nights, as you did before, for that one because it's a spy story, we wanted it to feel like a classic film from the '60s so wherever we could we took out the sodium vapor in the nights. It was the opposite of *Harry Brown.*

LC: On *The American* you commented that the natural events of the day influenced what you shot. It does indeed have a very organic-seeming look. Could you comment on that?

MR: On the earlier film I shot with Anton, *Control*, we had story boards, or shot lists. On *The American* we didn't have that in the beginning. Due to time pressures, we did start doing it a little later. We had those beautiful Saturdays where we went out and shot basically second unit stuff. That was so nice exploring the Italian landscape, which is of course where the film is set. Have you been to Italy?

LC: I have seen lots of films *shot* in Italy. (*Laughs*)

MR: In Italy, when you go to bars, they are really lit in an ugly way. They put fluorescents in, they don't care, but that was where I took the colors from. The village was very orangey, and so we used a lot of orange colors in the nights, but when the guy chases him and he sits in the café we used cool, bluish light. I think I saw that in Wong Kar-wai's films. Chris Doyle did that in *Chungking Express.* I always loved that. It's a very strong color, but it doesn't feel contrived, or staged.

LC: I am glad you brought this up. The look of your color films, following your black-and-white film *Control*, has always been vivid, dynamic. What is your color philosophy?

MR: I hope there is none. I would love to be able to change it every film. Not get stuck in one look. I would hate that. To get stuck in the look of *Harry Brown*. Or the look of *Control*. That's why I tried to do things very differently. I went from *Control* to a sixteenth-century period film in color. Then *Harry Brown*. If you want to talk color philosophy, then start from real life. Watch it because it's so rich, so beautiful. Take that over. Use that to make it believable. I hate when films are so self-aware. Some cinematographers are so self-aware in their use of color that it really just becomes a way for them to put their stamp on a film, rather than to reflect some kind of reality.

LC: When Jack, the George Clooney character, has sex in the brothel, the light is very red, saturated, in *The American*. This is naturally a comment on the fact that the scene is occurring in a brothel, but the red is very rich. Is that an example of you starting from reality and then taking it to a more romantic, expressionistic level?

MR: The director, Anton Corbijn, of *The American* is a photographer. He is very aware of light, framing. His photography doesn't use many lights. We talked about it quite a lot. He loved the idea of the red light. Then we just made it very strong, to be honest. Very pure. It's a simple thing. There was no big philosophical thought about it. It was just "that's it, that's how strong and pure it should be."

LC: So, it was color for its own sake?

MR: Sometimes it's hard to say where things come from. We knew we would use red light for the brothel scene, then I used a little bit of orange light coming from the street. Anton really loved the idea of red, and we didn't want to contrast it with anything. That was not thinking of the effect for the audience. It started with Anton's vision. And when we saw it, we knew it didn't need any contrast. We were very fast in making that decision, and sticking with it.

LC: In terms of the gray of the slate in the village, it contrasts very nicely with the red of the brothel scene. Did Anton want to establish some kind of a contrast in the larger visual design of the film?

MR: It's part of the character of the landscape. It's part of Abruzzo. It's like a forgotten place. The villages are very empty. In the village, there were 200 houses and only 10 or 20 were actually lived in. It was very bleached out. The landscape was bleached out. Also, we started shooting in late September and we went into autumn. The streets don't have color. But what I felt strong about was when you go into nights and you have this strong color. You have orange, from the street lights, or the bluish, greenish color I described. You can add colors, but they are still based on what you observed there.

LC: What about backlighting, such as when the prostitute Clara is nude at the river? That seems to me a scene lit and shot in a way very conscious of the beauty of the image.

MR: I love backlighting. We chose that time of the day to shoot it, and really kept it quite natural.

LC: There is of course the flip side to that. There is a scene of Michael Caine undressing in *Harry Brown*, and the lighting is arguably unflattering. It's very clear to see that he is an old man. What is your approach to lighting the human body?

MR: It has to come from the story. In *Harry Brown*'s bathroom, it's a studio scene but . . . he's aware he's just killed someone, he's undressing . . . I was actually grateful with Michael Caine that there was no discussion, he didn't want to look at the monitor to see how he looked . . . but I just felt that this was how it should be, it should be real. It shouldn't be too nice. I think it's how a council house would be in the night,[5] and so it's very intimate, lighting from above. There is the side shot of him where his head is against the wall, I think it's a very intimate moment.

LC: The actress for Clara in *The American* [Violante Placido] is classically beautiful, classically voluptuous. Do you and Anton seek to reference any particular works of art in how you framed or lit her?

MR: No. It's interesting we never watched many films together. A lot of people noted what they saw as a Melville influence on *The American*, a film like *Le Samourai*, but Anton didn't even know that film. Anton wanted her to be a real woman. A believable prostitute. And the film is really almost like a western. The Clooney character comes to the village and befriends a priest and a prostitute. In some ways, it sounds very clichéd. That's what he loved about it.

LC: In an ironic sense?

MR: In the sense that a lot of the great stories are very simple stories. But there is strong conflict there. A guy trying to escape his past, he falls in love, then things don't work out.

LC: Do you see *The American* as a tragedy?

MR: I'm not sure. For me *The American* is almost like a meditation. I think it has . . . It's a thriller, a meditation, it's almost like a very old-fashioned archetypal film.

LC: *Harry Brown* could be black and white in terms of the monochrome effect you achieve. And of course, you shot *Control* in black and white. Do you have a preference for monochrome, or very full range of color? I ask because, given that you are early in your feature film career, it feels as though you are in the process of working out your aesthetic preferences.

MR: I like to jump between these worlds. When we shot *Control* I wasn't really aware that it was a big deal to shoot black and white. We talked about it. I was excited that Anton had asked me to shoot it. Anton had shot Joy Division in black and white at the time the film is set. Anton is known for his very grainy black-and-white photographs, but we talked about how we didn't want that. That style is very much identified with period photography, and we wanted something which would feel more contemporary, but also root you in that period. So it's different from what he usually does in his stills. I wondered, for a bit, if I should use filters, but then I thought no, Anton doesn't do that in his stills, so I decided I was not going to do that. We should keep it natural. We shouldn't use extra red or blue lipstick.[6] We didn't want that.

LC: Again, an interesting aspect of your films is their simultaneous visual sophistication, and simplicity. I suppose this leads to a simple final question: Do you believe in visual metaphors, or do you believe in telling the story as simply as possible? In short, do you believe that imagery should be symbolic?

MR: Oh, I don't think I've used them very much. I have used them, but it is a thin line. If it's too much on the nose, then it feels as though you are lecturing people. You don't want to do that. You want to tell the story. If there is a symbol for what you are trying to express, then it is nice, but you have to be very careful with that. For *Harry Brown*, we shot an end scene where he goes into a tunnel, and there is a light at the end of the tunnel. That did make it into the film because it raises the question "is he going to God?" "is he dying?" and how the film ends with life just going on is much stronger. It's nice to have visual metaphors, but you have to be so ingenious in how you go about it. You have to make sure that nothing goes wrong in the execution.

~

Ruhe's discussion of lighting for the scene holds true when strategies for blocking and filming scenes are considered. In the nighttime scenes where Clooney sits in the café, the choice of the cool fluoros is naturally pervasive as a lighting approach. Using fluoros to light from above, and therefore being the major source of light for a nighttime interior—with limited external light penetrating the café—Ruhe sets his lighting strategy up such that the fluorescent light must dominate. Wherever the Clooney character moves in this lighting environment, or however coverage is used in such a scene, he will always be in this specific lighting environment. This in turn helps reinforce the scene's mood of loneliness, and isolation, setting up his later move toward a romantic relationship with a prostitute he meets. In the case of the film, an element of contrast is established by the external sodium vapor lighting of the street lamps, but these are not dominant light sources in the frame. In a scene from the Ruhe-filmed *Control*, a biopic of singer Ian Curtis, Ruhe and director Anton Corbijn blocked out the final scene between Curtis and his wife, Debbie, such that Debbie would stand in the well-lit living room and Curtis would speak to her from a dark kitchen. This is in turn a lighting choice indicative of their relative mental/emotional states. He commits suicide shortly after, while her perspective is essentially more upbeat. As such, very much like the fluoro-lit scene in *The American*, particular lighting conditions dominate the scene, its narrative content, and its thematic portent.

The significance of lighting for the scene may be judged as a method to signpost aspects of the theme of a scene, and in turn help the viewer intuit how cinematography aids in the development of mood and story. This method is not a catch-all. As Ruhe observes, cinematographers often err toward lighting faces. This fealty toward portraiture can aid immeasurably in characterization. In a film such as Ingmar Bergman's *Persona*, Sven Nykvist entirely commits himself to lighting faces, sometimes to the point of abstraction and disengagement with anything in the environment other than the characters. Such an approach is every bit as deliberate as what Ruhe describes in lighting the scene. It is simply worth noting the different outcomes they may produce.

Notes

1. Mercury vapor is a metal halide discharge lighting source very common to industrial/civic lighting. The lamps are connected to ballasts that power them, giving a large amount of light for relatively low wattage. Mercury has a bluish-green cast.

2. Sodium vapor is similar to mercury vapor, but it has an orange-green cast. Both of those sources have a high green spike that is difficult to neutralize.

3. Master Primes is a series of lenses made by Zeiss for Arriflex. They have a maximum T-stop opening of 1.3, are very sharp, and are quite large. Depth of field relates to the amount of focus that any lens will hold at a given T-stop. The wider open the iris, the less depth of field. For instance a 35mm at T 1.4 has a depth of field of 1' 4" when focused at 10'. The same focus distance at a T 11 has a depth of field of 14' 9". This is useful for deciding on selective focus and images.

4. The ASC award is one of the several awards for excellence in cinematography given annually by the American Society of Cinematographers.

5. A council house is the British equivalent of section 8, or HUD-subsidized low-rent housing in the United States. They are usually in multistory apartment buildings.

6. In black and white photography, the makeup is done differently than for color. Depending on what color filter is used on the camera, the red or blue lipstick would either accentuate or minimize the lips.

Javier Aguirresarobe

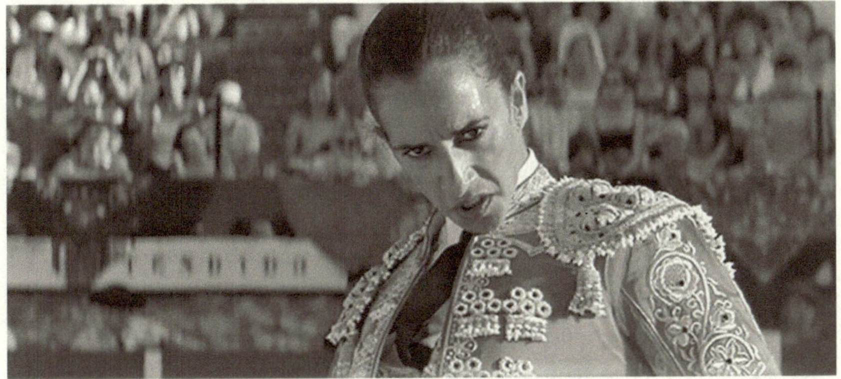

Image 22. Lydia González (Rosario Flores) awaits her bull in *Talk to Her* (Almodóvar 2002).

Javier Aguirresarobe ASC AEC is a prolific cinematographer who has collaborated with Woody Allen on *Vicky Cristina Barcelona* and *Blue Jasmine*, also shooting two of the Twilight movies, *New Moon* and *Eclipse*. His collaborations with Woody Allen have been among the more consistent for that filmmaker. Where longtime Allen collaborator Gordon Willis favored a starker aesthetic, Allen's collaborations with Aguirresarobe have been remarkable for their fulsome embrace of a richly romantic aesthetic. Aguirresarobe himself can favor a subtle, meticulously evoked naturalism, evidenced in his work on *The Sea Inside* and *Talk to Her*, as well as monochromaticism with the bleak Cormac McCarthy adaptation *The Road*. No genre snob, Aguirresarobe can elevate franchises with his confident sense of an audience's response to color and movement, as evidenced by the potent aesthetic reinvention he exhibited in the *Twilight* films.

The following interview was conducted between Ricardo Aronovich and Javier Aguirresarobe in July 2013.

Ricardo Aronovich: Let's start with examining how you feel you exist as a collaborator with your director, given that you have worked with some of the most famous ones. Some cinematographers feel they are like co-directors. Do you feel that way?

Javier Aguirresarobe: No, no. I am in service of the story and director. I like to collaborate, to have creative input, but I serve these two.

RA: Claims are made that Woody Allen does not really contribute to the visuals of a story. What was your experience?

JA: He always proposes where the camera should be, how the framing should be. He is not always super specific. He talks about how it should be, and if he doesn't like it, he will tell you.

RA: In turn, sometimes your work can incorporate authorial elements from sources alternate to the director. The choreography of the dance which opens *Talk to Her* was by Pina Bausch. How did you hope to distinguish it from the rest of the film?

JA: The choreographic sequences of Pina Bausch were shot on theater stages, and I had to shape the light that was already there, with no chance to make many changes of my own. So filming those sequences was a real frustration for me, especially the first one. I would have liked to work more on each shot and get a personal touch on the light, but it was not possible. There was no time for it, and it was not the appropriate moment to create major complications. Moreover, this first sequence of Pina Bausch is seen in the theater . . . I shouldn't give more importance to this issue but, whenever I see it, I still feel bad because I don't like the color contrast, limited by the use of tungsten theatrical lights. However, I prefer the second sequence, at the film's end, where there is not only the theatrical light but also a light coming from the ground.

Finally, in the dance sequence—the credits one—I've got at least a good overhead light, which makes it more attractive.

RA: Sometimes your work, even with a strong, auteurist director, can be influenced by a given film genre or convention of shooting. *Talk to Her* features a silent film in its middle section. How closely did you study the conventions of silent cinema for this, or were you aiming for a more unique, non-academic approach?

JA: This black-and-white silent film embedded in *Talk to Her* was quite difficult to shoot. On the one hand, Pedro Almodóvar wanted a look that exactly matches the one of silent films we all know. So this part was filmed with a different camera speed: I think I remember there were seventeen frames per second. And that wasn't all: the actors had to move with impulses. Then, there was the issue of the male character whose size was reduced to a height of nearly fifteen centimeters. There are some shots taken in a huge set, and others on a green background. I had to be careful with the light when the shot was covering two different spaces. The truth is that we didn't want to create a rather different look from the one of silent films. Our intention was to imitate, as closely as possible, both movement and texture of those eternal silent movies, exactly as if the sequence *The Shrinking Lover* was an existing title from the silent period.

RA: Briefly, can we diverge to discuss some of your other celebrated examples of genre cinematography? *The Others* is a period film and a ghost film. What influences did you draw on for the film? How would you describe its period look, particularly give your use of lamps in the film?

JA: Honestly, in preparing for this movie, I didn't find any other film that could help me as a reference. I worked with Benjamín Fernández—the production designer—in order to create a neutral environment with both walls and household items, and that helped me a lot to come up with an eerie atmosphere. For ghost and horror movies, the books about lighting recommend the conventional use of strange lights. . . . This visual concept seemed to me wrong in relation with *The Others*. So in this movie, I tried to revive my feelings, my memories as a child when my house lights went out. Remember those deep shadows created by the moonlight, or by the street lights in the hallways or the rooms. Moreover, given the disease of both children, the light takes on a vital importance in this movie. It becomes a fully fledged actor of the movie. Therefore, I wanted to create a more realistic light than the ones usually used in this type of movie. I also wanted to be true to the light diffused by the oil lamps of that time. So there were small lamps concealed in the base of those "oil lamps." When Nicole Kidman was walking through the house, I didn't succeed to do it, even though I was prepared for it. And the preparation of the "pencil of light" and of its wiring was very complex then, with the actress moving all around the house. I remember having used only once a Fresnel projector in such scenes, and I took great care that the shadows on the actress's body could not be seen.

RA: You have also of course filmed pure dramas. I am thinking of *The Sea Inside*, and *A Better Life*. *A Better Life* is a simple story of love. How did you approach creating a visual style which would not overwhelm the story?

JA: When the story of *A Better Life* was proposed to me, *The Sea Inside* immediately came to my head. Although the stories are different, both are touching reality. In this case, it is the life of an undocumented Mexican gardener in Los Angeles, who gets back his son, who is about to be lost in the maze of Hispanic gangs. Therefore, it's a fiction that brings us to a documentary treatment. We could not fall into artificiality. Both movies have an austere look, with real nights and credible images. I think that photography should never exceed the other message: the reality of lives that are settling; moreover, in very much known and highly recognizable areas, as in this case, a neighborhood of Los Angeles.

RA: Can you elaborate on what makes for credibility, in relation to *The Sea Inside*?

JA: This movie had to be credible. That was the priority. So I had the idea of creating a documentary-like visual treatment for this movie. Its main protagonist was a real person who was injured in the same place of the beach where we shot the fictitious version of the accident. They had to put makeup on [Javier] Bardem for about six hours a day as he had to physically look like Ramón Sampedro, the real man who was the subject of the film. . . . All these elements led to light, color, and composition parameters far from any artificiality. I remember that each time before starting the camera, I was looking at the frame exhaustively to confirm that what my eyes were seeing was as real as life can be. Javier Bardem is amazing. And the music also helps.

RA: Even with the realism of *The Sea Inside*, much of it is very beautiful, particularly your seascapes. What is your experience of filming the ocean?

JA: I live close to the sea and I have shot a lot of movies where the sea is present. I remember that my first documentary films were about seafarers or fishermen. Many years ago, I have also shot a documentary film in Calcutta and we have been sailing for several days on the Ganges. . . . I remember, too, a movie entirely shot on the sands of an Almería [Spain] beach. In *The Sea Inside*, there are stunning sunset images, because we wanted the ultimate vision of the main protagonist to be an extraordinary picture of a beautiful horizon, as the sun slowly disappears into the waters.

RA: Returning to *Talk to Her*, that film also features some very strongly visual scenes which are a really showcase for your gifts as a cinematographer, genre cinematography aside. What of the bullfighting scenes in *Talk to Her*?

JA: The scene in which the heroine is trampled by the bull, a dummy was used. It didn't quite work, so that needed to be fixed in post. Also, shooting in the ring was very complicated because the light changed throughout the day. We had to wait for the most opportune moment of each day to collect a shot specific to the light conditions of each period of the fight. Shooting with real bulls was complicated in terms of the laws of Spain also. If you use a bull, it cannot go home, it must be killed. The first bull just jumped over the dummy rather than hitting it. The shot didn't work, but they had to still kill the bull. The second bull hit the dummy, then ran away. The third bull completed the job. Three bulls died.

RA: The use of slow motion is quite agonizing. How did you decide on the frame rate for that scene?

JA: We used several cameras, one with slow motion, others not. Slow motion was introduced to one of the cameras in post. It is such a dramatic moment we couldn't just have a simple shot. It is central to the rest of the film. This was why we used slow motion.

RA: Another aspect of the film's cinematography which is intriguing is that much time is spend gazing on Leonor Watling, a convalescent patient of the film. She is subject to the camera's gaze. How did you avoid exploiting her nudity, as there are a number of scenes in which she is nude or partially nude?

JA: An elegant aesthetic was required when her body was shown. The saturation is a little greater in those scenes. The brightness is higher, the contrast is softer. Also, the hospital setting lends her a more virginal feel.

RA: Do you judge the characters you film, such as Javier Cámara's character Benigno, who has sex with the comatose Leonor Watling's character off screen?

JA: Of course. It is important to understand the character. I accept what the character does. He is a controversial character. He is seemingly a good person, who at the same time violates this woman, yet he also brings her out of her coma. He is the key of the whole story.

RA: *Talk to Her*, despite its range of differing imagery, does seem to form a stylistic whole. Do you feel you have a style?

JA: Of course. The way source light enters the room, the level of contrast, how I always present blacks, the natural sources of light, these are all things which define my style, and can be found in all of my films. Even if they look different these elements are entirely consistent. The color might change, but I enjoy keeping these elements. Interestingly, my style can sometimes clash with what is favored by a director. Pedro Almodóvar films are generally brighter, more colorful. *Talk to Her* was done in a style closer to what I would say is my own style.

RA: The approach which you describe taking would seem to be very different from that of Affonso Beato on *Live Flesh*. Affonso shot this and also the film immediately before *Talk to Her*, *All About My Mother*. His aesthetic favored a much higher level of saturation of color.

JA: Almodóvar was very happy with Beato. He would often say, "More like Beato, more like Beato," while we were shooting *Talk to Her*. José Luis Alcaine also worked very well with the instructions of Almodóvar. I didn't like it. He doesn't like my work. There was a scene in *Talk to Her* where I favored a more soft light, and he was definitely not happy with it. *Talk to Her* looks very different from his other movies.

RA: Given that you have a distinct style, do you feel every cinematographer has a style?

JA: No, not at all. I think over time certain cinematographers fall into a pattern of picking projects which better complement the way that they work.

RA: One final thought on "style." It is interesting that you have discussed certain lenses as being "noble," and suited to you in a particular way. Could you discuss your use of "noble lenses" in *Goya's Ghosts*?

JA: To qualify certain lenses as noble—in comparison to others, that we call "ignoble"—is a matter of argot, of slang. And in this argot, we qualify as noble shooting movies with lenses with a focal length range from 27mm to 75mm. With these ranges, the perspectives are not distorted, and we get through the lens a view close to the human eye's one. *Goya's Ghosts* is a movie that sails into these waters of "nobility" in the perception of its fiction.

RA: We have discussed Allen and Almodóvar. Julio Medem is also a great storyteller, and certainly a very accomplished visualist. How do you feel his vision complements your own?

JA: Julio Medem is always very original, always trying to establish a creative way of telling a story.

RA: It's interesting that you've only worked once each with two of the finer visual storytellers of Spain, Medem and Almodóvar.

JA: Julio called me again for the next feature, but I wasn't available. I would guess that Almodóvar was not happy with my work on *Talk to Her* because I didn't hear from him after that film.

RA: *Earth* has a very strong, evocative look. What do you think is Medem's approach as a stylist and visualist?

JA: For Julio Medem, *Earth* had to be a film made out of pure, saturated colors, and with a strong contrast. For this movie, the basic locations were the Aragon lands; close to the place where Buñuel was born, and where grapevines are planted in stunning red-colored grounds. Red is a key color. Think of the inside of the bar . . . and even of red moon nights. Julio always wants his movies to develop a poetic language, a visual, interpretive language. . . . I was very excited about making this movie. And during the shooting, Julio's passion was contagious. For *Earth*, I dared to work with polarizing filters, with skies saturated by an intense blue, with unusual contrasts. It was a wonderful experience, and I owe it to Julio Medem.

RA: *The Road*, in contrast, has a limited color palette. What challenges did this present in terms of communicating different moods in the film?

JA: The main challenge for *The Road* was to film on location, and in a land without any sun; in a land where the green color is gone; in a land where ash is a substantial element of the environment. Therefore, the color palette was already reduced to very few colors. And the actors' costumes were chosen according to the same rules as well. Besides, for this movie, I applied a technique that delved into the criterion of getting the lesser chromaticism. I worked with film (Kodak 5218) which I pulled two stops on in the development. With this system, I could even lower the color saturation and contrast. Finally, for the DI, we worked to come up with a look which we felt matched the spirit of the source novel by Cormac McCarthy. We tried to reflect this sprit visually. Shooting *The Road*, we all worked with the same idea. It was an extraordinary experience. We were aware of the risk we were taking, making such a special movie, so real, so harsh. Audiences are not often very open to such a story, especially if the story seems so probable, so close to reality.

RA: The reds are very strong in your work on *The Twilight Saga: New Moon*. How would you describe the specific color approach you were attempting, and what emotional tone were you hoping it would evoke?

JA: For *New Moon*, both director Chris Weitz and I wanted to get a different look from the first movie of the series, which was a cold, bluish film; perhaps because vampires were its main protagonists. So with the script in hand, we came to the conclusion that the second part of this series—*New Moon*—was a romantic movie. There was action, there were still vampires—who led a normal life among students—but there was basically this girl and this guy in love. For those reasons, we changed the tone and built a film with a normal contrast and slightly warm colors. In *New Moon*, there is a space for "vampires" and there is another area for "wolves"—two different communities—but this was not a reason good enough to differentiate them outrageously by the means of color. So we settled for a warmer tone to the "wolves" and a slightly more neutral one for "vampires." I don't know; it was an option. Over time, I consider it successful.

RA: Did you find that the producers tried to influence your work on the *Twilight* films?

JA: No, I didn't feel any pressure. The main goal was to change the look of the first film. This was requested by the producer. They realized that they were doing a love story, not a vampire film.

RA: They didn't know that on the first film?

JA: They knew that, but the first film favored a more clichéd action/horror look.

RA: The camera moves around Kristen Stewart when she is in her room and the seasons are passing. How was this evocative shot in *New Moon* achieved?

JA: It's a much simpler shot than it looks. There was no motion control for the shot. It was a duet dolly. They shot the whole thing in three hours. There were lights attached to a dimmer board. The lights changed as we moved the camera. It was a normal shot. The only postproduction was on what was outside the windows, which of course featured the changing seasons.

RA: In the past you spoke of frustration with regard to the scenes on *Eclipse*, your second *Twilight* film, shot with another cinematographer. How much do you take authorial credit for that film's look?

JA: About *Eclipse*, I don't feel like making any comment. I couldn't intervene in the DI. I find it especially painful to see this movie. I don't like its color and texture at all. There is a scene that I didn't shoot myself. I was busy when reshoots were made. But it doesn't matter. I am responsible for the light, though I am not for its final look, which I find lamentable. For *Eclipse*, we shot nighttime both with "day for night" method and during real nights, and with a very warm light I liked a lot. The dailies were really great. Both director David Slade and I wanted to break the cliché of blue moon nights. Finally,

> *Eclipse*—with the exception of a few action sequences—has lost its photographic personality. This movie remains in a place that leads nowhere.

~

Aguirresarobe's final thoughts highlight the issues for cinematographers in their attempts to claim authorship of the image in the era of digital cinema. Cinematographers largely are attracted to projects that enable them to work on a big canvas. Detailed lighting schemes, cranes, complex rigs, the ability to create artificial lighting environments on a broad geographic scale or alternately on sets. Naturally, such a visual scope is a fit for epic narratives, stories that require logistically complicated schedules to be filmed, as well as often lengthy schedules, or alternately dramatically truncated schedules. In such scenarios, few professional cinematographers are able to see through their work, beginning to end. Thanks to audience test screenings, focus groups, and the influence of those in marketing, reshoots are often required for major films. Studios may independently insist on including new elements. Deadlines for films in a franchise may similarly loom, with thought only being given to the pragmatic requirements of meeting a deadline. In such instances, the visuals of a film may represent the lighting choices and camera placement of two very different artists. The resulting edit may put emphasis more onto one sequence and off another. Aguirresarobe's final comment would thus best be interpreted as meaning that the film does not represent his own developed style, a style he can expound on at length. Also, it means that it does not have a unitary style, or a clear visual personality, caught as it is between two "voices."

Although this interview represents exclusively Aguirresarobe's own, it is worth noting that in the history of film there have been significant cases where mixing two or more cinematographers on a project has resulted in disputes as to authorship. For *Days of Heaven*, cinematographer Néstor Almendros won an Academy Award. During a portion of the production, Haskell Wexler replaced him. For the decades, Wexler maintained that his contribution has been significant enough that he deserved credit as coauthor of the film's visuals, and in turn of its great influence on filmmakers in the period since. Thirty or so years separate the productions of *Days of Heaven* and *Eclipse*, but the theme of mixed or contested authorship of a film's cinematography is still potent.

Claudio Miranda

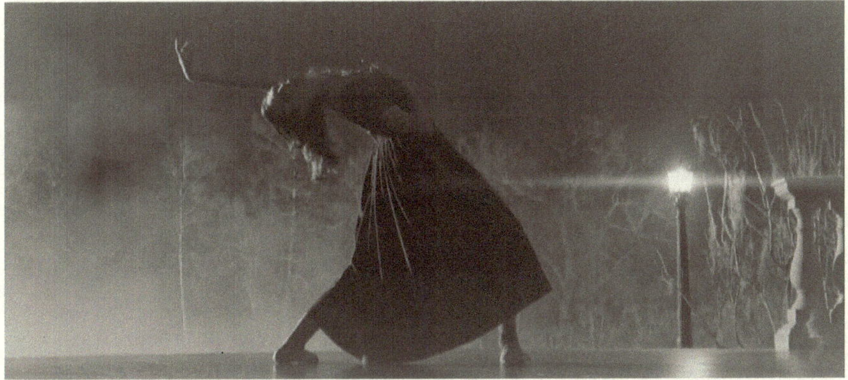

Image 23. Daisy Fuller (Cate Blanchett) dances for Benjamin in *The Curious Case of Benjamin Button* (2008).

Claudio Miranda ASC has come to prominence in the world of cinematography in the past decade thanks to his tasteful lighting and flawless work in postproduction. Early films of his include *TRON: Legacy* and *The Curious Case of Benjamin Button*. In 2013 he won an Academy Award for his work on *Life of Pi*. A close early collaborator with both Janusz Kamiński and Mauro Fiore, as well as a gaffer for the legendary Harris Savides on earlier David Fincher films, Miranda's pedigree is significant. Fearlessly embracing the new digital age of cinematography, his work is ever subtle, conveying an intense understanding for how his plates, lighting, and camerawork will integrate with both the DI and visual effects. It is perhaps worth noting that aside from an early assignment on the romantic comedy *Failure to Launch*, Claudio's films have been high-budget spectacles, often set in the past or future, and have been located in fantasy worlds far removed from our own, worlds where his unique aesthetics find fullest expression.

The following interview was conducted between Roberto Schaefer and Claudio Miranda in November 2015.

Roberto Schaefer: Going back to your early career, when you were a gaffer and working with Harris Savides on *The Game*, what lessons did he impart to you?

Claudio Miranda: Harris always spoke of the necessity to keep on looking, and to not be afraid of imperfections. You can fuck it up. You can let light bounce around, or watch it get panned off. You can be really simple at times. Just because you've made a plan doesn't mean you are slave to it. I have been with Harris where he turned off a bunch of lights and just brought in a bulb! You are there to tell the story. If it's one bulb and that works, then you should go with that. I feel kind of guilty actually, when I was Harris's gaffer I would hassle him about ordering lights, and then not using them. It was interesting seeing him transition to digital. He was a such a film lab expert. My career started around the inception of digital, but he was truly experimental in the photochemical world. He had an oven, he baked his film, he did special flashing. Sometimes you do the tests he would do and just get lost in the process. He had a way of knowing the right recipe for everything.

RS: Speaking of your entry at the start of digital cinema, you worked with a camera which has since become less popular, the Thomson Viper. It really had a brief life span. What do you feel was its contribution, as a camera, to *Benjamin Button*? What did it contribute to early digital cinema?

CM: Fincher called me early on about the film. He wanted me to come and look at the camera. I learned as much as I could about the Viper in the two hours before going in to test it. I was trying to make it fail by sticking practical lights in the shot, having a bulb next to someone, things like that.

The Viper, to its credit, held on. I was doing horrible tests to it. I did a commercial with it and I believe it was the first digital camera to shoot a Clio-winning commercial. I wasn't sure if I was going to shoot *Button*. Harris had shot *Zodiac* but wasn't available for reshoots, so I did uncredited reshoots. *Zodiac* was of course also shot on the Viper. I wasn't sure from that if I was going to do *Benjamin Button*. I think I was the last person hired on that film. Having said that, I had eight weeks' prep, which was helpful. It really was a big movie, with a 150-day schedule. Typically, David Fincher has storyboards and prep tech books which we might access, but *Button* didn't have any of that. This really left me feeling a bit raw and naked. The battle on the boat was prevised, but nothing else was. I went and shot stills, using natural light, at the main house of the film. I made a book with that and gave it to David Fincher. We used it as a bible, but I would say that David Fincher favored more the last eight hours. From the Viper I took stills, had a web page which David Fincher and I would look up, I'd sometimes do rough grading, and that, along with the book, was a key reference. I think the look of the film holds up. We were always working with ten to zero on that camera, working within that box: low light and practicals. I think given those constraints the camera held up pretty well. I think the tone, the color, the softness, really holds up well.

RS: The hotel interiors on Benjamin Button feature some very evocative lens flares. What particular effect were you going for?

CM: Truth be known, the camera didn't flare that well. There were a couple of shots where we turned on a work light and noticed how great the effect was. There was a shot with Benjamin and Oti talking, and this bulb was off to the side. That worked really well. I think the production design really helped, having great tones on the wall. Having a simple bulb, not needing a thousand cutters and nets, really ended up working well. I believe flares were added in post to the scenes in which Daisy dances in silhouette for Benjamin.

RS: What lenses were on the rig which you shot?

CM: We shot with DigiPrimes.[1] They didn't flare well. All of the flares which were noticeable would have been added in post.

RS: The lovers' montage in the film featured some impressive day-for-night.

CM: It was day-for-night, the scene of them on the beach. We actually shot that sequence on film. We went to a really beautiful beach. At the time, we needed huge hard drives to record all of our footage. We wanted to be simple, so we shot with film instead. There is also film in the red dress scene, where we shot slow motion. There was no slow motion on the Viper. I believe we shot forty-eight or sixty frames per second. I think the limit on the Viper was thirty or thirty-two.

RS: All of these details are fascinating. Your knowledge of what can be added to a captured digital image is impressive. Some of your peers have noted that you excel in post. Do you feel this is a misperception, or accurate?

CM: I do understand that perception. I shoot with an awareness for post. If, for instance, I were to shoot with flares, then knowing that they would need to be erased in post for a plate, I'd take that into account. I wouldn't do it. I have a good understanding of what they, in post, need to do. If you don't understand their process, if you're not in sync, the end result will look terrible. *Pi* was successful because we coordinated with one another so well. I'd specify the time of day a particular shot was evoking, pass that on to post, and then stick with it. We all had references of what the scene was going to look like. I lit it like that. The magical night had tons of warmth in the light, then offset by cool skies. That helped for the cinematography to integrate well with the VFX. I don't think it would have been possible to integrate without an awareness of what the extension is going to be. They work off our light, they do an HDR, and mimic that in their library. They will of course expand it out in space, but it comes from that direction.

RS: I feel if previs is not on the correct level with the DP, this can lead to many issues. I think previs, camera department, and postproduction must all be working in accord.

CM: I always aim to have a dialogue about what is the rough style. I will say, for instance, "medium shots at 27mm, close-up between 50mm and 75mm, maybe 40mm, but depending on what the background is." It could be better to go wider or closer, or hold a two-shot. Sometimes the previs can be wacky. Once I saw a wide shot with a 150mm lens! (Laughs) It felt weird, false. I feel for some productions if you give good guidelines to a lead person in post, then it will work out. The people on *Pi* really understood. On *Oblivion* I got better at making the rules, better at communicating my intentions.

RS: It's interesting you bring up *Oblivion*. It seemed as though your feeling for the camera, for what could be done in post, had evolved. How do you feel the camera you went with on *Oblivion* complemented the textures of the landscapes of Iceland, where you shot?

CM: Joe [Kosinski], the director, wanted a 4K release on that film. On the Sony F65 there is such small, minute texture. If there is a blackish stretch of terrain you can see all the tiny shades actually within it. A softer camera would not have captured that. There is a lot of beauty in the subtlety of Iceland. The shades are very subtle. The F65 is very well suited to the subtleties of texture. The blacks and grays of that film, the "end of world" stuff, is what we were going for on that film, and Iceland was a perfect location. Joe and I both wanted the range in those low, sensitive areas.

RS: Not being released in 4K, instead in 2K, do you feel that subtlety was lost?

CM: It might have been lost a bit. It got crunched down. Oblivion is one of the film sets I'm most proud of. There were people, higher up, discussing the shift from projection to bluescreen, back to projectors, feeling it was an expensive process. We had twenty-two projectors which had to seam across all of these borders on the set.

RS: Do you think having a projected environment, which is what you got with the projectors, helped Tom Cruise and Olga Kurylenko play their scenes?

CM: I think so, I think it seemed totally real to them. The images were moving. It seemed quite immersive. I have to admit there wasn't the luminance you would come to expect from being outside. Even though we were at T2.[2] I had to map it down to the budget. We couldn't have shot film, or anamorphic, just because I needed to be operating at 1/3 (T1.3) and still hoping for more, I wanted to blow it out more. In terms of the choices we made with the set, we were able to keep all of the glass in, we were able to use shiny chrome, all the materials you could ever want. We did things beyond what I thought would work. Using projectors enabled us to make choices based on what would translate, whether a reflection might look like a real location reflecting off glass. If it had been with bluescreen, well you can always use your imagination, but it certainly helped me in my work on that film. We didn't need anything to light the screen themselves, there was more than enough light coming off them. Maybe I used a little bounce light, but that was it. It ended up saving a ton of money. It felt like a true victory. There were contingencies of course, so we set up some bluescreen, but the set just disappeared. It was like it wasn't even there. It would have looked terrible and cost a lot in VFX to fix.

RS: How much of your lighting in the water tank on *Pi* was based on mood, compared with lighting for the reality of time of day, and so forth?

CM: Ang Lee, my director, really wanted the boat to travel from east to west. So, that was a little bit influencing me in terms of the direction of the "sun" and also what would be the position of the sun for that time of year. Ang would say things like, "I feel it's 10 o'clock." Then I would translate that into my own feeling. A lot of times I'd look at real light in noon, just where you are really protected. So I sometimes made it as hideous at noon would be, a light blasting down from straight above.

RS: And that really works!

CM: When the characters are uncomfortable, you need light like that. Also, I do believe there is pacing of beauty in a movie. I think if you are looking at beauty all of the time, it just becomes mundane. So it makes sense to set up a contrast between shots of beauty, and those which take on a more bleached look. We were very conscious about those rules in terms of the sun.

RS: Did you have a script supervisor, indicating the day, or likely time of day, of action?

CM: No. I kind of had a system. We had blackgrids, or full grids. I could open to the real sun. We couldn't do it for long. Shooting a full scene would take six hours, so that would interfere with continuity. Also, we could open up a portion of the studio to true west. We opened the doors up, and there was a real sunset. So we used a few shots, here and there, of a real sunset hitting the tank. It was nice to have a tank which was that flexible. It was great to put a black down one end, then a white, then another black, and give the impression of a storm coming, or a little cloud break. Playing with the way of opening up the black and grids was great. The scene where Pi is yelling at the zebra, the sun is mainly past set. But it wasn't hard light. So I black off everything in front of me. The far grid I kept a bit open. It was still natural light, but it felt like it had come from that sunset. You're trying to think about what it would normally be, and then figure out how to make it last long enough to do the scene. It always feels better when you work with the sun and bend it, rather than force it.

RS: Were the lights on the barge for the festival scenes early in *Pi* tested or did you respond in the moment?

CM: I tested them. They were wick candles. We had about 2,000 people lighting them. That worked amazing! It was an amazing day! There was so much beauty outside that was captured in the camera too, which was amazing.

RS: Was there a particular effect you were aiming for?

CM: Sometimes I wasn't as brave as I should be, kind of reverse engineering my lights, knowing the DI was coming. It was a huge set. You're lighting as the sun is coming down, and as you get into the scene, things get a bit more obvious. So I knew I'd have to go back and fix it in the DI. I was trying mainly for candles. In a scene like that, the barge on the water lit with candles, where is the light truly coming from? I had to be responsible, to make sure the actors were showing up, so I also had available a few chicken coop lights. I spent a lot of time really using the candles, using bars of candles. They might be off-camera, but we succeeded in lighting the actors with just the candles. It was still a 3D rig, and an extra two-thirds more.

RS: Of course, I forgot you captured in 3D!

CM: We did, and for a good reason. There was no real way that we could have postconverted so much of the footage based in the tank, with the water. It made more sense to capture in 3D, and not postconvert. I mean how would a computer know how to divide water into layers in the postconversion phase? I can see it working with people, or objects, but not water.

RS: Don't you think, given the incidence of digitally rendered water in a film such as *The Perfect Storm*, that they would have an algorithm for water which they could use to reverse engineer the postconversion?

CM: They probably would have just completely replaced all of the water. It would be easier at that point, and that is exactly what I was hoping to avoid.

RS: I would also say that the postconversion of human faces results in the faces always feeling very flat, and two-dimensional, to me, in comparison with other elements in the postconversion. They can look like pop-up books. Did you discuss much how you hoped for your plates and footage to blend with the VFX work supervised by Bill Westenhofer?

CM: Bill would send me notes about skies, what worked well with what. Without a team effort, it wouldn't have worked. We had a good long period of prep.

RS: What were the challenges with achieving focus in the tank, given that you were working with a 3D rig?

CM: The water on the lenses was a nightmare. Ang wanted to start and then shoot in sequence. That meant starting in the tank with the hardest sequence, which was the ship sinking. We had cable cam, the 3D rig flying around on cables above the tank. We had an air knife system with two tanks which were fifteen feet tall and eight feet wide, the compressors were purpose-built, which ran 200 pounds at high volume. There were five fire hoses aimed at the camera, with these massive air blades. They would physically lift the camera off the ground, just because the pressure was so intense. Spinning rain deflectors could not be put on the camera. A little water, in 2D, is fine. It might even feel good. On 3D having water on the lens is like being struck in the face. On the first day, we didn't get a single shot we could use. In terms of focus, with digital, the benefit is you can check both "eyes" to see if they are in focus. There was talk about shooting on film for *Pi*, but I think there would have been a lot more reshooting. For me, it was difficult because it was Ang's first digital, and first 3D, film. The lenses were tough, though. Luckily, we could do playback, due to it being HD, and check whether we had things in focus or not. For operating with 3D there can be a delay, so that was a challenge. You also need to try to work to minimize strobing, because in 3D it is much worse than it might be in 2D. In 2D if someone is walking, if they are strobing, you can instinctively operate for it, to compensate. In 3D, with waves, that is just impossible. Sure, you are keeping things in frame, but it is just crossing the screen all over the place. Plus, the strobing gets exaggerated. We calmed some of that by going to 270. That made the strobing less of a big hit. This helped create more intraframe motion blur and resulted in less strobing. Some projectors, I think, do left-right, left-right, but it feels like a 270 is equal to a 180.[3] There's overlap, but then there is also the on-off between the two eyes. I didn't mind the 270 in 3D digital as much as I do in film. I would guess I shot quite a bit of 270.

RS: Were you trying to get more exposure?

CM: I was trying to less get exposure than to make the 3D feel less harsh, softer. I experimented with that because Ang saw a film in 3D which was terrible. It was more of a hip-hop style of filmmaking, with 45- and 90-degree shutters. Ang really panicked. There was no real attempt at 3D at all. They shot in Real 3D, the overs did not match, the stereographer did not keep a 3D pace note. The same over would have a massive difference for the two eyes, one shallow, the other extremely deep. Sometimes it was all set to eleven, with a tight shutter angle, and people were just strobing across screen. It was the worst thing I've ever seen. I said, let's experiment the opposite direction, and open things up. We discovered that the ocean stuff worked well with 270.

RS: How did you go about achieving the phosphorescence on *Life of Pi*?

CM: I did some tests. The tests were amazing, but a little bit toxic. *Laughs*) I had two lines running to a person's hand. I then injected a mixture of chemicals, one for each hand, and as it mixed in the water as the person was placing their hands in the water. It produced this incredible glow. It was so cool! It worked in a smaller tank, perfect phosphorescence, perfect illumination. But it became to be a bigger deal because we would have needed a greater volume for the bigger tank. So we ended up just going with standard underwater lights. We flickered them, and ran them in series.

RS: And yet even after *Pi*, you have continued to embrace bigger and bigger challenges! The continuous camera move upon Casey's entry to Tomorrowland, in the film of the same title, is incredible! How did you go about planning and executing such a series of camera moves?

CM: That was real difficult to plan out in my head, because I'd have to backtrack from when I would be shooting in Spain, when she lands on the final bridge, and where the sun would be two months after we had finished shooting the other parts of the sequence. We figured out we needed to be there at 11 o'clock, when it would still be relatively low, but still high enough. Part of the scene was shot on both interior and exterior stages in Vancouver. So, I knew we had to match the 11 o'clock light from Spain. There were sections in Florida which were on interior stages. It just went all over the place. We had to be very conscious when it came to the direction of light. The traveling of the train was done on an interior stage, and again, we had to be really careful with the direction of light. There was also a section of the sequence which was cut.

RS: What were the camera platforms?

CM: Well luckily it wasn't 3D. We had a bit of Steadicam. There was some crane work where the camera had to flip around and then right itself. Also, it is worth noting we had to take into account two sun positions. We had it all prevised. We worked on previs on the time of day, position of the sun, direction the sun would be shining on the set, on the action. We also had to determine from the previs where the cuts would be. We used the F65 on the film, and it worked out fine for the sequence. Some of the fast stuff, stuff for crash cams, we went to F55, for fast motion. They matched well. The blacks are better on the F55, the image is sharper. Brad Bird, the director, really wanted IMAX 15 perf sharp. There is nothing as sharp as that camera for that purpose. Brad wanted to mix formats between 2.34 and 4:3.[4] We did initial test with 1: 3 anamorphics,[5] turning them, rotating them ninety degrees to change the presentation format. I was hoping with the turning, we would have vertical or horizontal flares, for

Tomorrowland, or the real world. The tests were cool, but the 1:3 lenses were a little soft.

RS: What would you say were some of the major contributing visual elements to the crisp and upbeat aesthetic of *Tomorrowland*? It is a film quite unique in its look for modern films, and quite distinct from your sci-fi work on *Oblivion*.

CM: I like a lot of environmental lighting. I work with the props department to get props as bright as possible. The house in the film was soft-lit by the glowing ring. Scott Chambliss and I worked hard on that. I'm not really big on having a lamp, then putting an off-camera light above the lamp. I'd rather have the lamp work for itself. I always feel if I am on a set, and it looks as though I am lighting it, that the result will not be a good one. The gaffers are always amazed that I never use traditional lighting. When the ring goes over the people, that is providing the light. When the guns fire in the film, the props would actually emit a light. I had a bright ball at the end of the guns. I always feel it is strange when the flash of a gun comes from off-screen. The way we did a series of LEDs on the guns, which would trigger, and then the end would light up. We'd then remove the outer apparatus in post. I thought having it feel as though the light were emitted from the gun was important. Sometimes, in effects work of that kind they will just brighten up a particular part of the image. They may need to do that, but it is good to have a lever to start it. It feels more impactful if you have in-camera lighting from the right place. I would say on *Tomorrowland* they were really helpful, in terms of the VFX. They even allowed smoke and blue screen. Wow!

RS: Let's come to something which is probably important to discuss and pertains to a controversy which developed around your cinematography on *Life of Pi*. Christopher Doyle made some critical remarks on your cinematography on *Life of Pi* which went viral, around the time of its release, and your winning the Academy Award. What are your thoughts on that situation?

CM: I felt depressed, really disappointed. Some people said I should stand up for myself, but in the end I just said, "I'm sorry he feels that way." I didn't feed it. It felt like people maybe wanted us to get into a confrontation. But *Pi* could not have been shot on the ocean. There was a lot of work which went in on all sides to the end product. You can't put a tiger and a kid in a boat together in the middle of the ocean. There was negative media toward me at the time. I really respect so much of Christopher Doyle's work. There has even been an argument in the ASC as to there being separate categories for work involving a heavy amount of CGI and old-fashioned cinematography. In a way, I was thinking, if someone is in charge of creating a beautiful image, then it doesn't matter how it was created so long as you are struck by the lighting and composition of it. So in the end, that is where I stand.

~

Miranda's career, even putting aside his major achievements, is interesting. His career ascent from director of photography on his first major feature, the romantic comedy *Failure to Launch*, to an Academy Award nomination on his second film, *Benjamin Button*, to a giant effects production on his third film, *TRON: Legacy*, to an Oscar win on his fourth, *The Life of Pi*, followed by successive visual dazzlers since then, is meteoric. Yet when his pedigree is accounted for, it is hardly surprising. A point worth noting of Miranda's career is his involvement as gaffer in significant cinematographic achievements at the tail end of the photochemical era. He was able to apprentice with not only Harris Savides during a period of high productivity and invention for that cinematographer, but also David Fincher, a director truly and uniquely gifted in his insights on cinematographic techniques. Working as gaffer on 1990s productions such as *Se7en*, *The Game*, and *Fight Club*, with Savides, Darius Khondji, and Jeff Cronenweth, as well as logistically and technically dizzying Tony Scott productions such as *Crimson Tide* and *Enemy of the State*, Miranda was attracted to projects during this period of genuine visual ambition.

By his own account, Miranda pushed to collaborate with technically gifted directors, and in so doing often found himself paired with stories that required his pushing not only against the standard techniques of cinematography but also above and beyond what would seem to qualify as conventional cinematography. As such, Miranda's achievement is in his clear understanding of rigs, lighting, lenses, and camera formats and in his ability to understand how a mastery of cinematography might allow for the effective extension of those techniques into other departments, be they editing, visual effects, or indeed anything that would complement visual storytelling. In this respect, for instance, what would otherwise be considered a classic "mistake" of cinematography, a lens flare, might be mapped onto the image during his supervision of the postproduction phase. This artificially created effect produces the simulacrum of the classic "flaw" generated in the process of capturing the image, ironically a desired visual element cherished by many cinematographers. Miranda's facility with the rudiments of conventional cinematography and an understanding of the new dominance of the postproduction phase, has allowed for his being in a constant process of refining the images he produces, well beyond what he captured photographically on set or location. The balance he strikes may be sufficiently unconventional to garner attention. The span of his engagement—from a clear grasp of the requirements of visual effects, to a fascination with emerging digital cameras, to an appreciation of how visual elements or manipulations of the image are layered on to produce the final image—is comprehensive.

Notes

1. DigiPrimes are lenses manufactured by Zeiss Optics.

2. Here he refers to the lens aperture opening at a T2, later noted as T1.3.

3. Here he refers to the angle of the camera shutter in degrees. The standard film camera shutter for movies at twenty-four frames per second is 180 degrees. At 270 degrees, the exposure time is longer. In addition to admitting more light per exposure, it allows for moor intraframe motion blur. This is the case for movies shot in the United States and anywhere where the electrical grid is running at 60 Hz. In Europe the grid is at 50 Hz so, the shutter angle is usually 172.8 degrees or 144 degrees. If the shutter angle is incorrect for the electrical system, the images will flicker when lit with artificial lighting.

4. 2.34:1, or 2.35:1, 2.39:1 or 2.40:1 are the ratios of the frame size for anamorphic widescreen projection. 4:3, or 1.33: 1 is the common academy aperture ratio and also the standard definition TV frame ratio.

5. "Anamorphic" refers to a lens that has a 1.3× squeeze ratio versus the classic 2×. Used with a 1.33:1 frame, it produces a projected ratio of 1.78:1, commonly referred to as 16:9. When used with the 16:9 frame capture, such as the normal HD TV format, it produces a 2.40:1 anamorphic projected image.

Seamus McGarvey

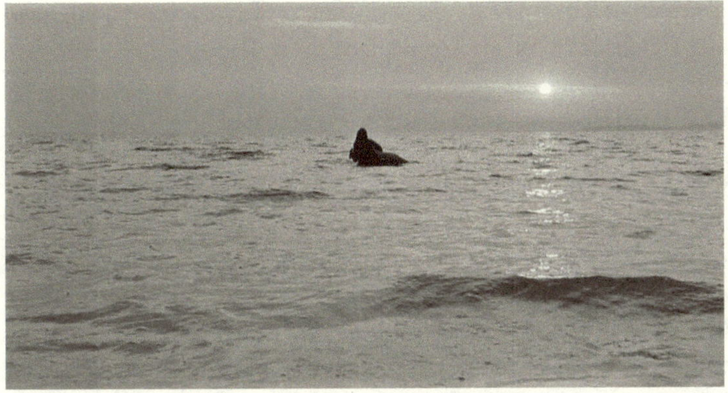

Image 24. Mi (Saskia Reeves) holds the dead body of Eu (Amanda Plummer) as the tide comes in in *Butterfly Kiss* (Winterbottom 1995).

In the 2010s, Seamus McGarvey ASC, BSC, ISC consistently shot some of the more provocative and popular films to come out of Hollywood. Following his breakthrough in 2007 with the drama *Atonement*, he went on to shoot *The Avengers* in 2012 and *Fifty Shades of Grey* in 2015. This rise to prominence was no overnight fluke. Typically, the rise to director of photography is gradual and may take a decade or more, gradually working through the various aspects of the camera department. McGarvey was a voracious learner in his youth and rose quickly to the position in his twenties. From there, he tackled one challenging project after another, working with cinematic provocateurs such as Michael Winterbottom and Lynne Ramsay, fostering strong partnerships with talented directors of spectacle like Joe Wright. In time, he graduated to straightforward studio fare, shooting logistically complicated films such as *World Trade Center* for Oliver Stone and the Matthew McConaughey film *Sahara* by the mid-2000s.

The following interview was conducted between Lindsay Coleman and Seamus McGarvey in October 2012.

Lindsay Coleman: When you first became a DP, you were so young. Was *Butterfly Kiss* your first feature?

Seamus McGarvey: Pretty much. I'd done shorts before that, but that was my first, really proper feature. I did a BBC feature film called *Look Me in the Eye*. But it was my first real film, and Michael Winterbottom's first as well.

LC: I believe you were twenty-eight then?

SM: It was 1992, so I believe I was twenty-four, or twenty-five.

LC: The final shot on the beach, where Amanda Plummer is being drowned, was that difficult to capture? It certainly looks like it, with the actors surrounded by water, and the operator too, by the looks of it.

SM: It was hugely difficult! In all seriousness, we all nearly died in shooting that shot. It was on a beach at Morecambe Bay. You can actually see the water rise in the shot, very, very quickly. It's an extremely flat beach. The water rises extremely fast. It's the place where those Chinese cockle pickers all drowned. The water rises a foot every minute. The camera was on a tripod, and I just felt the water rise and rise and rise. In the end, I just had to unclip the camera and hand-hold it as the water rose. The water had submerged the tripod, I was freezing. We barely made it to the shore! I was holding the camera above my head as the water was lapping around my mouth!

LC: Was it near dusk? It seems to be last light.

SM: It was.

LC: The film places huge emphasis on performance. It would have been one of your first experiences of that level of performance I imagine. Amanda Plummer's commitment to this psychopathic character she plays is extraordinary to see!

SM: It was. It was very intense. I'd always grown up with a focus on lighting, composition, so forth, but this was almost an experience of something like wildlife photography. Michael wanted to preserve the spontaneity. We had to almost shoot in a documentary style that was fused with something with a bit more consideration and grandeur. It was an unusual mixture. I tried to do something similar with *The War Zone*, which was really shot, effectively, on the hoof, yet still trying to preserve something more resounding, confessional.

LC: What strongly comes through is the visual influence of Winterbottom's forebears. Did you feel influenced by British director Alan Clarke with *Butterfly Kiss*?

SM: Absolutely! He's a huge influence. Definitely with *The War Zone*. Alan Clarke was our touchstone, director Tim Roth and I. Obviously, he had worked with him very closely in the past, on *Made in Britain*. I love Alan Clarke's work. There was somebody who took the realist tradition, something the UK is famous for in cinematographic terms, the documentary style. Yet Alan Clarke's work sits outside of that. He still maintained the language of cinema, mise-en-scene, composition. Clarke coalesced all of it. He's a singular filmmaker.

LC: It's interesting to note, as of course he was one of the first filmmakers to really refine the use of Steadicam for narrative effect. You of course have worked with Steadicam in a celebrated fashion in *Atonement*.

SM: Oh totally. Films like *Elephant* are phenomenal, featuring that sort of disembodied eye of the Steadicam. In some respects, it's perfect for a story on the horrors of Northern Ireland, the hovering depersonalized eye which the Steadicam can be. I'm not a huge fan of Steadicam, but he used it brilliantly to express the clinical eye.

LC: We've discussed *Butterfly Kiss*. Another major film of your early career was of course *The War Zone*. Apart from Alan Clarke, what were the visual influences for *The War Zone*?

SM: We looked at a lot of documentary photography. Roger Mayne. Nan Goldin, I suppose. Not in color terms, but more in terms of the apparent nature of the setups. We didn't want to strive for anything ornate. The visuals had to be apparently haphazard. Yet they had to communicate this profundity, either with the light, or the scenarios which were depicted. Tim worked hard to create this inner sanctum where we could all work very closely. Where emotions could breathe. We had a crew that was very lithe technically, that could work fast enough to capture these unfolding moments. To that end our crew was very small. Once the setup was lit, and lit in a very broad way, Tim would sequester himself and it would begin. There was no hullabaloo on the set. It was a very, very silent set.

LC: There is a tableau look to some of the shots.

SM: We shot 35mm with anamorphic, on these great old lenses which had actually been used by Chris Menges on *The Mission*. They had lain in a dusty box in Panavision for years. Because we had such a low budget, Panavision said, "You can't use the Primo Anamorphics, but you can use these little lenses." We shot the entire movie with them. Necessarily, for those landscapes the anamorphic and 2.40 ratio was really well suited, using the foreground for composition. I think the choice of those lenses were twofold. For the interiors, the domestic landscape, we could push the characters to the edge of the frame. I think it allowed the use of negative space to become really expressive.

LC: I am reminded of a shot, even after seeing it around fifteen years ago, in which on the one side of the frame you see Ray Winstone and Tilda Swinton having sex in one room, and on the other side is another room with Lara Belmont hearing this happening.

SM: Yes, it just shows what you can achieve with the format.

LC: Moving forward in your career to the films which really cemented your reputation, *Atonement*, it is striking in how much it features some quite unusual shots, unusual images.

SM: There is a shot of the back of James McAvoy's head near the film's beginning, I like to call in my Magritte shot. I pulled focus on the back of his head and it sort of slides into frame, like a realization. I love looking at the back of people's heads. You feel like your entering their brains. Before the shot you feel at a dispassionate remove from them, then suddenly you are the person. It's a subjectification of the image.

LC: David Fincher does that a lot.

SM: Yeah, it's a wonderful technique. You think you're kind of safe in your cinema, then you're suddenly just flung into someone else's head.

LC: How do you transition from *Anna Karenina* to *Atonement* to *The Avengers*? So many varied styles in all of them, each with their own totally unique set of images.

SM: It's just a bit of a workout really. I'm learning as a cinematographer. I think after *We Need to Talk About Kevin*—which was extremely low budget . . . The internet said it was $6 million while it was more like $1.2 million. It was shot in twenty-four days. By the time I'd finished *We Need to Talk About Kevin* I had just gone through a divorce, and having to take off time surrounding that, I was really broke. So I called my agent about some work. I've never used my agent up until this point. Every other job I've had came via other means. But anyway, I realized I was totally skint and paying alimony. *The Avengers* came up as an offer, and I was terrified, because of the large visual effects nature of the film, visual effects that I didn't know about. Effects had expanded, and improved, over the last few years, and it was a really high-end movie in that kind of way. I found it one of the most rewarding films I've ever worked on. I learned so much, for a start. I learned, and I earned. Because we shot 103 days, and there was four months prep, it really felt like a workout where I got into a sustained rhythm. We were shooting in a desert. There were no distractions. It was almost like a monastic cinema experience. You'd go into the studio and have big, big, expensive shots to do, and its really very humbling. Going with the monastic metaphor, you're in this huge studio like a cathedral, all of these big, big actors. There's a sort of silence there, too. Also, this huge responsibility means that you are properly scared. It reminded me of growing up in Northern Ireland, and being at church and that kind of fear built in there. There was no socialization, we weren't going out at night. It represented this return to a rhythm in my life that I hadn't had in a very long, long time.

LC: What were some of the bigger challenges on *The Avengers*? I mean, where to begin?

SM: Joss Whedon, the director, came to me and said, "I'm building all of these major sets and I want to be able to shoot 360 degrees on them." I knew that this would be a major challenge, and it meant that I had to work very quickly with the production designer, James Chinlund. The only way to light a space the size of the bridge set of the flying boat . . . is to make sure that it has a clear logic in terms of the placement of its practical light sources. We built effective light sources, not just architectural accents, though we did do that as well. Light that would light the actors, lights that would produce ambience in both day and night scenarios. LEDs were used on the consoles, they became the architectural accents. The set was like a charcoal gray. It was a slightly reflective paint surface. But it was incredibly difficult to light. I knew I needed hot spots to define the lines, I think because I didn't want to bang a load of light at it. So I asked James to introduce a little bit of reflectivity into the paint so I could use lower reflective surfaces that I could just drop out of the ceiling and bounce light into, so that if somebody was in silhouette against a bounce light the gray would be a slightly shinier gray. Throughout the various layers of the set I had various MR16s which were harder sources, so it was a real mixture of overall ambience and then these pings of hard light coming through. Of course, when the characters came in I found I could use a Chinese lantern on bean poles, moving it around and then out of shot, and then bring it in for the key light. That become my key light for close-ups.

LC: Did you do much to create directional light coming in from the windows of the ship? It would seem to be necessary to sell the fact that the flying boat is passing above the clouds.

SM: The set was huge, so big it was virtually touching the walls and the blue screens. We were a little closer than I would have liked, so I didn't want to pump light at the blue screen itself. For the daytime scenarios, I needed fast ambience up top. So actually, the spill from my space lights just above the set that was creating light bounced off clouds and the light from underneath, that was lighting with the blue screen naturally.[1] It may not have been as precisely even as I would have liked, but it served its purpose.

LC: I guess it is also the sort of film where you don't expect to have the sense of natural light pouring through the windows.

SM: Yes, true. There were daytime scenarios where characters were looking out the windows. In those situations, I had big softboxes outside of the window pumping light through the window.[2] They replaced the glass digitally so we didn't have to worry about reflections. Like I said, it was a huge learning experience for me!

~

Seamus McGarvey's career, particularly in the 2010s, is a testament to the particular blend of talents that cinematographers must bring to their work. On one hand, they must be highly conversant in the history of cinema, in the database of images that has helped evolve the grammar of visual storytelling. McGarvey is part practitioner, part scholar, in the sense that he is aware of how particular techniques, such as the use of a Steadicam or pieces of equipment, such as the lenses from *The Mission*, assist in conveying cinematic sensations that echo down through the history of visual storytelling. The particular ineffable quality of a given image, in short, is the place McGarvey will work toward, using his own poetic sensibility, a firm historical understanding of cinematography's evolution, and a practical appreciation for the methods needed to capture images of these particular qualities.

Simultaneous to this is the practical application of state-of-the-art technology to the basic requirements of visual storytelling. The flying battleship of 2012's *The Avengers* is a set. Via careful lighting, and integrating subtle—and sometimes not-so-subtle—visual effects, the audience must believe that such a piece of technology might exist, cruising high up in the clouds, and be functional. To sell this story point, to ensure this scenario is a fiction that audiences are willing to engage with, McGarvey must use lighting to evoke that this is a working piece of ultra-sophisticated military equipment. He must allow the audience to subliminally grasp that this giant ship is passing beneath and through clouds, that sunlight is shining through the windows, and that it is constantly moving through the atmosphere. This work speaks powerfully to the ongoing importance in the work of cinematographers to engage with their aesthetic interests and fascinations and with the very pressing concerns of selling a narrative's setup, tone, and individual story points that will allow the fiction to, literally, fly.

Notes

1. Space lights are specialty fixtures used for broad overhead lighting of large spaces. They are usually hung from the ceiling of the stage or set and covered with silk curtains.

2. A softbox is a usually large lighting structure made to hang from a ceiling of the stage that has any of many types of luminaires to create a very large and soft top source light. They can be skirted or teased to keep the light off of walls or from spreading horizontally across the set.

John de Borman

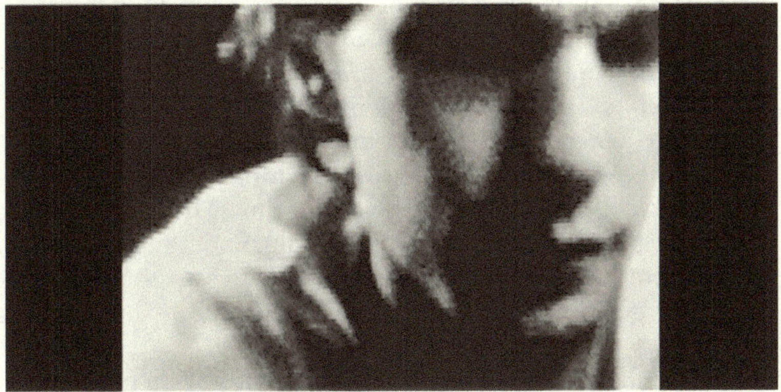

Image 25. CCTV footage of Hamlet (Ethan Hawke) in *Hamlet* (Almereyda 2000).

Working mostly in the British film industry, John de Borman BSC has been responsible for some real gems: *Hideous Kinky*, *The Full Monty*, and *An Education*. He has also worked in typically independent American fare, on films such as Ethan Hawke's iteration of *Hamlet* in 2001 and the strange *Passion of Darkly Noon* in 1995. Though often not specifically singled out for his cinematography, de Borman is a model of consistency and taste and has strong instincts for powerful stories and scripts, along with a knack for capturing memorable performances using an often sophisticated visual strategy.

The following interview was conducted between Lindsay Coleman and John de Borman in May 2013.

Lindsay Coleman: I was speaking with a cinematographer recently who shot a major Australian comedy. He was saying that no matter how good you get the lighting, you are always stuck with a two-shot, because that is where the comedy lies, in the interaction. Looking at *The Full Monty*, is that something you agree with?

John de Borman: Well *The Full Monty* is really more of a five-shot. I think that when it comes to filmmaking, there really are no rules. There are different types of comedies, different ways of making things feel and look funny. Obviously close-ups don't make things more funny, often they make things less funny. The physicality, the physical acting which you get in a wider shot is a big part of where the comedy is found. If you do close-ups, you don't see people's bodies. Often that is true. Certainly, on *The Full Monty* it was five-shots, and then reverses, and then all sorts of other things. We shot an incredible amount of angles on that film. You'd start the day with a rehearsal and the scene was hilarious. By the end of the day we'd done the scene so many times, from so many different angles, it really wasn't funny anymore. But that was the director and his style. I think it is better to stay wider, and only go in when it is the right moment.

LC: The film is social realism of a kind, but it wasn't perhaps ideal to go too much in that direction with your lighting. How did you strike the right balance?

JDB: It was an incredibly low-budget film. We had very little money. We had just enough money for tracks, and a dolly, and were shooting six-day weeks. The producer and the director both said that they didn't want the photography to take you out of the story. They wanted it to feel real. It wasn't, as you say, a documentary. I wanted to push it a little, more to the type of look found in *Kes*. That would have been a more beautiful approach to it than what we had in the end. The producer and director wanted it to be about the characters, and the characters only. I think there was a bit of a compromise between the two approaches in the final result. It looks nice and composed, and not too gritty. England often has a reputation of making documentary-type films which are gray, and horrible, and depressing. We didn't want that. Basically, it's a social statement of depression, but we didn't want to make it look depressing. You had a combination of talking about something which was depressing, yet also was very funny. It was universally depressing for people all over the world, but we made it human and funny. I think that is what comedy is, it's humanity. If you can filmically get the humanity of a situation, then that gets under people's skin, and they can relate to it, and that's probably what makes comedy work.

LC: Looking at *An Education* and *The Full Monty*, there are many scenes of social realism that build up to scenes of outright glamour. What do you feel is successful about such an approach?

JDB: I remember what people were like in the 1950s just before *An Education* is set, even though I was very young then. I remember the weather, there was a lot of fog then, how flat things were, the people. I remember there was a lack of cynicism in those days. There was a postwar acceptance of things as they were. There was very little cynicism. It is the sort thing you have to convey in the period. You convey the period in the feeling of that time photographically. That is what we tried. We all got very close together, the costume designer, the production designer, to help the director Lone [Scherfig] visually, on *An Education.* We needed to get the sense of the young girl's perspective on this glamour.

LC: You talked about using older lenses to give it a period look.

JDB: There are these lenses called Cooke S2. You'd light the set as you would light it anywhere. Then you put these lenses on and suddenly, automatically, it gave you a 1950s look! The field, the dropoff, it gave the image a certain softness which was very much a 1950s look. I am a believer that just because things are sharper it doesn't make them more beautiful! In fact images, more often than not, get ugly when they are sharper. I am not a fan of this whole HD thing!

LC: So you are not a fan of the Arri Alexa? This is surely one of the finer digital cameras.

JDB: I am a fan of the Alexa. But I'm not a fan of super sharpness. I like portraitures. And with portraitures you'll find that more and more it is getting harder to do that on HD. You look at *The Hobbit* with forty-eight frames a second and you see the makeup, you see all the stuff on their skin. It's hideous! I love the portraits of the '40s and '50s where there is a falloff of focus. There is a certain softness in the image, and that makes the image poetic. That's what I am interested in, I am interested in what makes the images poetic. I cannot stand images that do not have a painterly feel.

LC: I spoke with John Mathieson and he was relatively unique in discussing how he evoked paintings in his cinematography. Would you say that you are also influenced by painting?

JDB: Yes. I mean I came from art school. I didn't really go to film school. I was a sculptor. I always go to exhibitions . . . [Edward] Hopper, Francis Bacon, Lucian Freud. I'm constantly looking at paintings and stills photography. I'm having to write an article for the BSC magazine asking about my influences . . . well it's hard to say, but definitely paintings are an influence because that is the tradition I originated from. Images are about more than image. They are about the three-dimensionality of the image, the emotional pull of the image. I don't think cinematography should be a straightforward representation of what is in front of you. There should the representation of an implied other. There should be something behind the camera or off-screen which influences how you go about capturing and producing that image. I think that is what painting is. It is about the feeling behind the image. It means something more than the image itself.

LC: Interestingly, you can sometimes be quite low-fi, less painterly. Going to *Hamlet*, you mix CCTV footage in with film; how do you feel about striking the correct balance between those formats?

JDB: Well, going back to it, I have to say that I loved it. Those children's cameras that the director had, they only shot black and white, and it had a quality of being quite contrasty, rather beautiful. In the same way as John Mathieson with his Bacon film, it had the same quality of looking through glass and playing around with the images and things like that. That was shot on Super 16, in five weeks, a lot of it was handheld. The director had worked with David Lynch, again very much an artist . . . a really, really tough shoot. We had two lights we could afford to rent. The rest was just lighting with light bulbs, and fluorescent lamps, and finding practicals. In a way, the confines of making that film created a look which was rather challenging. It went up for a cinematography award, so really it worked.

LC: How aware were you of trying to distance yourself from Alex Thompson's work on the Kenneth Branagh version of *Hamlet*, shot in 70mm, and released about five years before your *Hamlet*?

JDB: Oh, completely. For one thing, this version was a modern version, unlike the Branagh version. Second, a lot of the play was cut out. We're in the middle of New York, so I wanted to have a lot of shots of the characters looking up into these huge skyscrapers. We got to use reflection and glass, and we had views of New York in all of the rooms we shot in. So it was very New York–based, quite original. Branagh's was very much period, he was anamorphic; we shot super 16. We wanted the grain. We wanted to feel more active or real.

LC: How much did Shakespeare's language inspire your approach? Surely it was quite inspirational.

JDB: Very little. I'm sort of dyslexic. I find it hard to understand Shakespeare very well. I do get it, but it doesn't visually inspire me. But this version was truncated in that it was coming from a very different place. It wasn't really his play as he wrote it. The director changed it. For the better, I believe. I think that's probably one of my best films yet, probably, the lowest budget of them all.

LC: Do you feel it is the best technically, or the best reflection of your own philosophy on cinematography?

JDB: I don't think it necessarily reflects my philosophy on cinematography, but I think it had the most challenge of all the films I've done in terms of how much we had to do in so short a time. I felt very much on my own. The director hadn't made a film like this before. It was massively challenging. We had an amazing cast. They were all slightly worried that they couldn't do the Shakespeare, yet they were extraordinarily good, as good as any British cast. It was a challenge to them, a challenge to me. And I suppose, any time you make something which is interesting it makes for a good memory.

LC: You've talked about the importance of composition—in the film, there is quite limited coverage.

JDB: More often than not, that is what I like. Of course, it depends on the film. Maybe people who make comedies don't like to approach comedy in that way, but once again I don't think there is a rule for that. I do a huge amount of work with the designer and the director to come up with a distinctive look for each of the films I do. I take real pride in creating a different look for each of the films I do and never repeating myself if I can help it. I try very much to do that. You start off on a master, and then let it happen, and then cut where you need to cut. The important thing for me is that the close-up is very special, very precious. Some films are all close-ups. If you use it too much, then it doesn't have any impact, any relevance. If you use a close-up rarely, it has more relevance. We had used that in *An Education* where we would push into close-ups for really important moments, and then stayed back when you wanted to see the sets, and the people within those sets and their physicality. It creates a style. If you stay back, you create a style. I'm afraid that American films often shoot everything. Wide reverse, close-ups, midshots, wide, and so on, and then you work it out in the editing suite.

LC: Cara Seymour, as the mother, gives an amazing performance in *An Education*, and it is all in midshot and long shot.

JDB: Yes, that gives it a style. That film, which may be my favorite, is great at getting the period stylistically. The editor who I worked with, I've worked with four times in a row now, he was terrific. A cinematographer's greatest ally is the editor. Anyway, he really used the footage so well. I used two cameras at ninety degrees, never side by side, that way you get different angles on exactly the same performance so that you can do action cuts which are really specific. And he stays back for the most part, except for a tiny little bit. That is so rare. That really helped create the style. You know you have to work out who the editor is on your film because if you give them too much material they'll use everything and ruin the style. I know it's not really my deal, it's the director's, but I am conscious of it.

LC: Do you feel an audience is aware when cutting is happening on the same performance, on the same take?

JDB: I think they probably don't know the difference. Editors, cinematographers, directors, yourself, would know how to pick an action cut.

LC: Does it make a difference for performance or just continuity?

JDB: Performance as well. Some actors need to build themselves up to a certain point so that once they get there you want as much coverage as possible because you know they can't repeat it. Or you have inexperienced actors who don't get it every time, so you want as much coverage as you can get. It frees the actor much more to know two cameras are on them.

LC: There are moments in the film where Carey Mulligan almost breaks the fourth wall and stares directly into the lens. Was that a deliberate approach?

JDB: Yes, yes. She's looking at the audience. She's looking at herself, in a way, and she's also looking at us. I have a tendency to like that when it's an intimate moment, or a very emotional moment, I like the eyeline to be very close. I don't like to see people looking off because then I feel you become disconnected from the character. As close as they can look that makes you in the audience feel more connected to them as a character. You're looking into their eyes. I like to put a little ping in the eyes. That's the connection you get. It comes from looking into people's eyes.

LC: One thing they say about the camera is that it is like a microscope. It sees, to some level, who the person is who is performing.

JDB: I think if it's used properly, that's what it should be doing. It is probably more the actor than the character. You position the camera favorably to the actor, and to the performance.

LC: Some of Carey Mulligan's performances have come under fire since *An Education*. What do you feel you succeeded in capturing of her performance in that film?

JDB: I think I helped create an intimate setting, along with the other filmmakers. That is maybe not something in bigger-budget American films, which can be more cold. There was certainly that. This was a small film. We were all together. This was her first leading part. I was operating myself, and was very close to her. I would sometimes ask her to do things again. At the start, she was nervy and quite giggly, and I tried to get her to concentrate a bit more. She told me that she hated me at the beginning because I kept telling her she needed to calm down, control herself. I would say little things like that. In a way, she needed to slightly control herself. At the end of the film, she told me that by the end she realized I was trying to help her find a way to communicate with the camera, and to find a way of seeing the camera so that there was a communication between her, and the camera, and [me]. She needs to be slightly aware of where we are, thinking of what is the camera's point of view, not the actor's point of view. Some people might slightly disagree with that, but you have to have a slight relationship with the camera. You should be able to turn the sound down on any film and still get the basic idea of what the film's about. If we've done our jobs properly, you should be able to understand what is happening without any sound at all. In the emotional moments, you should know what is the emotional state of that person. That is what we do as cinematographers, as imagemakers.

~

De Borman's discussion gravitates toward the way a film's visual style may evolve from certain simple rules being set with respect to the use of the camera and lenses. Appropriate lenses, he notes, can ensure an optimal dropoff, which in turn signals (even if subliminally) that *An Education* is a period film with a period-appropriate look. Camera placement and key decisions in terms of the kind of coverage options to provide the editors naturally allow for a given style to develop.

The ramifications of these extend well beyond the decisions de Borman describes for a camera department. For one, actors calibrate their performances based on how they are framed and how much they might move around the frame. A performance such as that of Cara Seymour in *An Education* is all the more notable in that it occurs near the edge of the frame, due to the choice to opt for midshots and masters for the family scenes. In this respect, true to her presence in the family as a diffident mother, a quieter presence when compared with Alfred Molina's more gregarious father, Seymour's performance does not naturally dominate the frame. However, a fully rounded portrait of this character emerges from Seymour's series of gestures, postures, and interactions in the frame that will pass on to the audience most everything they need to know about the character. This necessarily affects the film editing. To allow shots to match well and hone in on nuggets of performance, the described footage from the film will necessitate a particular rhythm of cutting, as well as a necessitated remove in terms of the final style. In this respect, a careful set of choices for framing and camera placement with respect to the actors can result in a style entirely appropriate to the story being told.

Affonso Beato

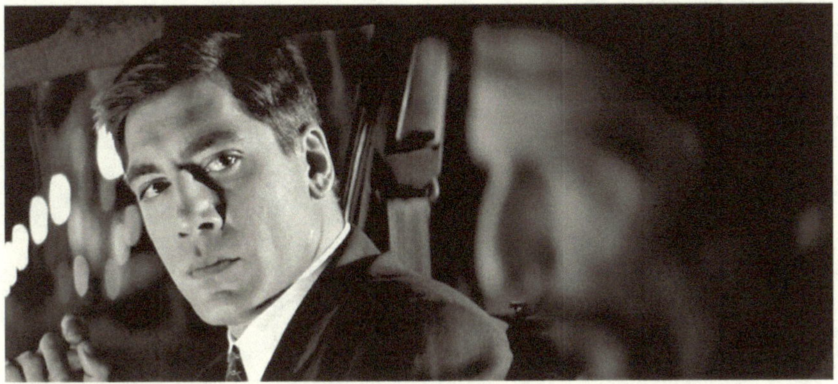

Image 26. David (Javier Bardem) has a guilty secret in *Live Flesh* (Almodóvar 1997).

Affonso Beato ASC, ABC has enjoyed a successful international career as a cinematographer since the mid-1960s, working on celebrated films such as *All About My Mother*, *The Queen*, and quirky indie films such as *Ghost World*. He is notable for his long-running collaborations with the likes of Jim McBride and Pedro Almodóvar. A particular skill Beato brings to his work is an ability to simultaneously shoot naturalistic stories, based in relatable, specific scenarios, while his camerawork and lighting slide toward expressionism. He can expertly carve up the screen space of *All About My Mother* with his compositions, creating a film world where the spatial orientations of characters toward the edges of the frame tell their own tale of loneliness, grief, and hope, layered on top of the overt melodrama of the picture. Equally, in *The Queen*, a similar tale of family grief, a massive helicopter shot of the British royal family can powerfully expand the intimate scope of a domestic drama to remind the viewer of the import of Princess Diana's death to the world.

The following interview was conducted between Lindsay Coleman and Affonso Beato in November 2012.

Lindsay Coleman: When did you experience your own awakening to cinema?

Affonso Beato: Very young. Me and my siblings were raised Catholic. My father would take me to mass on Sundays. We would take a trolley to downtown. We had theaters back when there was no television. There would be newsreels, features, nonstop. I think my father really tried to pair up in my religion and film, religion and film. It was kind of a gift he gave to me every Sunday. There are different kinds of intelligence. I think I have a visual, spatial intelligence. And I connected immediately with that. My mother wanted me to be a navy officer. My father wanted me to join his industry. I did that sort of thing for a while to please them, but then I said, "To hell with this," and got into the fine arts. And then I stayed there.

LC: Let's look at your second major collaboration with Almodóvar, the film *Live Flesh*. When Javier Bardem first appears in *Live Flesh*, you shine a very specific light, what appears to be a kind of yellow light, on him as he rides in the car with his cop partner. What led to such a specific kind of lighting?

AB: I think it's a nice question. Almodóvar is very intelligent. The yellowish, or yellowish-orangish light, which comes from vapor mercury, comes from another concept. It comes from a desire to realistically depict the street lighting of the different periods the film takes place. When Penélope Cruz gives birth to the film's hero, we needed to separate the night scenes of that period from the period which we then transition to when the character has become a young man. It became about public lighting. In the early scenes, I used particular filters on the public buildings they pass in the bus in which he is born. Later on, we pass the same buildings in the next section of the film where the cop played by Javier Bardem is shot and rendered a paraplegic. Now the lighting has more of that yellowish tinge found in modern Madrid. Everybody that is in the street or in the windows gets this kind of lighting. So I wasn't trying to reveal anything particular about the character. On *Live Flesh*, we didn't have a DI. I didn't have the freedom or the possibilities which the DI gives. Everything was created by the filters I used and electing for the particular color of given sources. Even though we didn't adjust the light for given characters, in the color correction phase we did make adjustments dependent on the situation of the scene.

LC: The scene following, when Francesca Neri is introduced as a wild young woman, the color is very saturated in that scene.

AB: Correct.

LC: Did you discuss with Almodóvar the color palette for each scene?

AB: Absolutely! In the '60s there was a Brazilian director whose name was Glauber Rocha, who was like a Pasolini of the Brazilian cinema. I shot a movie for Glauber called *Antonio das Mortes*. This movie got a critics award at Cannes in '68. The photography of this movie was considered revolutionary. A modern equivalent would be *Amores Perros*. All of the directors who came to me afterward, this is the film that drew them to me. All of the English directors I have worked with love Almodóvar, or love this particular film. Mike Newell, who I shot *Love in the Time of Cholera* for, also loved the earlier film. In '68 I dared to push the original negative two stops. I knew I would have an incredible color saturation. It was so unusual that we needed to change the printer's light to print the movie! The normal printer's head could not deal with such a dense negative. Because we shot in the north of Brazil, we had beautiful cinematographic colors, but very clouded days. I said, "No, this is not good enough." We need to push the negative. So yes, to answer your question, we discussed the color palette a lot! Almodóvar believes a lot in preproduction. That is what cinematography design is about, to plan and plan and plan.

LC: Almodóvar is famous for his love of the color red. Did he discuss with you much about what the color of red means to him?

AB: Yes. Basically, the Iberian Peninsula. Spain has brilliant cinematographers. He had worked with them before. I worked with him after *Kika*. Why did it happen? According to him *Kika* was a problem in terms of writing and presenting . . . It was a crisis in his career. Within his universe he went to an absurd place in terms of how he designed his characters. In terms of lighting it also represented a kind of "artificialism." The critics and the public rebuked him. He wanted to change, because of this crisis. Almodóvar felt, at that time, that Spanish cinematographers were influenced by cinematography to their north, by French cinematography, by English cinematography. This cinematography is really colder. The Iberian Peninsula, though, is nearly tropical! The peninsula has all of this tradition of red and yellow. Their flag! Goya! Basically Goya. Almodóvar felt nobody would translate that. A mutual friend said, "Why don't you speak to Affonso?" And because he loved the film *Antonia das Mortes*, we had an interview. We had an incredible meeting, talking about color, talking about everything. Our first movie, *The Flower of My Secret*, is really more of a "shy" collaboration with him. *Live Flesh* is a film I love more in his career, and perhaps mine also. Color, I think you spotted very well, is his main concern. And color is my middle name. *Dark Water*, a film I shot with Walter Salles, is a film I am not very happy with in terms of the design. It was shot in New York, New York covered in rain, enveloped in rain! In that instance color was not really explored.

LC: When Cecilia Roth weeps and grieves for the loss of her son in *All About My Mother*, to the point of it almost being unbearable for the audience in seeing her pain, what is it like for you to capture such a powerful performance?

AB: Almodóvar's relationship with the actors in the set, it is amazing to see. They get into the characters. Things are very emotive on an Almodóvar set.

LC: Javier Aguirresarobe mentioned that when he was shooting *Talk to Her*, Almodóvar kept complaining that he was not lighting and shooting like you. Of course, the film before *Talk to Her* was *All About My Mother*.

AB: (*Laughs*) Oh really, he never told me that!

LC: How do you feel about that?

AB: I feel proud. He's an incredible cameraman.

LC: Given your connection to him, aesthetically, why have you not worked more with Almodóvar?

AB: Well, I became expensive for him. I am in the middle of my career. I love him. We are friends, but we are not close friends. We see each other once a year. What happened, in terms of what you ask, is that his approach is more like a "family" production. His films are very low-budget. You get to the middle of your career, you have other offers, and so on. I had my collaboration with him, I'm the only cinematographer who did three films in a row with him. I'm the only one who did that!

LC: Let's discuss your collaborations with Jim McBride, *Great Balls of Fire!*, and *The Big Easy*. *The Big Easy* was very famous for its love scenes, at the time of its release.

AB: Jim always wanted to include the sexual, the sensual. And why not? The camera can actually see more of the sensuality of given moments than we might see when we are shooting. It really captured that joy of life in a special way.

LC: In relation to that some people say that the camera can easily see the basic nature and personality of the individual. Is this true?

AB: It is absolutely true! I did a movie called *View from the Top* with Gwyneth Paltrow and Mark Ruffalo. These actors were not in love in real life, they played a couple in the movie. At the end of the movie they kiss, but it was basically like they were not kissing in terms of what I was seeing through the camera. The camera sees more than you can see with your eyes. People's eyes are not as objective as the camera. The camera is showing in such objective terms what is happening that perhaps you can actually analyze beyond the image. The whole point of the movie is that these characters are going back and forward on whether they love each other and want to commit. At the end, they commit, but this just does not translate in terms of what the camera records. The critics complained that it didn't seem that they loved each other in the movie. They didn't "love" each other in real life, and that translated on camera. You mentioned the love scenes in *Great Balls of Fire!* There was something going on there in those scenes between Dennis Quaid and Winona Ryder. Nothing sexual, but something in terms of acting and friendship. And that really translated. In *View from the Top* they are not really grooving. The same can be true though for actors and directors. Sometimes they don't get each other. Terry Zwigoff on *Ghost World* didn't really get how cool Scarlett Johansson was. She is an incredible actress. I believe, as a cinematographer, I am in a position to really see, objectively, what is occurring in front of the camera.

~

The issue of the camera being able to objectively capture action is more ambiguous a question than many might imagine. During a screening of his film *Se7en*, director David Fincher was accosted by an audience member who believed he had actually included a shot of the actress Gwyneth Paltrow's severed head in a box. This was not the case. During a scene in which the villain describes placing her severed head in a box, there is a brief flash-cut to her face in close-up, still very much alive. The effect of this striking edit was to make it seem as though the horrific shot described had been filmed and included by the director. Conversely, the ethnographic eye of the documentary camera allows for much to be seen that in our socialization, we would feel compelled to avert our eyes from. The documentary camera may record that which we might be afraid to stare at in our everyday lives, be it a dead body, family violence, or act that typically produce shame. In short, depending on context, there is a lingering question on what can and cannot be captured by a camera.

To Beato, the camera is extraperceptual, objective to the point that we acquire more information and insight into what is happening in front of the camera than our eyes would otherwise afford us. Of course, slow-motion photography, infrared photography, and myriad other techniques do offer great insights into physical phenomena, but what Beato describes is the camera capturing normal human activities, with no special techniques involved. Paltrow and Ruffalo are capable actors, able to construct a characterization for the camera, and despite this the camera penetrates said artifice and captures what Beato seems to identify as a hollowness. The actors' craft can seemingly not seduce the viewer to believe that they are two people in love as, per his description, the objective eye of the camera captures too many details that assure us this is certainly not the case.

Ellen Kuras

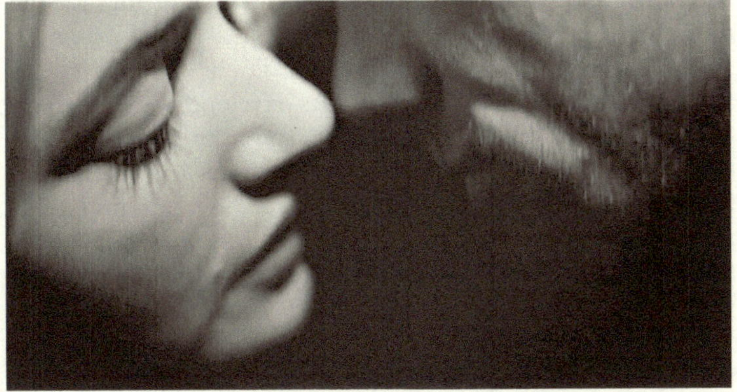

Image 27. The memory light is focused on Clementine (Kate Winslet) and Joel (Jim Carrey) in *Eternal Sunshine of a Spotless Mind* (Gondry 2004).

A successful director and cinematographer, Ellen Kuras ASC has unapologetically forged a vivid, flashy style in her cinematography for films such as *Summer of Sam*, *Eternal Sunshine of the Spotless Mind*, and *Away We Go*. Major early breakthroughs include the indelible stamp she brought to the black-and-white Sundance hit *Swoon*, a true crime story of the infamous killers Leopold and Loeb, and her smart work as a neophyte cinematographer to the world of high fashion in the documentary *Unzipped*. Her work on the period indie biopic *I Shot Andy Warhol* embraced the distinctive visual world of Warhol's Factory in a way that is yet to be repeated. In the 1990s, 2000s, and 2010s, multiple partnerships sprang up. Kuras collaborated with the likes of Jonathan Demme, Spike Lee, Michel Gondry, Sam Mendes, and Alan Rickman in his final film as director. Her documentary, this time working as director and cinematographer, *The Betrayal: Nerakhoon* was Oscar-nominated as Best Documentary in 2009.

The following interview was conducted between Lindsay Coleman and Ellen Kuras in December 2012.

Lindsay Coleman: You had many impressive features you contributed to in the '90s. A particularly impressive one was *Summer of Sam*, in 1999. Could you talk a little bit about the radical style you adopted on *Summer of Sam*?

Ellen Kuras: For me, *Summer of Sam* is one of my favorite films, both in how much creative freedom I had in making it and the final outcome on the screen. Director Spike Lee, a filmmaker who constantly pushes the envelope both creatively and politically, gave me a lot of inspiration to experiment cinematographically. He would challenge me to try different things. Drawing from his penchant to use cross-processed, reversal stock—a new approach at the time but familiar to Spike since he and Malik Sayeed used it on *Clockers*—we played with two kinds of reversal stock on *Summer of Sam*. We also experimented with the shutter angles, since we were filming with film cameras. For the murder scenes and for some of the mentally deranged scenes with the murderer (the flies on the peanut butter sandwiches on Berkowitz's apartment, the scenes where he was going crazy), I had a third camera standing by, an ARRI III, which I operated. On this camera, I used the swing and tilt lens system, also called swing shift. It is a type of lens system derived from the bellows system used in front of a large-format view camera. The lens can be moved in the x, y, and z axes from the film gate, as well as tilted off its central axis. This can help create selective focus planes, and also shape distortion. These systems were very popular in the '90s, especially in adverts and music videos. Some of the manufacturers were Clairmont Camera, P&S Teknik, and Arriflex.

Using these lenses, I wanted to bring more painterly elements into the film, rather than just capturing the narrative in a straightforward, traditional manner.

I also wanted to capture the hot, humid atmosphere of that summer, which to me meant open blacks, so I preflashed the negative before we rolled it through the cameras. I had experimented with the in-camera flashing system, but it gave me too many double reflections in the filter glass.

My greatest challenge on the film was how to light the huge exteriors during the blackout.

LC: Did you feel at all influenced by other cinematographers on that film?

EK: As mentioned, Malik Sayeed had done some of the preliminary work with Spike with the color reversal film, so I was continuing that experimentation with the cross-process reversal. I have to say that there were influences in painting and photography like Saul Leiter that influenced me more than other films; there wasn't really another film precedent to quote. I did get a number of calls from other cinematographers who wanted to talk about my work on the film—"Wow, how did you do this?" "How did you do that?"

LC: The photography of the film does bring attention to itself. Some cinematographers say that they wish for their work to be invisible.

EK: I don't think there is anything wrong with making the visual part of the film speak strongly in the language of the film. Why not? The visuals have a story to tell as well as the words, the design, the acting. In the visual world, visual metaphor works to tell the story. Early in my career when I was working on the film I directed, a documentary, I found that documentary filmmakers put themselves in a text versus visuals box—where text is tantamount and the image is merely slapped on afterward—as illustration of what's being said. Everyone seemed to stay in this box without questioning the approach or the paradigm. As a visual artist, I asked myself—how utterly boring is that? That approach was antithetical to the idea of the image having any meaning other than its literal meaning. I believe that the image can tell its own story inherent in the shot. Every shot has a beginning, a middle, and an end. For example, when I was shooting a film with Rebecca Miller, I sent the Steadicam operator to shoot a series of shots to open the film. I explained how I wanted to create a story with these shots to set the scene for the film and to give some backstory to the characters. When the dailies came back, Rebecca was the first to view them and said to me, "You should look at these, I think you are going to want to reshoot them." I was surprised, but okay. When I took a look at the footage, I immediately understood what she meant. The shots were beautifully executed, but they were just shots; they lacked a sense of intention and story. To me, that is the key. Whenever I am looking through the camera I am always thinking about the meaning of my actions—should I pan left to reveal this object, or if I rack focus to the background I'll reveal that character looking furtive, etc., etc. Whether in working with narrative or documentary, I find that I always want to know what the director wants to say in the scene—his or her intentions. What is the scene supposed to say? There's an inherent reason the scene was written, otherwise it wouldn't exist. And that in turn gives the scene a meaning, which in turn helps me know how to shoot it, and most important helps me to advise the director on how to *block* it. All of this comes because you create meaning with the image, and so blocking has to do with visual metaphor. It always comes back to the meaning.

LC: Bruno Delbonnel, the cinematographer of films such as *Amélie* and *Inside Llewyn Davis*, said that he feels that scripts need to be more descriptive of the visual aspects of the film.

EK: I think Bruno and I ask ourselves very much the same question. Bruno is thinking about those elements of meaning. The quality of light bears on the meaning of the scene. It can be found in the light, whether it is hard light or soft light. Or low light, or high light. All of this has to do with how one perceives and reads the scene, which is probably influenced by culture. So it is really interesting if you hit a universal tone. What is that universal feeling which comes out of things?

LC: What about the personal element of your cinematography? How do you figure in all of this, your personality?

EK: When I shot *Personal Velocity*, I really didn't want to shoot it in digital, as digital was in its very early development. I especially did not want to shoot with small consumer cameras that had little resolution and lenses with no optical integrity. I tried to convince the producers to shoot super 16, even though we had very little money. I knew that I could make the budget work. Yet shooting with these consumer digital cameras was conceptually important to the production; this was one of the projects initiated by InDigEnt (Independent Digital Entertainment)—which was started by Gary Winick to give indie filmmakers the basic means to make smaller films which they had found hard to finance. So I accepted the way we had to shoot, given that I was committed to Rebecca and wanted to enable her to make the film she envisioned. That said, I decided to think of the film as a series of short stories, thus reshaping my expectations of the film; short stories have a different scale than epic novels. I also decided to follow my intuition on how I wanted the film to look, given that I knew very little about the cameras and about the early digital medium with the exception of *Bamboozled*. On *Bamboozled*, I learned that the lenses were ghastly in wide angle (they had virtually no resolution and looked out of focus when the film was blown up on the big screen) and the digital could only handle a very, very small dynamic range, meaning that the highlights all went white and the blacks went totally black unless the light was completely flat. Admittedly, I was not enthusiastically embracing the challenge ahead of me. So I sought out what was the approach of the indie filmmakers to shooting digital at that time. I received a lot of advice, both technical and artistic, but in the end, I really went against the so-called norm on *Personal Velocity*. I used film filters to trick the color/white balance in the digital cameras,[1] I asked Rebecca to consider shooting only in flat light, and I set the shutter to 1/25th instead of 1/50th.[2] The norm at the time for shooting in PAL (a tad higher resolution than NTSC) was at what was considered standard speed—1/50th. But making the comparison to my eye, I decided to shoot instead with 1/25th, even though I would lose one field of information per frame. What that meant is that when we would transfer the digital to film, we would lose some of the minute information in the image. It was a minuscule difference to me. What was more important to me was the particular feeling I wanted from the image. And at the alternate rate of speed—the 1/25th—I felt like the image was more filmic. So in spite of everyone's admonitions, I went with my gut.

When the film came out, everyone commented on how beautiful it was, how no one knew such a look could be achieved with that camera. I laughed, remembering all the flack and the warnings I had heard. I could only be true to what my truth was in searching for how to make the film in the way I wanted it to look and feel. That "feeling" is hard to articulate, and also very hard to teach. It is where intuition comes in. This is what makes each cinematographer unique.

LC: Some cinematographers feel visual metaphor is dangerous territory. What kind of an internal barometer do you have for the inclusion of visual metaphor?

EK: Dangerous territory? Given what I've already said about visual metaphor, I see it as an opportunity for a cinematographer to create meaning in the image. Otherwise, it's just a shot. I would imagine that some cinematographers only want to deal with the technical side of the making of an image, leaving the ideas, and the creation of meaning to the director. On my side, I find the ideas part of it intrinsic to how I envision the image. I want to work beyond the literal, to sometimes speak in poetic terms. Working with the ideas is very exciting to me.

LC: Speaking of visual metaphor, there are many visuals in *Eternal Sunshine of the Spotless Mind* which are quite loaded. In the climax of the film, the hero's final memories of his lost love disappear. Remarkably it looks as though the whole scene is lit by a torch/flashlight!

EK: That was a really challenging scene to shoot for many reasons. First off, Michel Gondry was still influenced by the relative disappoint in the reception of his previous film, *Human Nature*, and wanted me to go "organique"—which was his way of saying "don't use film lights." *Human Nature* was shot in a studio. It was all studio lighting. It was all very artificial, which was of course the point of the movie. Michel chose to do everything opposite on *Eternal Sunshine*. He wanted everything to be shot on location. He just wanted everything to be as it existed, to use natural lighting, even if the sets were not representing what we consider reality. But given what we were doing and how we were doing it, that was impossible, especially because we were shooting film (digital wasn't even an option then). I had to come up with some imaginative solutions to ensure that the lighting was sublime. The house in Montauk was on the historical register, and we were not allowed to rig anything or touch anything. We couldn't put tape on the walls. We couldn't hang any lights. We couldn't put any rigging inside.

The scene at the beach was equally difficult and challenging. The dunes outside were part of a protected beach with stringent restrictions about walking on the dunes. We weren't able to run a cable across the dunes. We couldn't put lights anywhere near the location unless it was a battery light. Forget about putting any lights on stands anywhere near the beach. If you are shooting something outside, in the deep night on a beach, with no lights, on film, *it will be dark*. That is just simple physics. I had to find lots of creative ways to light the scenes. I said that it's impossible for me to light this location unless I have a condor.[3] So I managed to get that concession and we staged a condor in the driveway, which of course happened to be far from the beach, with a couple of Maxi Brutes to give us a base illumination. The rest of the lighting was hand carried by the electricians—the PAR cans, the 2Ks, the KinoFlos. I used bicycle lights and PAR cans rigged with car batteries so that we could put them out on the beach.[4] Inside the house, we had what we call "memory light." It's akin to "the light at the end of the tunnel." We used the memory light throughout the house, as well as when Joel's in the house and the water comes into the house. We actually duplicated a portion of the house with a set piece to create a space for the water to come in. But again, I had to light it. No less complicated. Thankfully, *Eternal Sunshine* is a film that has moved many.

LC: Your work often features a very vibrant use of color. Would you say you have a color philosophy?

EK: I would say I do. My color philosophy was shaped by one of the first films I shot. I was lighting in an apartment building hallway that had no open doorways for sidelight, so we switched out the fluorescents above. They were warm light fluorescents, so we had them switched out to daylight for the daylight scene. Back then, it was sometimes hard to see the distinction between warm and white fluorescent light by eye, so I missed a fluorescent which hadn't been switched out. Of course, this was the one that was situated above the actor for the most important part of the scene. I saw the mistake in dailies the next day—the actor was enveloped in all green top light only in that area,[5] and there was nothing I could do to change it. That time was long before we could rely on the digital world to make changes within the image itself. I was in the photochemical world, before the DI was introduced, so there was nothing I could do in post. I could only change the color of the scene overall. If I made the scene less green, it turned magenta. Regardless, that one area of the hall never matched the rest of the hallway. Whatever I did, the green was always green to me.[6]

So on the next film, *The Mod Squad*, I decided to embrace the green, which had caused me so much tumult. I decided to try and mix the light as much as I could in that film and really just experiment with primary green and the secondary colors like cyan. By mixing light, I mean using tungsten, uncorrected fluorescents, cool lights, warm lights, and daylight all in the same scene.[7] Even though *The Mod Squad* was a studio film, I decided to push my experiment, especially because the director was excited to do something cool. So I came to like green a lot. Now I use cyan against yellow a lot. I like that color contrast, and the way that color can separate various aspects of the image.

LC: There is a lot of cyan in *Be Kind Rewind*.

EK: Yes, I put a lot of cyan in shadow areas of *Be Kind Rewind*.[8] I chose to expose Fuji film stock, because I liked the cyan green inherent in the emulsion of the shadows. Some proclivities are hard to shake.

LC: What about when you are dealing with color in the real world, in a documentary like *Dave Chapelle's Block Party*?

EK: Since we have been able to transfer film original negative into a digital signal, we have been able to make changes within the image—on certain parts of the image—whereas we could only make global changes to the entire image when in the photochemical world (the world of negatives, developing baths, film stock, and analog color timing).

During the prep of *Block Party*, I was able to determine what colors were going up on the outdoor stage—the backdrop, the lighting itself, the time we were shooting. The same was true of the interior green room where the musicians hung out. But at a certain point, there is only so much you can do in production when you are shooting from the hip and a hurricane rolls in the morning of the concert.

I knew I could take some control of the image through the grade/color correction. In documentary, there is much more we can do than before. We have more creative choices now in the digital world. I start playing around with secondary colors, with shadow areas, with highlights, with the midtones, in a way that we never could when we finished photochemical. I always preferred to shoot film original then transfer it to manipulate it in the digital realm. Going from a film original negative to a film print always seemed to have more depth to me. Now digital technology has developed to the point where I don't feel the flatness of the image as before. The dynamic range is much greater, and the highlights don't disappear into white as fast as they once did. I can still feel the difference, however. Recently I did a test with a film and a digital camera, placing them side by side. To some degree, the images they produced looked very similar, depending on the manufacturer of the digital camera, but to me, the difference between them was evident, particularly with the exteriors. I would like to say that film still feels different from digital; film emulsion still has a certain warmth and roundness in the image.

LC: Let's look at the bigger picture, that of emerging formats. Cinematographer Mauro Fiore says that cinematographers are trying to make digital look like film, but they need to let digital finds its own expression.

EK: I totally agree. That is exactly what I realized in making *Personal Velocity*. I had to see the digital as its own medium, with its own integrity. Today, people are far more used to viewing a digital image, so much so that they are always expecting a super-sharp image and think that something is inferior when not. They are getting used to a hyper-sharp hyperreality.

In part, the digital revolution has taken hold due to film schools, and also partly due to economy, which is why film schools use digital gear. Films schools could not afford to use film, so they switched to digital. Students often want to work in digital because that was what they were taught and what they know. Shooting digital gave the studio, the producers, the space to question costs of film versus digital not only in post but on set. It's almost always about saving money—"Can we use fewer lights?"

The latest obsession is resolution. A while back, I had to make some still prints off of a 16mm print of my film. I made some TIFF files to enlarge for some C prints. What came back from the lab was that the files were not high res enough. This was a 2K file from a 16mm film. It had 2,500 pixels and they wanted 7,000. They said, "This is going to have film grain." And I laughed, "That's exactly what it is."[9] Most are now not used to film grain. How we see and what we interpret as the norm is really a learned way of seeing. Time and money play a big interest in the changes.

LC: Some cinematographers are proprietary about their work. Others see themselves as just hired hands. Where do you see yourself?

EK: I am *very* proprietary. In terms of what I am doing on the film, I want to be involved in the ideas/realization all the way to the end.

LC: Do you feel you're the author of the images you create?

EK: To be naive enough to think nowadays that we are the authors of our own images, I pause. Unless I am hauling a camera, lenses, wardrobe, and the set all by myself, and am the only one in the edit and post room, and am the only one making final decisions on where and when and how the final product will be viewed and sold, I have to say that in many instances, the images are a result of sometimes a grand collaboration, or sometimes a cacophony of voices—technical or otherwise—who want/need/feel obligated to put two cents in. Cinematographers are lucky now to be able to see their images through to the final phase of release, or they have good agents that secure firm commitments from the producers for their clients' input. What took years to learn through experience may now not have the same importance it once did in the photochemical world. After all, everyone, anyone can make a movie with a phone now, no? That's where the vision comes in.

So the question becomes, where does one draw the line? If you take the time to shoot a film, part of the understanding is that you get to shape it at the end. In the commercial world, it's becoming more and more common that the agency takes over the material and the rest is up to them, including the grade/color correction.

LC: Above all else, I would have to say I admire your ingenuity. Do you ever feel a task is impossible?

EK: As cinematographers, we become engineers. We are problem solvers. That's part of our job. My father was an engineer and so I'm akin to that way of thinking. My father did frequently say that God was an engineer!

~

The question of where an image derives its power might stump even the sphinx. Images may be as rough and blurry as the Zapruder film and haunt us, or shot in 4K, with a dazzling color space, and be instantly forgettable. They may derive power from the lighting, the movement of the camera, the balance of the frame, or perhaps the duration of a given shot. Equally, a shot may be of no particular beauty or resonance but may serve as the climactic image of an emotionally rousing point in a film. Hence, editing, performance, music, and visual effects may lend an aura to a particular shot in a film, in a way the viewer is unaware of. The impression that is left may be of a the image's power, but the exact balance of elements that produced such an effect may be elusive for easy categorization or quantification.

To champion the significance of a visual metaphor in storytelling is the prerogative of the cinematographer, but it is not necessarily a prerogative all cinematographers seize upon. Images may acquire significance given their integrated position in the larger dramaturgy of a film or television series, acquiring power based on how they accent a given moment in the story. In the interview, Kuras exhibits a curiously dualistic attitude toward visuals that acquire greater significance in a story, what might be called visual metaphors. She points out that for a cinematographer to claim authorship of a film's images might seem presumptuous, especially given the range of people involved in crafting those images. At the same time, she argues, "I find the ideas part of it intrinsic to how I envision the image. I want to work beyond the literal, to sometimes speak in poetic terms. Working with the ideas is very exciting to me." Hence, from her perspective, the investiture of the image with significance, and even symbolism, is still possible. This paradox is intriguing. It will surely continue to preoccupy not only cinematographers but those who love and consume visual storytelling.

Notes

1. Once the white balance is set, the overall color tone of the image can be altered by placing colored filters in front of the lens, making the shot warmer or cooler. Our brains process visual color information so that we perceive object colors as they actually are (red apple as red, green leaf as green, etc.) more or less independent of the color of the light illuminating the objects. This is a pretty impressive feat, achieved without any conscious input on our part. Professional digital motion picture cameras can be set (by adjusting the white balance) to render a particular color temperature of illumination (e.g., daylight, tungsten light) as neutral, thus producing color reproduction roughly as we would see it in life. The white balance can be adjusted to make the overall image warmer or cooler.

2. Because a film camera has to physically pull down and reposition each frame for its exposure, the shutter has to remain closed for a period as this mechanical work is done. Once the new frame is stationary and in position, the shutter opens, the exposure is made, the shutter closes, and the cycle repeats at

twenty-four frames per second. A digital camera has none of these mechanical restrictions; once the exposure is recorded, a new one can start almost immediately—so the 1/48th of a second that was previously devoted to the pulldown is now available for exposure. We can allow a longer exposure of 1/24th (or 1/25th in the case of twenty-five frames per second) of a second. A further consequence of this is increased motion blur.

3. A condor is a mobile variable-height articulated work platform with a boom arm. It is usually truck mounted. It is used in the film industry to mount and position large film lights in inaccessible places.

4. PAR cans are traditional stage and rock and roll lighting fixtures that can be wired to run on twelve-volt batteries.

5. Fluorescent lighting fixtures have long been a source of pain and suffering to cinematographers. Many have a discontinuous spectrum that result in a large green or magenta spike not readily perceived by human vision but very apparent, when recorded on film, as a severe green or magenta cast over the scene. Recent improvements in the Color Rendition Index of fluoro fixtures and the development of the KinoFlo fluoro units have considerably reduced this problem.

6. It was not possible to fix or correct the green color cast in the color timing or grading process.

7. Of course, these harsh color casts can be embraced and used aesthetically (see particularly the final diner scene in *Fat City*) as can the deliberate mixing of different color temperature lighting sources (see the teal and orange color scheme of pretty well any tentpole movie from the first decade of this century).

8. Cyan is a green-blue color. In digital post color correction, different color casts can be added to blacks, darker tones, midtones, and so on. So blacks and near-black tones can be given a blue or cyan or warm color cast independently of the other mid- or lighter tones.

9. Her point is that the lab had become so used to very high-definition grainless digital images that they saw a digital scan of a 16mm original as hopelessly lacking in resolution and encumbered with objectionable random film grain.

Uta Briesewitz

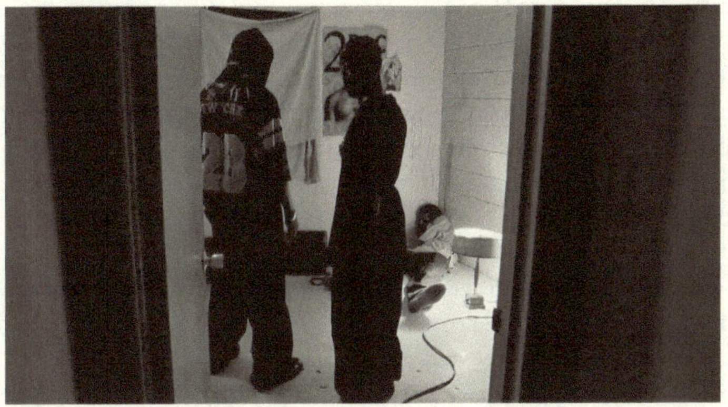

Image 28. Bodie (J.D. Williams) and Poot (Tray Chaney) stand over the dead body of their friend Wallace (Michael B. Jordan) in *The Wire* (Simon 2002–2008).

Uta Briesewitz ASC is an accomplished cinematographer who has worked in both television and film. Her most famous work is probably the first several seasons of *The Wire*. She has also shot for the series *Hung* and film comedies such as *Walk Hard: The Dewey Cox Story* and *Arthur*. In the years since she has moved into directing, working extensively in the series *Orange Is the New Black*, *Jane the Virgin*, *Hung*, *Lethal Weapon*, and *This Is Us*. There is an epic quality to Briesewitz's work on *The Wire*, and an intense sense of visual fluency found in how her camera adapted to a panoramic view of the city of Baltimore. Somehow, be it the projects, the docks, or the police halls, Briesewitz's mobile camera, dynamic lighting, sense of shadow, and composition expertly complemented the ambitions of this series.

The following interview was conducted between Lindsay Coleman and Uta Briesewitz in May 2013.

Lindsay Coleman: Let's start, if we may, with getting some sort of idea as to how you relate to images as a cinematographer. Each episode of *The Wire* begins with a montage of images from the season while the credits play, really without there being given any context for said images. How would you say you relate to images?

Uta Briesewitz: Images have always spoken to me more. When I was growing up in Germany, I was a painter. I was an avid museumgoer. I would look less at photography and the cinema, more at paintings. Now, my interest has drifted more to photography. I think, with the iPhone, it is especially easy to indulge my interest in photography, in taking photos myself. Pictures reveal something deeper to me from the moment you just experienced, they capture the feeling of that moment perfectly. It can also help you see something distinct from the moment that you missed. It is an ongoing search really.

LC: Do you feel you were sometimes more attuned to images on some projects over others?

UB: When I see a great performance, it makes a great image. On *Thief*, a series I worked on, I think I was allowed to shoot it the way that I felt it. Not only the locations and sets I'm given, but also the performer I'm filming will influence how I shoot a scene, or a single shot. I felt I had a great connection with Andre Braugher, the lead on that series. Shooting on 16mm, I was much closer to him than I otherwise would have been on 35mm. Just that proximity, being close to him, really feeling that performance, was inspiring for me in terms of how to shoot him.

LC: Do you feel an affinity for the performer, or do you feel you are witnessing something which achieves its own reality, and therefore it is happening independent to you?

UB: There were times when I felt I witnessed something great, and was a part of it. I felt it was a privilege. It was a responsibility to capture the performance as best as possible.

When I shot Andre Braugher in *Thief*, there were several moments where he breaks down crying. If you are standing close to him, and see him lose it close up, it shakes your body. It sounds girly, but in those scenes, I could feel waves of pain coming off him, literally feel it, and I was crying into my eyepiece, crying along with him in the scene. When you experience somebody's pain, it surprises you, shakes you up. At such moments, my eyepiece starts fogging up.

LC: How do you feel the storytelling you engage in is important beyond creating product? I ask because a series such as *The Wire* clearly transcended its origins as "just another police procedural."

UB: I think you have to find the truth behind the fake facade you are dealing with.

LC: I think there are many instances where you created images which were particularly loaded, potent. When Frank Sabotka goes to his death in season 2 of *The Wire*, it is a very symbolic final shot we see him in. There is nothing, other than the specificity of that shot, to directly communicate that he will die. Do you like images to comment on the action, or record the action?

UB: You absolutely look for these images that have a deeper meaning. But also, on *The Wire*, it was an environment where you worked on the fly, off pure inspiration. Because I was the only DP, I didn't get to scout locations. We'd just arrive, and have to make it up from there. I would walk around, find the angles, give suggestions on how it could be blocked. We wouldn't rehearse with the camera, we'd always skip it. It was incredibly harsh on my assistants, they had to be top notch. Dialogue carries a certain power when it is said for the first time. I wouldn't want to waste the original emotion on what would just be a technical rehearsal. Words trigger emotions. Just saying the words triggers the emotions.

LC: You arrived in America as an adult, and certainly made your way becoming a successful cinematographer in rapid succession. Being an immigrant and coming from Germany, what sort of inspiration or perspective do you feel that gave you in shooting a series like *The Wire* or *Hung*?

UB: I think Americans give Europeans credit for always coming from an artistic vein, even if sometimes it is not justified. They make that assumption because of your background, that you are exposed to European art and movies. I think that there is certainly something to be said for the perspective we bring. *The Wire*, basically, was a case of observing Baltimore, as an outsider. I observed the city at night. That was the reason for using so much sodium vapor light. The nights really feature that orangish light. I tried to ground the story as much as possible. It was a carefully lit show, but it was also about always keeping it real. My approach is very much about realism, about knowing where the source light is originating from. If a yellow light is on someone where is it coming from? Instead of hammering someone with a backlight when they are up a dark corner, just because a backlight looks nice, I don't do that![1] Things have to feel real.

LC: Continuing further with that discussion of the loaded significance of your camera style, the camera is very mobile on *The Wire*. It is clear you weren't in favor of an approach which was too static.

UB: Producer Robert Colesberry loved when the camera moved. I think sometimes we overdid it. I always tried to find certain moments where I could utilize a very specific movement to underline the exact dramatic significance of what occurred. I tried to be subtle about it. Very often I was using a zoom at the same time, so it was as though I was moving on two axes instead of one. You would be slowly approaching a character. I think, subconsciously, this approach gave you the sensation of entering somebody's mind, or you have a great understanding of them. Because you are approaching a character, getting closer, and it's not necessarily in a cut, you have this creeping sense.

LC: A lot of choices when you were shooting the series, particularly in season 1, were striking. When the character

Wallace, a young teenager, is murdered, you don't really light his killers, Bodie and Poot, as villains in the scene.

UB: If you remember, Bodie and Poot take Wallace to an abandoned building. Whenever the characters are in environments where nobody is living, the question comes up, "How will they create light?" We agreed they would bring in a small light, which they would plug in. The whole lighting was motivated by the one practical on the ground. I think even when the body is eventually found the light is still shining?

LC: Yes.

UB: It was completely driven by the logic of things. What kind of light would be there? What kind of light would they bring with them? Also, the fact that the light was on the ground allowed me to light them from beneath, and add some drama to the lighting. It worked better than having an overhead light.

LC: What about making sure to capture all of the nuances of performance, tears for instance, in a scene which is set in a darker environment?

UB: I am always very, very religious about eyelights. Even if the shot is toplit, and you have deep shadows over the eyes, you still need to ensure that you have a little ping for the eyes, just so you can see if the actors are crying. I think the biggest support for the actors are eyelights. I might make a creative decision about a character who is keeping their emotions hidden, and not giving them an eyelight, but that would very much be an artistic choice. I want the audience to see the performance, and the subtlety of performance. If you don't light the eyes, then you miss that, in my opinion.

LC: The scene where Wallace is murdered, did you know that all of the actors would cry? I ask, because it is such a strange, tragic, murder scene. The three boys are friends, and all are heartbroken at this turn of events.

UB: I think it was quite surprising for all of us, to see that they had it in them. But it was also a moment where you step outside of your job and think, oh my gosh, this is brutal, kids killing kids. It was *shocking*. It really sinks in what a desperate world this drug world is when you are in it.

LC: Larry Gilliard, who plays D'Angelo Barksdale, in the finale of season 1 gives a really stunning performance in his confession scene. You used a zoom.

UB: I *always* use a zoom.

LC: Was the zoom timed,[2] or was it your instinct for the performance? Were you operating the zoom?

UB: I always operate the zoom. I have a control for the zoom. I have a Micro Force Zoom Control.[3] That is one of the reasons I like to operate. I watch the actors very, very carefully. When I feel that there is a moment that could benefit from being given that extra push, to go deeper into the actor's face, and read the performance better, I just do it right in that instant. I don't want to see it first in the performance, I want to act spontaneously. My relation to my dolly grip is important. We just work on hand signals. We have to be ready to go left or right at a moment's notice. The same is true for my camera assistants. The same is true with lenses. We have to be ready to change from a 50 to a 135.[4] I always work off headsets, so I can hear the actors breathe, so I can pick up even the tiniest details, so I can feel completely connected with the performers. I think you are connected when you look through the lens. You are the key audience at that point.

LC: Did Gilliard confer with you at all before the scene?

UB: No. All those things are between the actor and the director. We also had to move so fast there was no way to rehearse it. I enjoyed a lot of freedom on *The Wire*. I could do things which, according to my instinct, would help the scene.

LC: Why did you leave *The Wire* before it finished as a series? It is surprising, looking back, to see you were absent in the later seasons, of what is now celebrated as one of the greatest television series ever.

UB: When I was shooting *The Wire*, nobody was watching it. Nobody told me I was on a great show. It was at a time when, as an aspiring DP, I wanted to shoot more features. After the second season I was advised to leave, that it would ruin my career. My plan was to move on after the third season. In the end, after being wooed by certain producers and directors, I decided it was better to move back to LA, with a project which they had lined up, rather than to head back without any specific job lined up. I was worried that in the end *The Wire* would be the only credit on my CV. I wanted to show I could light not only drama. I think also that people assume that a "gritty" look is just about working with what you have in front of you on a location, rather than very carefully planning things, and developing a strong aesthetic. I wanted to show I could do glamorous cinematography, light a leading lady. I wanted to show my range, basically.

LC: Do you feel you succeeded in that?

UB: Well, now that I have done a lot of romantic comedies I wonder that I ever shot *The Wire*. I feel that dramas really give you more of an opportunity to be visually inventive.

LC: Let's move on to another successful HBO series you shot, *Hung*. Thomas Jane is conventionally handsome, yet *Hung* is a parody of masculinity. It mocks the male self-image. It is interesting, in that you were working with a more glamorous-looking cast, and the series seeks to make those leads desirable and sexy, yet at the same time you were subverting those same glamorous images.

UB: Yes, that comes through in everything. It comes through in his somewhat depressing job, the fact that he can't afford to really dress like a super-hunk. His sex appeal is really being taken down by his environment. He doesn't have a cool car, he's living in a burned-out house. All of these things damage and turn down his sex appeal. Yet you look at him with his shirt off and you get reminded that he is a real stud.

LC: How did you go about visualizing your episodes on the series?

UB: I think *Hung* was about a very grounded reality. Alexander Payne directed the pilot. We did all of these B camera rolls of Detroit in crisis, really capturing the recession in full bloom. To me it is all about context. If you put a guy in a run-down car, they become one and the same. If you put him in a convertible, then all of a sudden he seems very different. It doesn't matter how you shoot the guy at that point. The environment far more influences the impression which the character creates. My lighting on *Hung* was dictated by the reality of his environment. That is how I motivated my key sources, and everything.

LC: Some cinematographers say that comedy always comes back to a two-shot, that everything must ultimately be about the interaction, less about lighting and camera movement. What are your thoughts?

UB: I agree it does come back to a two-shot. Comedians playing off each other, it is great seeing them in the same frame. When it's in close-up you are just guided by the editing. Here the rhythm is more important. Two-shots, or even wider shots, are crucially important.

LC: Would you say that there are limitations in the visuals of comedy?

UB: I would say so. There is a limit to how much you can polish it. The directors I am working with, they say, "Listen, the actors are going to be improvising, we need to cross-shoot."[5] Everyone is there for the laughs, no one is going to be checking that the lighting is beautiful. No DP likes to cross-shoot, because you always sacrifice your lighting a little bit. But I understand how it helps with the comedy.

LC: You spoke of your instinct for dramatic performances, specifically in relation to *The Wire*. Do you feel you have an equal instinct for comedic performances?

UB: No, I don't. I feel, with comedic performances, that I am not supporting the performance as much with my camera. With drama, you have a specific single take, and you can plan around the requirements of that take. With comedy, they usually don't even stop shooting between takes, they just keep going again and again.

LC: Do you ever watch *The Wire*?

UB: (*Laughs*) I haven't watched them since then, but I should. I like to look forward. I don't like to look back. I think maybe I don't want to look back because, while I think I did good work then, perhaps if I look back I will start criticizing myself, criticizing my choices from that time. I suppose I like to let things be, so I can appreciate them for who I was at the time I did that work. I can beat myself up if I feel . . . Well, on the other hand, I would have to say that I never say that I'm ready if I am not totally prepared to roll the camera. It takes a lot of people to get everything in front of the camera. To capture that is a huge responsibility, and I take it very seriously. In any moment, I feel I have to be doing my best work. So, when the camera rolls I am at total peace, I have to feel I have done every last little thing which I could have done. It has to be perfect for me in that moment. It can never be erased once you have done it, it will be there for decades. So, I usually don't look back with regret.

LC: How do you feel about the amount you've worked in television?

UB: I always like a challenge. Back at the time of *The Wire*, I felt I'd rather do a series which was really special, and striking, rather than a feature which might not be as exciting a project. All I want is good, strong material.

LC: You happen to be the youngest cinematographer in this book. From our communications, I am aware of how much you appreciate spending time with your children, who are still quite young. How do you, or your peers, tend to go about striking that balance of family time, and what can be a very hectic schedule?

UB: When my children were born, my husband opted to be a stay-at-home dad. With the long hours I was working, this would often make me a weekend mom. I would be out all day, and only get to see them on the weekend. That's difficult, but you try to make the sacrifice in terms of trying to find work which will be near your home. I feel like my adventure days are over. If I got an amazing offer for a feature, I think we would pack up and make the adjustments so we could go on such an adventure. My husband has returned to his career. Somehow, we figure it out. When I have time off, I really get to dedicate it to them. I don't have a nine-to-five job which is a bad thing, but it is also a good thing because when I am there for them, I am really there for them.

~

An important aspect of cinematography that Briesewitz addresses in this interview is lighting, which is motivated by both the environment and the dramatic content of a scene. The potential for the lighting of a film or TV series to become expressionistic rather than realistic is always present, given that both are necessarily artificial and contrived in their production. The ability to control light, often in a studio but frequently on location, is a sufficient factor to many cinematographers that they pursue a lighting approach divorced from the presented reality of the scene or larger narrative. The light falling on actors may not match directionally with practical sources as presented in the scene. Similarly, it is possible that backlighting "rules" may be broken. A famous example of this would be a shot of the Bride in *Kill Bill: Volume 2*, seen from behind in a wide master, facing the sun. In the next shot she is seen in close-up, backlit by the sun. In the transition from one shot to the next, the sun races across the sky to backlight the character! In short, the quest for what is most expressive and most aesthetically pleasing may motivate cinematographers to light and sometimes position their camera in a manner that would not seem realistic or possible within the scene. In contrast to this, Briesewitz on *The Wire* always worked to ensure that the sources of light, and the position of the camera relative to this, made sense to the naturalistic style of the series and the specific reality the producers were hoping to evoke. This might include the position and practical source of light during a night exterior in the projects of the series. Or, as she aptly points out, backlight for its own sake makes little sense when an individual is framed backed into a dark corner. In short, the lighting Briesewitz promoted on *The Wire* was at least an approximation of what we might see in our daily lives, and the story benefits in turn from this, tonally and aesthetically.

Notes

1. A backlight is a light positioned out of shot from behind, and usually above, a subject to provide a rim of light that helps separate it from the background.

2. In a timed zoom, the zoom is planned and rehearsed to occur at a specific point in the action.

3. A Micro Force Zoom Control attaches to the pan handle, which enables the operator to vary the focal length of the lens—to zoom in or out—at a variable rate.

4. Changing from a lens focal length of 50mm to a focal length of 135mm changes the perspective of the shot, the depth of field, and the size of a subject at a particular distance—in this case, the subject will be a bit more than double and a bit less than three times bigger in frame.

5. A cross-shoot is shooting two or more subjects at the same time with two cameras and the same lighting set-up. It requires careful lighting and usually some compromise in that the DP is lighting for two angles at once.

Roberto Schaefer

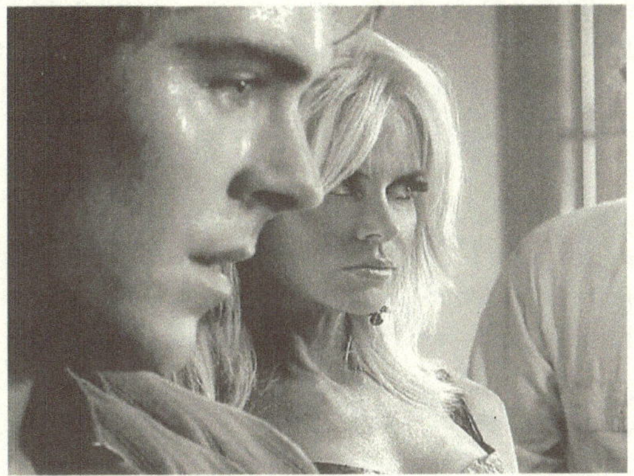

Image 29. The first jailhouse scene from *The Paperboy* (Daniels 2012).

FOLLOWING A SUCCESSFUL cinematography career in Italy, in the late 1990s Roberto Schaefer broke into Hollywood features. Since then, he has worked on productions both big and small, independent and studio films. Notable titles include *Quantum of Solace*, *Best in Show*, *Finding Neverland*, and *Machine Gun Preacher*. Schaefer has also worked in incredibly varied genres, from melodrama in *Monster's Ball*, to YA fantasy in *The Host*, to scandalous auteurist experiments such as *The Paperboy*. A tireless student of filmmaking and cinematographic technique, Schaefer is equally adept and qualified in the realm of visual effects. By serving on the American Society of Cinematographers board, Schaefer persists in communicating his passion for cinema and the art of cinematography.

The following interview was conducted between Lindsay Coleman and Roberto Schaefer in December 2012.

Lindsay Coleman: Let's start with one of your first major successes. *Best in Show* is labeled a comedy, but there are dramatic elements to it, and relationships exist between the characters which are overtly dramatic.

Roberto Schaefer: Absolutely. Lighting-wise I would say that our approach was to allow for a blending of different tones in scenes. I think the approach that we took was to make things seem naturalistic without becoming overly ugly, to basically avoid a feeling of the scenes being overly lit.

LC: How many hours of footage did you have with that film? It was a film which was improvised, within certain narrative parameters, hence I would imagine that there would have been a lot of takes.

RS: Well, we probably shot the film in about a month. But we shot a lot. On all of my films with Christopher Guest, that has been the case. *Waiting for Guffman* was single camera, except for the final performance they give. Also, *Best in Show* was single camera, except for the big dog show at the end. *For Your Consideration* was two cameras. It was fifty-four hours, the entirety of the footage on *Best in Show*. And that for a ninety-minute film. We had to shoot it so that it would cut together well, so that it would plausibly seem as though it was happening. We'd make sure to do things like never being in a room before a character arrived in the room. It was an exciting challenge. You have to be on the same frequency that both the directors and actors are. I have to join in their improv. I have to anticipate what they are doing without revealing that is what I am doing in the camera moves. I have to react for something that is said, as opposed to preparing for the reaction. It's a different discipline.

LC: Did you feel you knew the characters going in, or was it a discovery as you went about shooting?

RS: I would say it was a discovery. I knew something of the characters from the fourteen-page outline I received from Chris. I knew something of each character's background. But really, so much of it was brought by the actors. There was a lot of discovery in there, too.

LC: What was that like?

RS: It was an extremely creative experience. It can be an unsettling experience because I'm not always sure if what I am doing is appropriate to what Chris wants for the scene, in terms of coverage, framing, and so on. It is so mercurial within the scene, moment to moment. I don't know, at least for the first two takes, what the actors are going to do. After that they generally settle into a pattern. The unusual thing is that we start with the coverage, and then go back out to a master. Once you figure what your coverage is going to be you can jump back and create a master which will match the coverage.

LC: Christopher Guest plays a very unusual character in *Best in Show*. He is a loner, with a very particular perspective on the world. And he loves his dog. In terms of capturing that performance, you had to pay special attention to minute behavioral details, yet also to be certain not to editorialize with your camerawork, to not hint that the audience should look down upon the character.

RS: The character was an outsider to the world of dog shows. I tried, as much as I could, to portray and reveal him as that outsider. Yet when he's out walking in the woods that is another side of the character, where he loves and cares for the environment, and his dog. I think that was the only character who had a love affair with the dog he owned. The dog licking his face, holding him. The others, it was always about showing off the dog. For him, it was about showing off the dog he really loved.

LC: In documentary the feeling of the operator toward the subject can influence camerawork. Did you find that this influenced how you filmed certain characters on *Best in Show*, even though it is a mockumentary, not a documentary?

RS: I don't think consciously. I think, in addition to the characters they were playing, I also liked and respected all of the actors on the film. Chris prefers that the filmmaking be more observational, not commenting so much on the characters.

LC: Even so, the emotional violence of the scene between Parker Posey and Michael Hitchcock's characters is really striking when they are searching for their dog's toy Busy Bee.

RS: Oh, absolutely. We were all stunned when that happened. It was like shooting true documentary because none of us were expecting it, not even Hitchcock, the actor who instigated that verbal fight. After this scene we asked him where that incredible emotional explosion came from and he said he didn't know, this emotion just suddenly overwhelmed him and his performance. It happened also with Larry Miller when he talks about the jumper from the building, witnessing the death. Everyone was floored that he improvised that entire story. It just came out of absolutely nowhere. You try to keep shooting as an observer in the room. You then realize for later takes you might need accents on further takes, so you go back and get close-ups for the reactions.

LC: When acting is at its absolute best, it acquires its own kind of reality. When are the moments in your career you feel you've witnessed that? I would venture to say there is that transcendence in moments of *Best in Show*.

RS: Pretty much any moment in *Monster's Ball* where Billy Bob Thornton and Halle Berry were acting together. Or Billy and Heath Ledger. Pretty much everything in that film. Shooting on Death Row made everything real. [In] *The Kite Runner* there are moments that are fabulous. The actors at times are not actors, they become the character. *Stranger Than Fiction* is an odd one. Every time Emma Thompson was on camera, she was so real, so emotionally captivating. Generally, these moments were in the films I shot for Marc Forster.

LC: Reading on your work on *Quantum of Solace*, which you also shot for Marc, you don't seem to have any problem with visual effects. I think it is interesting you are as comfortable capturing intimate performance as you are amazing effects. Why would you say you have less of a problem compared with some cinematographers with visual effects?

RS: I love doing stuff in camera. A lot of stuff on *Quantum* was done in-camera, with some visual effects enhancement. A lot of the fire at the end the film was real. Chris Corbould, who worked with me on the film, is a genius at special effects. Kevin Tod Haug, who did the visual effects, dealt with enhancement beautifully. I want effects to feel organic and feel a part of the work we are all doing. To me it only makes sense to work with them. [In] *Stranger Than Fiction*, a lot of those effects were determined and added after we had finished shooting. I loved the dimensionality of the letters and numbers, which are superimposed over the image, the shading, I thought it was a brilliant touch. It really helped the audience get into Will Ferrell's mind. I don't think anyone would have a problem unless visual effects people would tell you to butt out, and that they were taking over. I think I've been lucky to have good collaborators in that respect. I have heard horror stories though. I have been lucky in that I've worked a lot with Kevin Haug and I've been able to pregrade any plates which I would pass on to the visual effects people and they would then adjust their approach to the grade of the plates. I've heard stories of visual effects people taking over, then changing everything. Once it's baked in, you can't change it or go back, or go in a different direction. To me it's just part of the collaborative process. Today every movie has some visual effects.

LC: Some aspects of [*Quantum of Solace*] felt very real though, like the boat chase.

RS: Oh, the boat chase was completely real! The car chase at the beginning was directed by Dan Bradley, shot by Shaun O'Dell, and was also done brilliantly. That was all real, practically done, with some enhancements. Rigs had to be painted out. There's some close-ups done against green screen with Daniel Craig spinning in the car. It couldn't be done safely with him on location. None of the film was really a complete CG construction. Even the shot of Bond and his adversary falling through the glass ceiling of the art gallery, that was a shot I had planned in reaction to *The Bourne Ultimatum*, I insisted that it be done as real as possible. It was shot for real, each element of these guys going through. There was gravity, even though there were wires present. There were physical bodies going through space. The glass in the roof wasn't actual, and we did marry shots together, but by and large it was all real. It looked real. It felt real. Marc sends shots back, time and again, if they don't feel honest.

LC: Conversely, *Finding Neverland*, a film you also shot for Marc, featured some very subtle nonnaturalist visual touches. I am thinking of the shot in which Radha Mitchell enters her bedroom door, which has a rim of darkness around it, and that of Johnny Depp features intense light pouring from its edges.

RS: When I am shooting, I always have the script on hand so I know what shot we are cutting to as the last shot, or the first shot, of the preceding and following scene. I am very big on organic transitions when they are due. Given that the next scene featured kite flying, it really seemed that this would be where his mind was, like a child, focused forward on the wonder of flying the kite. So his mental space was really in this other world. I was really gratified that paid off as an idea.

LC: *Finding Neverland* is a period film which does break the rules of period dramas in many aspects of its production.

RS: That was a conscious effort. Marc had emphasized the importance of that from the beginning. That was meant to be accentuated from the beginning, but the wardrobe and art department refused to play along. It was an interesting situation to be sure. Marc asked for anachronistic items, like a Bauhaus chair in Barrie's study, or a character wearing a suit jacket which was slightly out of time. He also did not want to shoot it like a period piece, which would bring the audience into Barrie's manner of perceiving things, which was certainly ahead of its time. In contrast, on *The Paperboy*, which I shot for Lee Daniels, we wanted the film to feel as though it was certainly rooted in the period of the '60s. So we forbade Steadicam, we used zooms in a way which was true to that period of filmmaking. We tried to make it feel as organic to that time period as possible.

LC: Do you feel Lee Daniels is underrated as a visualist? I felt, strongly, that the visuals in his film *Precious* were very, very strong. That film seems to have more of a reputation for its performances though.

RS: I do, I really do. I feel he gets harassed quite a bit by critics. I don't understand their shock and outrage over a scene such as the one in *The Paperboy* where Nicole Kidman pees on Zac Efron in a scene where he has suffered a jellyfish sting. It's not gross, or graphic. It's there for a reason. They never talk about the graphic violence and sex in the film. To me these elements also work in the film, but I think that critics have a hard time with Daniels. He's a passionate person, a passionate filmmaker. He's very much "of the moment." A lot of things he doesn't really plan out. He's very spontaneous, and also very true to his vision of how he sees things. I think he is unafraid to take chances. You could compare it to someone like Derek Jarman. *Caravaggio*, the film which Jarman directed based on the Italian painter, in the mid-1980s, was so radical in its time. Yet maybe Jarman was more of an intellectual, so critics could more easily digest his choices.

LC: Lee Daniels has come up through the industry, so people are less likely to acknowledge him as an artist.

RS: I think so. He was a producer, a casting agent. But he can be gregarious. Maybe he made enemies that way. I read an interview he gave after his film *The Butler* came out. He was under a lot of pressure for the project. After the film, Lee mentioned that it was the first film where he felt he had needed to compromise his vision. He was not comfortable. To say that before the film came out, and the potential effect that such a statement might have on the success of the film, I was surprised that he said it, but at the same time I was not surprised. He speaks before he thinks, but he's not ashamed of what he says.

LC: *Precious*, which you did not shoot, is very expressionistic on many levels, in terms of both the cinematography and the editing. People think of it as kitchen sink realism, but it really isn't.

RS: I agree. It has a lot more in common with *Finding Neverland*, in my view, in that both films depict this other world in your head. True, there is also plenty of harsh reality in *Finding Neverland*, what with the death of the Kate Winslet character. I see similarities.

LC: The look of *The Paperboy*, the film you shot for Daniels, is quite distinct. How did you come upon it?

RS: The evolution of the look for this film was a slow one that began with concept discussions at the beginning of the prep period. I was brought in to shoot the movie just a short time before prep began and didn't have any discussions with the director Lee Daniels before that. We sat down and started by discussing aspect ratio and what served the feeling of the story the best. Lee had some ideas in his head but was very open to discussion. He began by showing me some clips from past movies that he liked for one reason or another. As it turned out almost all of them were shot for wide-screen projection. I felt that this was a good choice for this film, being that it was a small budget that needed something to help it feel bigger and more expansive to show off the Southern vistas and flat emptiness of the small town. Also, as an intense personal drama, it would help for making better close-up two-shots. The most interesting and deciding factor that came out of viewing clips and some still images from Lee's selection was revealed by asking his true meaning of what he was saying to me. We watched very specific clips and shots that he wanted to emulate in the film. He showed them to me on an inexpensive LCD monitor from old DVDs and online sources. The images were very grainy, noisy, soft at times. When he pointed at the screen and said that he wanted his film to look like this, I asked if he meant just the framing, lighting, movement, or really like what I was looking at, that very degraded quality. He thought about it and said what he wanted was a film that looked like it had been shot in the late '60s or early '70s and was being seen today from a low-grade transfer on a cheap television. The movie from the negative. By shooting with 1.3× anamorphic lenses you use the entire 16mm negative, which is native 1.78:1 and get a 2.40:1 projection without cropping. This time I felt that we wanted to embrace the grain by shooting super 16mm spherical and crop the 2.40 image from that in post. It also allowed some wiggle room for reframing if necessary. We then went ahead and shot tests on several different Kodak stocks to see which would give us the desired results. I had previously tested every Kodak and Fuji stock for *Machine Gun Preacher* and retained those tests, so I knew that Kodak was better for the look of this film. Kodak had recently introduced a new 500 ASA stock called 7230, so I tried that for a few scenes but eventually decided that it was too grainy to use when we had large expanses of flat color like interior walls. We eventually ended up using a combination of 7203, 7207, and 7219. There were times when we pushed the processing to obtain even more grain and contrast.

LC: It sounds like a very immersive process.

RS: Yes, I think so. I think what is unique about that film is that it does not resemble a lot of "period" films set in the '70s. We weren't specifically trying to create a pastiche of that period. It was more a case of going in with similar tools and then creating our own aesthetic world.

LC: Returning to your work with Forster, the black and gold aesthetic you used on *Quantum of Solace* is amazingly consistent. Was that Forster's idea, or was it something you wanted to explore?

RS: I think it was the result of a collaboration between Dennis Gassner, the production designer, and myself, and Marc. We tried to approach the film as an homage to early Bond, *Dr.*

No and *Goldfinger* in particular, as far as set design, the overall look. We wanted it to have a retro feel, but to still be modern. We wanted to get across the feeling of the early Bond films, which we all loved. We had the desert, which was that golden color. We had the hotel which most of the action features in, which was its particular color. We also had Siena, Italy, which has those warm Siena colors. The counterpoint was the blue of the water, and some of the blue nights. Some of the opera, the Tosca opera, was very blue due to its existing scenography. I thought it worked well. The interior of the place had that warm light, then everyone attending was dressed in black. We had to deal with aspects which we couldn't change in the production in locations, and then produce some uniformity from it. In any case when I think of *Goldfinger*, I think of black and gold.

LC: I feel the film is a lot more emotionally rich than people give it credit for. What do you see as the connection between the emotions of the film, and the colors you are working with?

RS: I had not considered that before. If I was answering honestly, I would say that I am finding reasons or justifications for it. I think that aspect of filmmaking can be overly thought out. I think that in truth the matching of color and events or emotions can be very haphazard, just like life. You can see something violent, and horrible happen in a beautifully designed or lit shot. The opposite is also true. Part of our job is to transport the audience into a way of thinking or seeing. I can't say it was about the emotion. It was more about taking Bond back to the early, raw, lo-fi days.

LC: It is a heartbreaking story. In the film's climax, the Kurylenko character is overcome with grief and fear.

RS: Totally. That was a film where we had a minimal script. A lot of it was invented during preproduction and the shoot. If you look at all of Marc's films, they are so much about grief and the loss of a loved one, whether it be a brother, a son, a parent, a lover. Almost every one of his films explores the overcoming of loss or tragedy, becoming stronger through it, learning something. That was something Marc really brought to that script, to that story. I don't know that film critics got it. They saw *Casino Royale*. They loved it. I thought *Casino Royale* was better than the Bonds before it, but I also felt it was a little boring. I thought him getting his license to kill was great, so was the parkour. Marc was looking to bring a human element, to reveal the respective tragedies Bond's and Olga's characters had gone through. Being around the fire, as she was at the end, brought back all of these memories of the death and loss of her parents, murdered by this evil guy. I think it was really, really important, as important as the fight and chase scenes. I am mystified at the negative criticism on the film, only because I gave a year and a half of my life, and my whole heart to it!

LC: You spoke of Roger Deakins recognizing its strengths.

RS: Any time you get praise from other professionals, it definitely means a lot. Most of us don't praise each other just to be nice. To get that from Roger, while he was shooting *Skyfall*, meant a great deal. Bill Pope also really liked it. I've heard from others, too, who really appreciated it. I don't care what the critics say. I'm really proud of my work, and of the film itself. I hope it will get its due in years to come, people will realize what it really was.

~

The implicit stylistic question posed by many of the films discussed here might be summarized as, "What is the best way to evoke a particular kind of genre cinematography without falling into a pattern of shooting and lighting which would constitute a pastiche of that genre?" Schaefer describes, particularly in relation to *The Paperboy*, how he developed a style that was not aiming to carefully copy the visual style of the film's influences. Rather, it is an original style tapping into a similar vein of visual exposition, camera style, image texture, and so forth. The same might be said of Schaefer's operating on *Best in Show* and *Waiting for Guffman*. Both belong in the mockumentary genre, however it is worth remembering that at the time, before *The Office*, the format was still relatively underexplored. As such, to effectively coordinate with the films' actors in lengthy improvisational takes, Schaefer needed to be aware of both the conventions of documentary, those established by earlier mockumentaries, and the specific requirements of coverage for the scene. His style was more of a hybrid, given that he knew roughly what the actors would say and do in the scene, as compared with a rawly responsive approach as found in documentary. In turn, Schaefer's Bond picture was designed to be evocative of the Sean Connery Bond films, while capturing his own Bond, Daniel Craig, while also working within a design and color scheme reminiscent of the 1960s Bond. In short, camera style can be reminiscent of earlier approaches without explicitly re-creating them.

John Seale

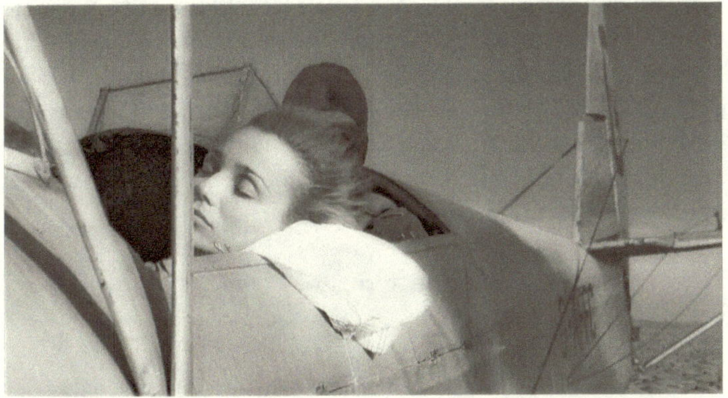

Image 30. Katherine (Kristen Scott Thomas) lies dead in front of her lover Almásy (Ralph Fiennes) in *The English Patient* (Minghella 1996).

An Academy Award-winner for his cinematography on *The English Patient*, John Seale ACS, ASC has been working on the international stage since the mid-1980s, starting with *Witness*. Equally at home in intense films such as *Children of a Lesser God* and action blockbusters like *Mad Max: Fury Road*, Seale's recent work has seen him come out of retirement to further acclaim. The earliest phases of his career saw Seale rise through the ranks of the Australian film and TV industry to become a respected camera operator, a legend to this day, who worked beside Russell Boyd and Don McAlpine. Operating on films such as *Gallipoli* and *Picnic at Hanging Rock*, Seale eventually transitioned into being a full DP on major Australian feature films such as *Careful, He Might Hear You* and *Caddie*. The international phase of his output began with *Witness*, and this was followed by a career full of major commercial and critical successes: *Rain Man*, *Gorillas in the Mist*, *The Mosquito Coast*, *The Perfect Storm*, and *The Firm*.

Lindsay Coleman spoke with John Seale on three occasions in 2012, 2014, and 2015.

Lindsay Coleman: Going back to early in your career when you were operating, a film such as *Mad Dog Morgan* has really lovely compositions. Was that the influence of Mike Molloy, your DP, or your own input?

John Seale: Mostly Mike. Mike was dominant as to what he wanted. He was working more in the commercials side of the business and was using more of a "commercials" compositional approach. I was more coming from TV shows. I was more locked into a realistic look. He took it more into a fantasy look with wider angle lenses. That was a trend at the time, and he was on the wave of the trend.

LC: Who schooled you in terms of composition, or do you feel you were self-taught?

JS: Nobody. There's a lot of times when a cinematographer may influence you. They influence you usually for one scene of a movie. Sometimes I'll say to a gaffer, "Let's do this like Bob Richardson." Put a search light in the roof, we'll bounce it off the table, and it will look like Bob Richardson. That might seem appropriate for a scene. I always only regard it as one scene. I'd never do it for a whole movie, as maybe Bob has for a whole film in the past. Yet another DP may have influenced the lighting in another scene, in another a DP may have influenced the operating. I look to everybody as a mentor, rather than one. That also opened the door to the director and myself to develop our own look. We always needed to find a unique look.

LC: You have a wonderful history as an operator in your early years in Australia and then beyond. What are your thoughts on the experience of being an operator?

JS: You are the only one watching the film being made! You are monitoring composition and the movement of the camera to determine what best conveys the emotion of the story.

LC: Do you feel the operator is the eyes of the audience?

JS: I do. I feel that if a film favors subjective camera, as opposed to a more objective perspective in a film, the use of the subjective camera really is such a personal thing! You need to understand that if you are being subjective to one of the actors, you have to know the emotion of the film and in turn really work hard to capture the specific emotion and performance he or she is attempting to convey and get across. You also need to know what emotion the audience will be looking at that actor with.

LC: How do your own emotional responses to a scene or a performance translate into your operating?

JS: Sometimes you get it wrong. I remember a director saying to me, "Johnny, I love the stuff you're giving me, but it is too smooth. I need a little bit more movement in your operating to give it that visual energy." I'd listen, but I'd got it wrong. Not wrong, but I'd took it in another direction. You can't really find that groove until you start shooting the actors. I just viewed a film the other night. It was called *A Most Violent Year*. A powerful, fascinating film. Well shot in a very old, traditional way. But there is one shot in it in the beginning where Oscar Isaac is walking along the waterfront near some big fuel tanks and the camera is following him. It was handheld, behind him. The shot is showing what his dream would be. It's behind his head. It's wobbly as all get-out. I wondered, "Why did they do that?" To me it wasn't showing "this is this character's dream of buying and developing land." It looked as though somebody was stalking him, about to track him down, and whack him over the head with a baseball bat. Everyone at the screening agreed that this particular shot annoyed them. I try to never do a shot which takes the audience out of a movie. If you take them out of movie then they are back in the theater, eating their popcorn, and watching a movie. They are no longer playing a role in the movie. You then have to work to get them back into a movie, to absorb them so much they forget to eat their popcorn. That would be the greatest thing. To get them so into the movie that they forget to eat their popcorn.

LC: You had immediate success in America with *Witness*, gaining your first Oscar nomination. It was soon followed by a sudden change in subject matter with *The Hitcher*, a kind of a slasher film. *The Hitcher* is very contrasty in terms of your day exteriors, but the film does not feature obvious horror lighting.

JS: That was a very interesting approach by the director. I did *Witness* and Ed Feldman was the producer on that. I went to Australia for the postproduction, and then back to America for the release print timing. Ed Feldman asked what I was doing, and I told him "not much," that I was just reviewing my options. He handed me the script of *The Hitcher*. I read it and did not like it at all.

LC: Did you dislike the violence?

JS: It was written in a manner reminiscent of the Sam Peckinpah body dismemberment-type script. Even back then, at the start of what would be my international career, I just did not feel like doing a script which focused on slow-motion body dismemberment. In addition, this was with a young director who had not much experience aside from a film which he had acted on as his own cinematographer. I told him I was not very interested in body dismemberment. He talked to me for about forty minutes on the phone and laid out his vision, which was quite distinct from the script. At the end of the forty minutes, I said right, I'd love to do it. The film was successful, and has gone on to acquire a cult following. What was really scary and effective about the film was that the violence was more implied than explicit. The approach was one of innocence. It was an expression of the boy's innocence, in contrast to the weirdo killer character who just wanted to kill or be killed. His innocence influenced the overall look of the film. Adding horror lighting to the film would have crossed over against the young boy's character. We decided it would be an innocent portrayal of the desert, and the people in it.

LC: A lot of the characters in your films are innocent, and you in turn are portraying their innocent point of view.

JS: I think so. If you go start suggesting via lighting that something evil is going to happen, you take away the shock of when it actually happens. We were seeking to portray the desert, the desert this boy is traveling through and observing. Nothing is evil in the desert except this man who is hunting him. I tried to make the desert look very pretty as a matter of fact, using grad filters, pumping up the skies a little bit. I was just trying to make the desert look a beautiful place. Yet in the desert you can have evil people doing evil things. I think sometimes cinematography can get a little clichéd. I always think of a princess in a castle whose love is going off to war. She is sad so it is raining, or there is a storm, or the lighting is dreary. I think matching the lighting always to the mood of the character can be a bit much. By keeping the desert beautiful we were saying that it wasn't going to change just for the mood of the character, just for this boy who was being chased by this maniac. That tendency is always there in the films I make, yet it is always in agreement with the director, it is always in the service of what they want to portray.

LC: In addition to working well with directors you also need to work well with other departments. I watched a documentary in which Walter Murch was talking about his editing on *Cold Mountain*. It occurred to me that for him to have the number of options he discussed there would have needed to be major continuity between the various angles you would provide him with on a scene, in terms of lighting and so forth.

JS: Yes, absolutely. It was not always easy. For the opening battle scene of that film, it was hard to maintain continuity. It was a disaster. It took six weeks to shoot it and the weather kept changing the whole time. So we burned diesel in pots which created a haze and smog, which helped with continuity. It was always a heck of a battle to get it, but I think we did all right between first and second unit. I work hard to maintain continuity. It helps lull the audience into the film. If it gets broken up, audiences can become uneasy about it. I try to maintain continuity in all ways.

LC: We've been discussing style. Often your style can be low-key, naturalistic. Yet on *Lorenzo's Oil* you used quite extreme angles and also quite short lenses.

JS: That's all of director George Miller's thing. It was the same on *Fury Road*. He does like the short lenses, the wideness of the background. He doesn't mind dutching the camera over to an extreme angle. It is interesting because often your instinct is to keep the camera level. When I looked at it, I thought, yes, it does work. It doesn't take the audience out of the film. George wanted the audience's experience to be as true as possible to the emotion of the Odone family, which had to deal with the son dealing with his terrible illness.

LC: In the final big scene of that film, you have a two-shot of Susan Sarandon and Nick Nolte where he tells her their son may never recover. The light levels are very low, but it is still possible to pick up the tears she is shedding. If the light were angled wrong in relation to Sarandon's face, you wouldn't have caught the tears, given the low ambience of the scene.

JS: It's good to see the tears. If the angle of the lighting or the camera is such that you miss, then you are missing a lot of emotion. We always work to get a little light in so that it will glint off tears. The audience knows that physically and mentally she is in distress. George would want the camera to zoom in so that the audience could track into that intense emotion.

LC: Then, in contrast, *The Firm* ends with a very static, lengthy exposition scene, between the Mitch McDeere character and the mobsters he is working for. How did you feel about the particular approach taken there? In some respects it is quite similar to the lengthy final scene of *Absence of Malice*, another film also directed by Sydney Pollack.

JS: I think I learned a long time ago that it is the directors who really make the film. We can't and shouldn't be disappointed with the ways things end up in a final edit, the way it ends up flowing. We've all shot so many scenes that are so lovely, we are so proud of how they look, then we are told by the director that they didn't do anything for the movie. So they were removed. We're making film, not a photographic exercise to prove your ability. If something stalls the movie, regardless of how it looks, out it goes. I've had them use out-of-focus stuff! If the best performance was in that take, that is what gets put in.

LC: In returning to work with Peter Weir, after operating on *Gallipoli*, then shooting *Witness*, you went into *The Mosquito Coast*, a film with a truly unique look. The stock you chose to work with on that film had such an unusual texture.

JS: That was a perfect example of when we had three negatives to choose from in the old photochemical days. I remember the Agfa stock loved green, and it was more yellow as a base negative. It loved the jungle. I know Chris Menges was shooting *The Mission* around the same time, and he opted for the Agfa because it just loved the green. We tested Agfa for the jungle in our film but that was not what Peter Weir was looking for. He wanted a dirty, filthy, greasy black jungle. Nobody was supposed to love the jungle in that film, with the exception of the Harrison Ford character. The Eastman stock was clear and cold and blue. Of course we could change that, in postproduction, but we relied at that time on a negative for 80 percent of the final color and contrast. So the Eastman was a bit too clean and blue. We went to Fuji. Fuji didn't like the greens. It made the greens look very drab and olivey green. Peter liked that. It was starting to move in a color direction which he liked. It also had a touch of grain. It was also a 500 ASA honest stock. The Agfa was not an honest 400 ASA stock. On *Gorillas in the Mist*, which I shot a couple of years after *Mosquito Coast*, and was also filmed in the jungle, I found

I had to open up and open up and open up to get a good negative. I wasn't an honest 400 ASA. Fuji on *Mosquito Coast* was a completely honest 500 ASA stock. I actually used it for a couple of films after, it was such a lovely stock. You could set your meter on it and it would work. With other stocks the lab would come back to you and be asking for an extra half stop, they weren't getting the full negative. Then I'd be thinking, hang on a minute, I'm on factory ratings. That was how *Mosquito Coast*'s palette evolved.

LC: On *Gorillas in the Mist* and *Mosquito Coast*, both films from the '80s, did you have worries about how what you were shooting would end up developing, given that you were quite isolated on location?

JS: On *Gorillas* I was on Agfa, having tested on *Mosquito Coast*, as that was a story about a woman who loved being in the jungle. Like I said, I had to keep opening and opening and opening the lens. It's a big dark jungle, even at midday. It does give you angst, to know you'll be waiting four days to hear back from the labs before they can get and develop the negative. With the connecting planes, that was how long we'd have to wait. So your heart would be in your throat. Now you can watch dailies going home in the bus! Now you've got the DIT man, plus the video assist guy who can do a quick grade using a LUT.

LC: Just as you had to open up when shooting in the jungle, you have also had to deal with very harsh light conditions. Looking at your work on *Prince of Persia* and *The English Patient*, having shot in the desert, it seems filters were a major part of your toolkit in such instances.

JS: Yes, on films such as that I used them a lot. If you didn't use them, you never got your shots. You certainly couldn't put it in on an answer print grading. You wouldn't have the necessary control of color and density. Now in the DI, with a system such as Baselight, you can essentially relight your scenes. You can put all of the filters and colors in. You can also select a given film stock look, click a button, and it gives you a vaguely “film” look. So yes, I would need to put careful thought into how to deal with such a reflective, glary environment as the desert.

LC: Anthony Minghella was a celebrated writer for television and the theater in the ’80s. He was arguably self-educated when it came to film. How could his visual intelligence have evolved such that he could conceive of something such as the opening of *The English Patient*?

JS: As you say, Anthony was an incredible writer. He had an incredible understanding of characters and emotion. He was the most incredible director which I worked with, who could meld that together. *The English Patient* was his first film after going to America to make *Mr. Wonderful*, which was a film I don’t think he was that excited about. This was his first time with me, my first time with him. He okayed me to shoot the film without a meeting, which is pretty rare. I found it interesting reading the script. The bottom line was that I had an image of the opening. You can’t read a script without imagining how it might look. When he asked me how the opening scene should go, I told him it might start on the shadow of the airplane, then crane up through the wing of the fuselage to reveal the people inside the plane. He said, “Oh my God, that is what I’d love to do.” That cemented our relationship for the rest of the film. He was very much one who would lean on you, which was nice because you could throw ideas at him easily. He could analyze what you were getting at. Some rely completely on you, and that can be dangerous because you are creating the visuals. One director accused me of that, so I backed down very quickly and asked him what he wanted. But he didn’t know what he wanted. My ideas he felt were making the film not his. It’s very awkward, sometimes. The understanding with Anthony was set up with six degrees of separation. We were able to banter around about ideas for shots. We could talk about scenes and how they were covered on that film.

LC: Your visual imagination fulfilled the potential of his visual imagination.

JS: On that film. It changed quite markedly on *The Talented Mr. Ripley* because when he went through the edit on *The English Patient* he didn't have enough material. On *Ripley* he wanted more material. I think the editor requested more material. Ripley had a lot more coverage, as did *Cold Mountain*. I've learned it is very wise to have lots of coverage.

LC: One might say that being a good cinematographer is actually knowing about where the cut will come in the footage you have generated.

JS: Yes. And that is where I love operating. As a job in aiding in the construction of a film, it is essential. In the old days, the directors would rely on you to report on what had happened during the take, through the camera. You are the only bloke who is actually watching the film. Everyone else is seeing the cables, the walls of the set, you are seeing the actual film in your view finder.

LC: As it is.

JS: Yes, for sure!

~

The greatest lesson Seale may offer is on the practical nature of filmmaking and the necessities of effective collaboration it produces. If you are shooting on location in a mountainous jungle, isolated and far away from the lab that will develop your film, err on the side of caution and shoot for a thick, well-exposed negative or file. Control the exposure later in post. If your collaborator is a director more known as a wordsmith than as a technician, such as Minghella at the time, lean into that fact and offer support on the visual side of storytelling, your visuals complementing their gifts for dialogue and as a scenarist. There are many such instances to be found throughout Seale's career. Shooting on *Rain Man*, he devised a system whereby two cameras would be shooting at once, allowing for greater spontaneity and freedom in the noted acting partnership between the two leads, Dustin Hoffman and Tom Cruise. Charged by other cinematographers that this decision was compromising his lighting, he quipped that there was only a "20 percent" compromise in the final lighting of the scene. Similarly, his approach with lighting for multiple cameras and shooting with multiple cameras assists greatly with coverage and editing options. On *Dead Poets Society*, director Peter Weir wished to shoot a scene with seven people, using close-ups as well as wider shots of them. If group dialogue scenes like this were to be shot with a single camera, it is likely that the number of setups would be much higher than otherwise, taking more time and resulting in more necessary changes in lighting. Hence, Seale was able to deliver more footage, matching the specific needs of the editors and director, in less time than conventional single-camera shooting would have produced the same results. Seale's gift for grasping a practical solution has been a key to some of his most respected collaborations.

Anthony Dod Mantle

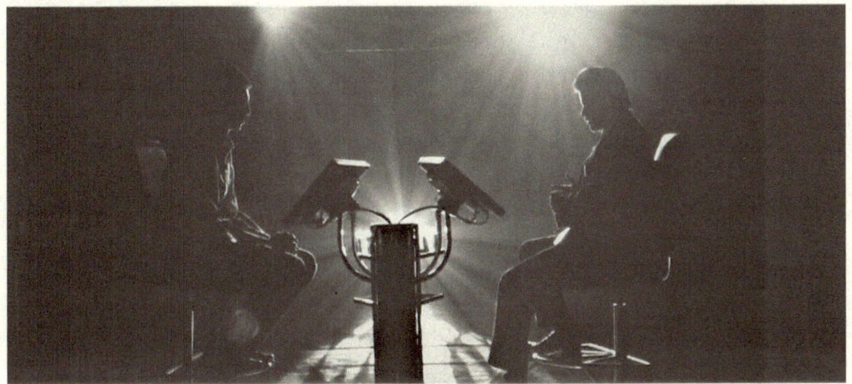

Image 31. Jamal Malik (Dev Patel) and Prem Kumar (Anil Kapoor) on the set of *Who Wants to Be a Millionaire?* in *Slumdog Millionaire* (Boyle 2008).

After an intriguing entry to cinematography prominence through his work for the Danish Dogme 95 movement, Anthony Dod Mantle DFF, BSC, ASC transitioned first to vivid collaborations with the likes of Danny Boyle on *28 Days Later*, then to a fruitful partnership with Ron Howard on *In the Heart of the Sea*. Winning an Academy Award for his cinematography on *Slumdog Millionaire*, Dod Mantle is seen as a pioneer of digital cinema thanks to his ongoing willingness to experiment with emerging camera formats. A noted collaborator, Dod Mantle has forged partnerships with Danny Boyle, Lars von Trier, and Ron Howard, and has shot Oliver Stone's biopic *Snowden*.

The following interview was conducted between Lindsay Coleman and Anthony Dod Mantle in July 2013.

Lindsay Coleman: Audiences will know you well for your featuring prominently in the documentary *Side by Side*. In that film, Danny Boyle mentioned he was glad you had gone digital for *Slumdog Millionaire*. Your aesthetic choices put you in a unique position of being the first cinematographer to win an Oscar for shooting a film digitally. Would you say that it is true you have "gone digital," or is that just how people see what you do?

Anthony Dod Mantle: I think it is true to *Slumdog* and the Oscars, I am very happy to get an Oscar for that film. There has been a gradual exploration of digital. I wouldn't say I'm an advocate for digital necessarily. I would say that if I am an advocate for anything, then it is for artistic license. I had been banging perhaps against the current rather than with the current of other cinematographers in the ten to fifteen years prior to *Slumdog*, advocating unusual formats. In my own way, I feel that it was nice vindication for a kettle that had been boiling for some time. I trained in celluloid though, I love my celluloid, and I miss it terribly at the moment. As far as Danny is concerned, he was attracted to me through my work on *Festen* [*The Celebration*], which was of course shot digitally.

LC: In terms of unusual aesthetics, you were of course a part of the Dogme 95 movement from early on. It was a movement designed to be unadorned, unglamorous. Yet if you look at *Mifune*, a Dogme film which you shot in the '90s, the lead actress is very much a star in how she pops off the screen. Dogme certainly had its share of stars.

ADM: Yes, it wasn't meant to, but there you go.

LC: Does star quality always shine through, regardless of the style of film is shot in?

ADM: Of course, star quality shines through regardless of the format or style. Regardless of the production. Of course, of course. That's the whole basic alphabet behind shooting a film. It's sad we spend time making categories for people. Your prior question is an excellent example of imbecile ideas where people place others in categories without even doing their research. They typecast everyone. I try to stay away from that.

LC: In *Festen* you turn the camera on its side and panned the camera around the room. I always wonder what made you make that choice?

ADM: God only knows. My personal shooting recipe was to try and retrain myself, to do what I wanted, to do what I could. I always have a private recipe. I shared it a little bit with the director of course. But on *Festen* I wanted to consider myself as a protagonist among these actors, throw myself among the actors so I could bodily and spiritually engage in completely irrational gestures. I used to do strange things like flick my wrist, which you can't do on a regular camera. On that film I just did what I wanted to do. I took on the costume of being the protagonist. I would allow myself to be physically surprised by the things that went on in front of the camera. I wanted to be inquisitive, abstract, outrageous, to turn the camera over sideways, all within reason of course. I haven't had that in my camera alphabet really since. I think the editor was great at picking up on that.

LC: Some of the films you have been involved in have certainly involved unusual, atypical approaches to production. In the documentary on the making of *Dogville*, there was a lot of tension demonstrated between [Lars] von Trier and the actors, some of them not responding well to his approach.

ADM: In reality, there wasn't much tension. There was tension between Paul Bettany and Lars.

LC: Do you feel the film is a representation of what was happening behind the scenes? [Michelangelo] Antonioni always said that films can be seen as a documentary of their own production.

ADM: I always try to maintain a good heart. I am very critical of my own behavior on the set. Unnecessary explosions of anger must be kept off the set. I work very hard myself to control it, and encourage it in my crew also, even though the work can be very stressful at times. The actors are the skin of the film, and they pick up on such things. As far as *Dogville* was concerned, it was the biggest experiment I was ever a part of with Lars. We were both nervous on that film. It was definitely out there. There were 900 lamps on the ceiling, miles and miles of cable. It really was high-tech, radical cinema. The actors loved it, as much as they were confused by the process.

LC: It was of course followed up by its sequel *Manderlay*, another film with a very impressive, high-power cast. Why did you go for such an overexposed look on *Manderlay*?

ADM: *Manderlay* was the second part. I was operating more. I developed things with Lars better on how to control our dramatic lighting more. Every single light was linked into lighting dimmer panels. I arranged for a private line between me and Lars because we were both operating, and I wanted us to discuss our work without others knowing. I operated more on *Manderlay*. That culminated in *Antichrist*, where Lars couldn't operate much at all. This was a problem. That became one of the issues of debate in the creative development of Lars and I. I think *Manderlay* looked cleaner, which was certainly good for the dramatic nature of it. There were less camera shadows. You have to cut them out anyway, so it's just better to avoid them on the whole.

LC: Bryce Dallas Howard has exceptional skin, and the effect of the light on her skin when she is nude is quite striking.

ADM: It's also the contrast against the black skin of her lover in the scene. *Manderlay* is so much more about racial issues. It was hyperobvious.

LC: Again, looking at digital aesthetics, your innovative approach to cinematography, and thinking about actors, the digital format can create complications for skin tones.

ADM: Early on, actors would beg us to switch back to film. The Sony CineAlta, which I had to use on *Dogville* and

Manderlay—because it was Zentropa gear—I'd always use Pro-Mists or soft/FX filters because digital could be brutal. Film still renders skin tones in a more beautiful way. Things have improved, thanks to resolution and color matrixing. There is a lot of differentiation in compression, camera to camera. I spend a lot of time in post—probably more than most cinematographers due to my experimenting with digital earlier—with various tricks of the trade to assist with issues surrounding skin tones. On *Slumdog*, the kids got off lucky. You can slam an HMI straight in the face of a kid, and they can take it. If you put an eyelight on me, I look like an anaconda. Some actresses or actors who have an inner beauty, it can really be enhanced by the lighting. I remember shooting *The Last King of Scotland* with an anemic James McAvoy in a two-shot with Forest Whitaker, playing an African leader, and it was very tricky. I had Forest wearing green makeup to balance out against the pink/magenta tone of James's skin, which is the result of his originating from Scotland. It really is a decision you need to make based on format, moving from 16mm to 35mm, then in turn to digital with the various resolutions, matrixing and color resolution capabilities. On *28 Days Later*, I chose a Canon camera not because they were the best tech spec-wise, yet we felt they were right for that film. So we worked with certain filtrations and diffusions to make sure we got the look we were going for. Cinematographers my age know our characteristic curves, our density programs, our gamma, the film stocks, latitude. New people who work less with film need to know different things, they need to know what compression is, what it does, color processing; the same things apply, it just got far more complicated.

LC: Beyond the specifics of a given camera you might work with, there is also a clear commitment on your part to a broadly evocative use of color. There is a great tradition of color in British cinematography. Is this something you are aware of in your work on *127 Hours*?

ADM: I don't see a conscious connection, though I am very much aware of that history. I feel incredible regret that I've never shot with a Technicolor negative. I mean I've shot what became a DI transfer in stills photography, developed it myself.

For the life of me, it pisses me of that we can't work out how to separate color in the digital domain in the same way as is found in Technicolor. Don't get me wrong, we can still do amazing things in post, but the primal effect of Technicolor, particularly in relation to the gorgeous skin tones it produced, is yet to be replicated. The primary colors in Technicolor are so clear and pronounced, it really is devastatingly beautiful. Working on *It's All About Love*, I did review Jack Cardiff's work on *A Matter of Life and Death*, so you are right, that imagery, that cinematography, is in my body. Getting color right is incredibly important. Getting the wrong colors is like the actor saying his lines backward. I don't like desaturated films, as a rule. I'd rather go for the right colors, and then push them. Ironically, on *127 Hours*, that was the one film where we shot with formats which were tough, cameras and lenses which were tough, all in order to get in close with a shot on our lead, James Franco, who of course plays a real-life individual who was trapped beneath a rock. Even though Danny and I had a pact as to where we were going to go with color, he sent me a letter explaining where we would need to pull back in terms of color. As James went further and further toward dying, Danny wanted the canyon to become dryer and dryer. I discovered, along with Danny, that some colors are wetter than others. That was why we had to desaturate some of the colors, and it really was a heartbreaker. But at the same time, it made sense, as Danny pointed out that the audience had to believe that Franco was dying of thirst. I had to pull back the yellows, and the reds, or the cavern wall to a magenta, a much thinner-looking color, and it didn't do the formats we had picked any favors at all. Yet we had to do it, we had to do what was right for the story.

LC: My understanding from Alwin Küchler is that you would both work as co-cinematographers on the film.

ADM: Well, Danny likes me to work with the actors, so I'd have probably have been the guy stuck in the canyon. I loved the idea. Then that shirker went off and did a film which I'd initially said yes to, and yet I instead opted for a radical yes to sharing with Alwin on our film with Danny. I love Alwin to death, but with Alwin being off it was a real shame. I've forgiven him. [Enrique Chediak], who took over from Alwin, was terrific, and we agreed it wouldn't be a case of good cop, bad cop. Instead we just worked hard to cover for each other. Sometimes he was in the canyon, sometimes I was.

LC: The overall look of *Antichrist* is very bold in its aesthetic, very consistent. The DI for *Antichrist*, were you going for a look in post whose beauty helped soften the toughness of that film?

ADM: *Antichrist* is a desperately hard journey for the audience. Lars and I were in agreement that certain images in the film needed to be artistically beautiful. Capturing them was incredibly difficult. I'm speaking of the black and white at the start of the film, as well the shots captured at very high frame rates. Lars and I were just overjoyed with what we captured! We took it as far as we could, and even further than that. For some of those scenes the takes are eight-hour renders! They are massive, massive pieces of work for that time in digital cinema. That said, Lars and I had a few problems. We worked hard to shoot 360 degrees on the set, yet at the same time Lars was often not very happy with the more naturalistic imagery of the shoot. Then other people got involved and it became a fucking nightmare. Our issues were about giving him has much freedom as possible, without it looking crap. Yet we also had to take into account special effects. You had to see the rain on windows because it is rain. The set was in Germany, yet we needed to have a sense of light coming from outside, of seeing the sky outside the window, feeling the rain, all of this had to come through. Otherwise what is the point of shooting it on a set, we could have shot it at Paddington Station! Lars was not at his best, and some of these points became very gritty negotiations. We got through it, the film is what it is. I think if you speak with Lars, that is where his frustration lies, with the quality of the imagery in the more naturalistic sections of the film. But he loved the beautiful elements.

LC: *Antichrist* ends with a very ambiguous image of a horde of women rushing at Willem Dafoe's character.

ADM: You can't work that one out, I can't either. I can't work out whether it is tongue-in-cheek, an intelligent release, or if it is saying "there is more to come of the violence between men and women." It's a strange, unusual image. But I never pressed Lars. Sometimes he's working things out, and he's not sure himself. That's what I enjoyed with Lars throughout our history, going all the way back to his documentaries, was how we developed things on the go. He's very specific about some things. He often storyboards. Yet there is also this room for improvisation. That is what is extraordinary about him. It came to a hilt on *Antichrist.* He was so poorly we were just struggling to get through. I felt, even going into the editing, there was a lack of respect from a certain group involved in the production toward the actual film itself.

LC: Was this coming from Lars?

ADM: No, I would say he allowed them to go on. At this time Lars was living in a world of turmoil. Because he was so absent, you have the issue of too many chiefs.

LC: How would you say your working relationship with Lars broke down?

ADM: Lars and I had a creative relationship which lasted twenty-five years. Our families knew each other. We would have a constructive debate. I would trust him. But the people who are around Lars now, I have enormous doubts about them as people. I was Lars's brother, and yes, he was an auteur, but I was also very much a part of the work we did, with my lights, the way I moved my camera. There are things which Lars does as a person which affected how I saw him as an artist. Usually, I could separate the two. But with films which are as author-driven as those of Lars, I can't easily make that separation. If something happens with our rapport as friends, then it becomes an issue and doesn't allow us to perform as a team on the film. I can't just do what he says. I have to have the right to question him.

LC: Are you still his friend?

ADM: No. After *Antichrist*, we just broke up. He is a visionary. He is also a child. I suppose you either get cynical, or laugh it off. I can't do either of those things. I just get in the hole with him. I still respect him as an important figure of cinema. Following the *Antichrist* period, things were said and done around him which were low in ethics, and I just wanted to pull out. He didn't want me around much more either.

LC: Would you work with him again?

ADM: Only if the air was cleared. I need him to help me understand the things which went on. I think he is too much of a child. He is too much affected by the strange world he lives in, packed in confetti. I haven't spoken to him since the premiere of *Antichrist*, where he behaved like a tit. It's sad really. I have to say Lars behaved weirdly as soon as I got the Oscar. I'm having more and more competent directors calling me. But you know I'm still very, very loyal to Lars. Whatever went on, they're based on childish things. And you know, I'm the shambles I was before I won the Oscar. Anyway, I wish Manuel, Lars new cinematographer, the very best.

LC: There were distinct aesthetics/looks in *Slumdog Millionaire*. A major segment of the film occurs in the studio for the Indian version of *Who Wants to Be a Millionaire?* On the *Millionaire* set for *Slumdog Millionaire*, you were shooting with practicals. Was that a new challenge?

ADM: The set was a replica. I was shooting about 150 ASA slower than the original program. We hired the original *Millionaire* crew, and they set it up on the set. Because I was shooting on SI 2K for a lot of the film, it's slightly slower than the original cameras. I had a little bit of bubbly grain to deal with. In some places I cleared it up, in some places Danny wanted it to stay.

LC: Sometimes the camera itself is very much responsible for kind of aesthetic you create. You used the Phantom camera for the super-slow-motion shots on *Dredd.* This camera can achieve incredible slow-motion footage.

ADM: Correct. I used the Phantom up to 3,000 frames. There's a suggestion of brown murk in the midtones and the blacks, but that is something which can be graded out. I think it's an incredible machine. Now like anything which comes to the industry, it gets overused. Every bloody toilet commercial will be shot using the Phantom! Seeing athletes perform using the Phantom is great, there is so much more visual information gained by viewers on how the muscles of the athletes work. So you see great examples of the Phantom, but also boring examples of the Phantom. I might have used it first on a commercial or *Antichrist.*

LC: Cameras themselves can come in and out of fashion of course. Why do you think, for instance, the Thomson Viper died out as a camera?

ADM: I can't tell you exactly why, but I know that there are corporate layabouts, who we depend upon to supply us, who seem more invested in creating waves than in creating equipment which can float up on the waves. We also know about the impact which the pornographic industry has had on formats in various parts of the world. Let's face it, I can't go into details on this, but you know who I am talking about! There is a lot of speculation. There is a lot of opportunism. All DPs can do is continue to liaise with these companies, continue to talk to them. Not the rental houses, rather those who actually make the cameras. I talk with a lot of people in the industry who can help me by producing more ergodynamic cameras. I have to admit, I can't really get my head around this rapid self-destruct on celluloid which is happening at the moment. Labs are closing everywhere. There is this race toward codex, raw digital imaging, and that's where things are headed. I'm not saying we should still be sticking with film projection, though I'd miss the beautiful blacks. For the life of me I can't understand why we can't shoot on film, then go to a DI, then go to a DCP.

LC: Would you say it is a conspiracy?

ADM: I can't call it a conspiracy without knowing, but there is something fishy. There is something going on which is very much about money. I think it relates also to a wide respect for industrial language. Some people might call it a conspiracy. It is a war about money. Who wants to invest in what? It can become an artistic argument, and we have these artistic arguments all the time. Sadly, more influential than that is the money.

LC: Interestingly, in shooting 3D on *Dredd*, the focal lengths you were shooting with seemed to be close to the human eye?

ADM: I would say I learned on *Dredd* when shooting 3D, 27–28 to 40 [mm] is where you need to be. That is where you get the maximum unanimous 3D effect, plus you get a balance, shot to shot. Even though the mise-en-scène changes, there is still a balance achieved. I have learned that from *Dredd*, which was much more anarchic. Now I can apply it to the new 3D film I am shooting with Wim Wenders. My stereographers were good on *Dredd*, I worked with multilayers, and I had a director willing to experiment.

LC: Looking again at overall aesthetics, when I spoke with Bruno Delbonnel about his work on *A Very Long Engagement*, he criticized his own visual strategy as cartoonish, switching between palettes for the various periods the story takes place. Do you feel such an adjective can be applied to cinema?

ADM: I don't know if "cartoonish" is the right word. It can certainly work for a story. In *Slumdog* the lighting of the television studio for the *Who Wants to Be a Millionaire?* segments and the exterior shots we had of the kids in the flashbacks worked very well to separate out the various parts of the story. All of these areas had to be clear for the audience, and we agreed to stick with particular palettes and lighting. This can result in an approach which might be noted as "simplistic," but I think, at the end of the day, you have to admit that the audience, in terms of IQ, need it all made pretty clear to them. They're stuffing themselves with popcorn, or gadgeting, multitasking at the same time. Sometimes, they will be watching something at home while they are doing other things. I've been to cinemas in Cuba where people are snogging or going up to get ice cream all through the film. It's the director's privilege or the director's hell to make these judgment calls. In the case of Bruno, who is a great cinematographer, it can obviously result in that feeling where you are ultimately needing to make things clear, or the director decides this, and you might have to adjust your approach. As cinematographers we often feel you can get away with more visually, but at the same time the director can get worried because they fear they are losing the audience.

LC: Are you ever feeling that your attempts to achieve a successful aesthetic fail?

ADM: (*Laughs*) Something fails every time. Failure is a big word. It's an equation isn't it? Success is there also. It's like yin and yang. In knowing how good it is, I also know how much better it could be. That's private though.

LC: Looking at your career as a whole, you seem unafraid to depict stories that can really reveal human suffering and cruelty.

ADM: My evolution as an artist has been such that a film I align myself with needs a social conscience, or a political conscience, coupled with a lyrical, artistic, or poetic gene to them. Stories I seek out need to have a balance of the two. Someone like [writer] Alex Garland, on *Dredd*, is a person who I would similarly feel an affinity for, knowing that we have similar priorities. He camouflages his stories in *The Beach* or *28 Days Later*, but it is clear he is dealing with stories which relate to all of us, to problems we all experience.

~

Dod Mantle's descriptions of his collaborations with Lars von Trier lay bare the close, essential relationship that may exist between director and cinematographer. In the case of von Trier especially, who is both a visually talented writer-director, a technically knowledgeable filmmaker, and an auteur with repeating personal themes, motifs, and storylines in his films, the importance of his close partnership with Dod Mantle cannot be overestimated. Von Trier was in a position where he might be constantly creative, unencumbered by the necessity to check in with alternate entities when it came to matters such as dialogue, action, and framing. In this respect, the necessity that Dod Mantle "be on the same page" became a make-or-break component of his work as a filmmaker. As co-operators on a film such as *Dogville*, they had to be in sync on matters of ensuring sufficient material was being collected, that their styles of capturing footage would mesh, and that Dod Mantle's lighting could allow them to fluidly capture all of the necessary footage without having to interrupt to reset or reblock a scene. *Manderlay* and *Antichrist* saw Dod Mantle move more and more toward being the dominant operator. In this respect, arguably, von Trier was placed in a greater position of needing to trust Dod Mantle's operating and how he worked to develop the film's aesthetic. In this specific paradigm, one of trust and pooling talents in the interests of creating a shared creative output, director–cinematographer relationships may languish or alternately flourish. Robert Rodriguez, a director who immediately embraced the potential of digital cinema to permit a new transparency in this process, is on record as to his disappointment in cinematographers who he felt had taken advantage of his trust in such instances. Conversely, the likes of Ingmar Bergman and Sven Nykvist achieved transcendent collaboration through Bergman's trust that Nykvist's work would not only be beautiful but also entirely appropriate to the canon of work that became their shared enterprise. This is undoubtedly one of the most alchemical and human aspects of filmmaking and will likely propel stunning, perhaps emotionally fraught filmmaking as long as cinematographers work and as long as directors have such intense need of them

Index

Aguirresarobe, Javier, 17, 195, 196, 205, 243; *Earth*, 202; *Others, The*, 197, 198; *Road, The*, 195, 202, 203; *Sea Inside, The*, 195, 198, 199; *Talk to Her*, 196–202, 243; *Twilight: Eclipse*, 195, 204, 205; *Twilight: New Moon*, 195, 203, 204
Alcott, John, 60
Allen, Woody, 195, 196
Almendros, Néstor, 205
Almodóvar, Pedro, 70, 82, 192, 201, 202, 239, 240–243; *Kika*, 242
Anderson, Paul Thomas, 1, 2; *Phantom Thread*, 2
Anderson, Wes, 179
Antonioni, Michelangelo, 156, 299
Argento, Dario, 153, 156
Aronovich, Ricardo, 17, 196
Arquette, Patricia, 102–104, 110
Arri Alexa, 11, 13, 16, 111, 140, 141, 152, 231, 232

Ballhaus, Michael, 3
Bardem, Javier, 199, 240, 241
Bausch, Pina, 196, 197
Beato, Affonso, 201, 239, 240; *All About My Mother*, 201, 239, 242, 243; *Antonio das Mortes*, 241; *Great Balls of Fire!*, 243; *Live Flesh*, 201, 239–242
Beebe, Dion, 15, 16, 116, 124, 125; *Collateral*, 120, 125; *Memoirs of a Geisha*, 115, 121, 124, 125; *Miami Vice*, 16, 120, 121; *Praise*, 116, 117
Bettany, Paul, 299
Bird, Brad, 217
Bouchez, Élodie, 37, 39
Boyle, Danny, 15, 186, 297, 298
Bradley, Dan, 277
Braugher, Andre, 262
Briesewitz, Uta, 70, 261, 262, 270, 271; *Wire, The*, 261–271

Cameron, James, 4, 15, 93, 94, 173, 176–178; *Abyss, The*, 93, 176; *Terminator 2*, 93, 176
Cameron, Paul, 125
Campbell, Neve, 101
Cardiff, Jack, 302
Carpenter, John, 14, 48, 50
Carpenter, Russell, 173, 174, 181; *Charlie's Angels*, 173, 178–181; *Shallow Hal*, 173, 180, 181; *Titanic*, 167, 173–178; *True Lies*, 173, 174, 176
Caravaggio, 149
Casino Royale, 283
Chediak, Enrique, 4, 303
Cheung, Maggie, 134
Chinlund, James, 226

Clarke, Alan, 223, 224
Colesberry, Robert, 264
Colin, Grégoire, 38, 45
Corbijn, Anton, 185, 188, 190, 193
Corbould, Chris, 277
Craig, Daniel, 277, 284
Cronenberg, David, 20, 26–30
Cronenweth, Jordan, 70
Crowe, Cameron, 73, 74
Crowe, Russell, 149
Cruise, Tom, 212, 294
Cruz, Penélope, 70, 240
Cuarón, Alfonso, 2; *Roma*, 2
Cundey, Dean, 47, 48, 62, 63; *Apollo 13*, 52–54; *Casper*, 58, 59, 62; *Jurassic Park*, 47, 48, 54, 60; *Thing, The*, 47, 48, 54, 60; *Who Framed Roger Rabbit*, 47, 48, 55–62, 88

Daniels, Lee, 279, 280
Damon, Matt, 73
De Borman, John, 229, 230, 237; *An Education*, 229, 231, 234, 236; *Hamlet*, 229, 232, 233
De La Tour, George, 149
Deakins, Roger, 5, 6, 69, 130, 131, 283; *Blade Runner 2049*, 5, 6; *Prisoners*, 7; *Sid & Nancy*, 5, 6; *White Mischief*, 7
Delbonnel, Bruno, 154, 250, 307; *Very Long Engagement, A*, 307
Deming, Peter, 1, 15, 97, 98, 112, 113; *House Party*, 98, 99; *Lost Highway*, 15, 97, 101–107, 110; *Mulholland Drive*, 97, 107–110; *Oz, the Great and Powerful*, 97, 111; *Twin Peaks: The Return*, 112
Denis, Claire, 38, 42, 44, 45, 46
Dod Mantle, Anthony, 2, 15, 129, 131, 297, 298, 308, 309; *127 Hours*, 301, 302; *Antichrist*, 300, 303–306, 309; *Dogville*, 299, 300, 209; *Dredd*, 307, 308; *Festen*, 298, 299; *Manderlay*, 300, 301; *Slumdog Millionaire*, 131, 297, 298, 305
Doyle, Christopher, 10, 16, 30, 127, 128, 130, 136, 189, 218, 219; *2046*, 128, 134; *In the Mood for Love*, 128, 134; *Limits of Control, The*, 128
Doyle, Peter, 11, 12

Edlund, Richard, 24
Elswit, Robert, 2
Eminem, 71, 72
Elvgren, Gil, 179

Feldman, Ed, 288
Fincher, David, 1, 4, 207, 208, 209, 219, 225, 244
Fiore, Mauro, 4, 5, 15, 16, 87, 88, 94, 207, 256; *Avatar*, 4, 5, 15, 16, 87, 88, 89–94
Forster, Marc, 276, 281

Garland, Alex, 308
Getty, Balthazar, 103, 104, 107
Gilliard Jr., Larry, 266
Godard, Agnès, 37, 38, 46; *Beau Travail*, 38, 40–42, 46, 62; *The Dreamlife of Angels*, 37–39; *Sister*, 37, 38, 44; *Trouble Every Day*, 40, 45
Godard, Jean-Luc, 15
Goi, Michael, 4
Goldin, Nan, 224
Gondry, Michel, 247, 252
Guest, Christopher, 274–276

Hanson, Curtis, 72
Hoffman, Dustin, 294
Horler, Sacha, 116
Howard, Bryce Dallas, 300
Howard, Ron, 15, 54, 297
Howard, Trevor, 7
Haug, Kevin Tod, 277

IMAGO, 154
Iñárritu, Alejandro González, 4, 14

Jane, Thomas, 267
Jarman, Derek, 138, 141, 279
Jarmusch, Jim, 134
Johansson, Scarlett, 244
Johanson, Ron, 17

Kar-Wai, Wong, 134, 189
Kamiński, Janusz, 11, 88, 207
Khondji, Darius, 18; *Beach, The*, 186, 308
Koirala, Manisha, 163, 167
Krasker, Robert, 148
Kosinski, Joseph, 211
Küchler, Alwin, 302
Kuras, Ellen, 247, 248, 258; *Eternal Sunshine of the Spotless Mind, The*, 180, 247, 252, 253; *Personal Velocity*, 251, 256; *Summer of Sam*, 247, 248
Kurylenko, Olga, 212, 282

Lavant, Denis, 38, 42
Ledger, Heath, 69, 77, 276
Lee, Ang, 14, 15, 66, 67, 70, 74, 75, 78, 80–83, 212
Lee, Spike, 247, 248
Leiter, Sam, 249
Lewis, Jerry, 4
Lucas, George, 4, 19, 23
Lucci, Gabriele, 154
Lubezki, Emmanuel, 2, 8, 9, 76, 133, 146; *Children of Men*, 2; *Knight of Cups*, 8; *Revenant, The*, 8, 9
Lynch, David, 1, 97, 98, 101, 112; *Eraserhead*, 101, 112; *Inland Empire*, 2, 112; *Twin Peaks*, 2, 107

Mann, Michael, 120, 121, 125, 132
Mary Poppins, 62
Mathieson, John, 137, 138, 151, 152, 232, 233; *Gladiator*, 137, 138, 143, 145, 149; *Kingdom of Heaven*, 137, 138, 148; *Plunkett & Macleane*, 137, 144, 146, 147, 151; *Robin Hood*, 139, 141, 142, 143, 151
Mayne, Roger, 224
McAvoy, James, 225, 301
McBride, Jim, 239, 243
McBride, Joseph, 2
McGarvey, Seamus, 221, 222, 227, 228; *Atonement*, 221, 223, 225; *Butterfly Kiss*, 221–224; *War Zone, The*, 223, 224
Medem, Julio, 202
Mehta, Ashok, 162; *Bandit Queen*, 162; *Kahl Nayak*, 162
Menges, Chris, 19, 179, 224, 241; *Mission, The*, 224, 227, 291
Menon, Rajiv, 162, 164, 165; *Bombay*, 161–170
Minghella, Anthony, 293–295
Miller, George, 290
Miller, Larry, 276
Miller, Rebecca, 250
Miranda, Claudio, 15, 16, 17, 128, 207, 208, 219, 220; *Curious Case of Benjamin Button, The*, 207–209, 219; *Life of Pi*, 5, 16, 128, 207, 216, 218, 219; *Oblivion*, 211; *Tomorrowland*, 218
Müller, Robby, 43, 135
Mulligan, Carey, 236
Murch, Walter, 289

Navarro, Guillermo, 4
Nykvist, Sven, 46, 194, 309

O'Dell, Shaun, 277
O'Leary, Bill, 150

Pace, Vincent, 4
Paltrow, Gwyneth, 243, 244, 245
Pau, Peter, 66
Phantom, 305, 306
Plummer, Amanda, 222, 223

Prieto, Rodrigo, 14, 65, 66, 82, 83, 132; *8 Mile*, 65, 71, 72, 76, 83, 84; *21 Grams*, 74, 83; *Alexander*, 65, 70, 75, 82; *Amores Perros*, 65, 74, 241; *Brokeback Mountain*, 65–69, 76–78, 82; *Frida*, 73, 76; *Lust, Caution*, 68, 70, 74, 78, 79, 83
Pullman, Bill, 102, 103, 107

Ralston, Ken, 56, 63
Ratnam, Mani, 162, 164, 165
Red Monochrome, 111
Red One, 2
Régnier, Natasha, 39
Richardson, Robert, 286
Rocha, Glauber, 241
Rodriguez, Robert, 1, 3, 4, 309; *Sin City*, 3, 4
Roth, Cecilia, 242
Ruhe, Martin, 15, 185, 186, 194, 194; *American, The*, 189–193; *Control*, 189–193; *Harry Brown*, 185–193
Ryan, Ellery, 17

Sarandon, Susan, 290
Savides, Harris, 3, 135, 147, 186, 207, 208, 219; *Zodiac*, 209
Sayeed, Malik, 248, 249
Schaefer, Roberto, 17, 208, 273, 274, 283; *Best in Show*, 273–276, 284; *Finding Neverland*, 273, 278, 280; *Monster's Ball*, 209, 273, 279; *Paperboy, The*, 279, 280, 283, 284; *Quantum of Solace*, 273, 276, 277, 281; *Stranger than Fiction*, 276, 277; *Waiting for Guffman*, 274, 284
Scorsese, Martin, 4, 14
Scott, Jake, 145, 149
Scott, Ridley, 1, 137–139
Scott, Tony, 219
Seale, John, 93, 119, 285, 286, 294, 295; *Cold Mountain*, 289, 294; *English Patient, The*, 285, 292–294; *Hitcher, The*, 288; *Lorenzo's Oil*, 290; *Mad Max: Fury Road*, 290; *Mosquito Coast, The*, 286, 291, 292; *Rain Man*, 286 294; *Witness*, 285, 288, 291
Seydoux, Léa, 44
Side by Side, 4, 144, 298
Soderbergh, Steven, 1–3; *Logan Lucky*, 2; *Magic Mike*, 3; *Knick, The*, 2
Spielberg, Steven, 4, 14, 59
Squyres, Tim, 13
Stone, Oliver, 4, 14, 15, 75, 82, 222
Storaro, Vittorio, 186
Suschitzky, Peter, 15, 19, 20, 33, 34; *Dangerous Method, A*, 28, 29; *Dead Ringers*, 20, 28; *Eastern Promises*, 20, 29; *Empire Strikes Back, The*, 20, 23, 24, 31, 33; *History of Violence, A*, 20, 27, 29; *Immortal Beloved*, 19, 20, 30–32; *M. Butterfly*, 20, 26

Taymor, Julie, 72, 156
Thomson Viper, 16, 120, 147, 209, 210, 306
Tovoli, Luciano, 15, 153, 154, 159; *Kiss of Death*, 153, 157, 159; *Murder by Numbers*, 158; *Single White Female*, 158; *Suspiria*, 153, 157–159

Vacano, Jost, 123
VistaGlide, 58
Von Trier, Lars, 15, 186, 297, 299, 308, 309

Watts, Naomi, 74, 107–109
Weir, Peter, 291, 295
Welles, Orson, 2, 3
Wenders, Wim, 15, 43, 307
Wexler, Haskell, 205
Whedon, Joss, 226
Whitaker, Forest, 301
Winick, Gary, 251
Winslet, Kate, 280

Woo, John, 175
Wright, Joe, 221
Wright, Joseph, 149
Zemeckis, Robert, 14, 56
Zonca, Erick, 39
Zwigoff, Terry, 244

www.ingramcontent.com/pod-product-compliance
Lightning Source LLC
LaVergne TN
LVHW050148080826
844660LV00002B/118

* 9 7 8 1 4 3 8 4 8 6 4 1 3 *